Eminent Buddhist Women

Eminent Buddhist Women

Edited by

Karma Lekshe Tsomo

Cover art by Margaret Anne Smith

Published by State University of New York Press, Albany

For information, contact State University of New York Press, Albany, NY
www.sunypress.edu

Production by Diane Ganeles
Marketing by Anne M. Valentine

Library of Congress Cataloging-in-Publication Data

Eminent Buddhist women / Edited by Karma Lekshe Tsomo.
    pages cm
  Includes bibliographical references and index.
  ISBN 978-1-4384-5131-2 (hardcover : alk. paper)
  ISBN 978-1-4384-5130-5 (pbk. : alk. paper)
  1. Buddhist women—Biography.   2. Buddhist nuns—Biography.   3. Women in
Buddhism.   I. Karma Lekshe Tsomo.

  BQ850.E65 2014
  294.3092'52—dc23
  [B]   2013022608

10 9 8 7 6 5 4 3 2 1

Contents

Preface

This book has been a labor of love, not only for me but also for the many dear friends and colleagues who have taken part in this wonderful project. Many have been involved from start to finish. First, I would like to express my appreciation for the selfless dedication of the team who created, sustained, translated, and documented the Sakyadhita International Conference on Buddhist Women in Ho Chi Minh City in 2010, especially to Christie Yuling Chang, Yu-chen Li, Thích Nữ Vien Ngan, Thích Nữ Như Nguyệt, Bhikkhunī Lieu Phap, Emily Mariko Sanders, Malia Dominica Wong, the Vietnam Bhikṣuṇī Saṅgha, and to all those who support the global Buddhist women's movement. Mere words are insufficient.

This heartfelt effort to document the lives of exceptional Buddhist women has come to fruition because of the kindness of an outstanding team of conscientious and astute editors. Boundless thanks go to Margaret Coberly, Rebecca Paxton, Bhikkhunī Adhimutti, Alison Hoffman, and Pamela Kirby for their diligence, expertise, compassion, and amazing turnaround time. Sincere appreciation also goes to Evelyn Diane Cowie, Anne Girard, Carol Stevens Gerstl, Constance Ellwood, Joy Fox, Karen Jensen, Kathleen Monaco, Mara Canizzaro, and many others who have helped along the way. Mahalo nui loa for your enthusiasm, encouragement, and friendship.

Immense gratitude also goes to the authors who so generously contributed their knowledge and insights. An international collaborative effort involving so many different languages and perspectives involves many risks— linguistically, philosophically, and politically. The contributors are to be commended for being courageous enough to venture those risks and for their patient cooperation throughout years of revision. In an attempt to preserve their original voices, I have retained their own use of either Pāli or Sanskrit (for example, *bhikkhunī* or *bhikṣuṇī*), with diacritics or without, and apologize for all errors in transcription.

It is a great joy to bring to light the stories of these extraordinary Buddhist women. Among others, I am delighted to preserve in these pages the lives of several of my own teachers, the *bhiksunī*s Khechog Palmo, Hyechun Sunim, and Shig Hiuwan. The book is dedicated to them and to all the wonderful, often unheralded women who have kept alight the lamp of Dharma over many centuries. May their stories encourage other women on the path to awakening. May they also inspire the continual discovery of other stories and achievements of eminent practitioners whose voices have not yet been heard.

All merits derived from these efforts accrue to this spectacular team, while all flaws are entirely my own. May the merits be shared with countless beings throughout time and space. And may all sufferings derived from gender discrimination and other insidious forms of oppression be banished forever!

Introduction

Karma Lekshe Tsomo

For centuries, women have been relegated to live, practice, and teach in the shadows of far more visibly-placed men. History is dominated by the deeds, thoughts, and influences of men considered to be eminent, with the value of human achievement determined exclusively by the standards of men, the unfortunate method of assessment until recent times. But eminence can be interpreted in many different ways—to define it as merely having visibility, power, and authority is to misunderstand the word. When the word is applied to the majority of women in Buddhist cultures, the definition expands to influential, important, notable, and superior. As in other spheres of life, women perform vital functions in religion throughout Buddhist communities in Asia and abroad.

For too long, the measure of what was true and valuable in the human experience ignored a crucial component—millions of women who have loved, worked, fought, compromised, suffered, and succeeded in realizing their own highest potential, but who remain unknown to us simply because their stories were never deemed worthy of recording. When eminence is predicated on a larger set of qualities than those typically recognized as marks of achievement; when eminence recognizes inner qualities such as sincerity, warm-heartedness, kindness to children, care for the weak and disenfranchised, wisdom, tenderness, patience, and compassion, then the term eminence includes a host of individuals who existed and flourished throughout history but were overlooked, ignored, undervalued, or invisible simply because they were women.

Now, in an era of greater openness and awareness, it is appropriate and timely to reassess the lives of exemplary Buddhist women whose stories have been hidden or ignored. We can bring to light narratives that teach us to reconsider the past criteria of eminence and compel us to question how

1

and by whom those criteria are constructed and controlled. In the Buddhist world, until very recently, the reputed knowledge holders have been male. Upon reflection, this is rather odd, especially considering the nongendered nature of Buddhism's primary values: loving kindness, compassion, knowledge, wisdom, authenticity, spiritual attainment, and liberation. In view of this apparent contradiction between the universal nature of fundamental Buddhist principles and unapologetic male dominance for more than two thousand years of Buddhist history and development, a reassessment of the lives and experiences of women within the tradition is imperative. For instance, why is the story of Mahāpajāpatī Gotamī and her five hundred noble women companions, who led the first march for women's rights in recorded history, not well known today, even in many Buddhist countries? It is essential to recognize the work of women and their inner attainments so that this knowledge and inspiration can be imparted to future generations. In an effort to elevate the status of all women everywhere, especially because the struggles of women in earlier generations still remain largely unacknowledged and unappreciated, it is essential that we begin to collect these stories and bring to light the bountiful accomplishments of women thus far. A review of Buddhist women's contributions is a long-overdue tribute to their determination, realizations, and achievements. This book is a step along that path.

Rediscovering Buddhist Women's Legacy

The Buddhist traditions are not bereft of feminine imagery and exemplars. The legacy of eminent Buddhist women begins with Mahāmāyā, the woman who gave birth to Prince Siddhartha. Without her, there would have been no Siddhartha Gotama and hence no Buddha Śākyamuni. According to legend, she passed away just seven days after giving birth to the young future Buddha. As often occurred in the day, Mahāmāyā's sister Mahāpajāpatī Gotamī stepped in to nurture the young prince. Later, after Siddhartha Gotama's awakening and the death of Mahāpajāpatī's husband, she renounced the household life and became the courageous progenitor of the Buddhist order of nuns (bhikṣuṇī saṅghā). The Buddha offered special teachings to Mahāpajāpatī when she was a layperson and also after she was ordained as a nun. Her leadership in advocating for the admission of women to the monastic order is one of the earliest recorded instances of what today is termed feminist advocacy. In fact, she could be eulogized as the first great Buddhist social activist. According to the story, the Buddha eventually acceded to her request but asked her to agree to certain terms of inequality consistent with the society of the time as a condition for her admission to the order. Mahāpajāpatī's attempt to reverse one of these conditions—the one that clearly subordinates nuns to monks—is evidence of her awareness of gender injustice and her determination to change it.

The legacy initiated by Mahāmāyā and Mahāpajāpatī continues today with the scores of eminent Buddhist women working as agents of social change. Not only did Mahāpajāpatī and her many disciples become liberated from mental defilements, but they also freed themselves from the prescribed roles that society allotted them. They blazed new pathways for women both personally and socially. Instead of being confined to the expected female roles of housewife and mother, thousands of women at the time of the Buddha became seekers, many of whom were publicly recognized by the Buddha as outstanding exemplars of spiritual attainment. Sujata, a young village woman who had offered milk rice to the emaciated renunciant Siddhartha and who sustained the fledgling Buddha in the crucial days leading up to his final awakening, was one of the first to enter his newly discovered path to liberation.

Mahāpajāpatī and the five hundred noble women who marched with her, traveling barefoot and resolute in their determined effort for women's rights, deserve immense appreciation and respect. Knowledge about this important chapter of history is long overdue. Mahāpajāpatī succeeded in founding the *bhikṣuṇī saṅgha* and skillfully guided its development until her death. Thousands of women became respected *arhats* and were recognized by the Buddha himself for their extraordinary attainments: Khema for her great wisdom, Uppalavanna and Patācārā for their exemplary monastic discipline, Dhammadinna for her proficiency in teaching Dharma, Nanda for her dedication, Sona for her energetic determination, and so on. Not only nuns, but also laywomen were acknowledged by the Buddha as eminent. Visākhā, the devout daughter of a millionaire, became renowned for her exceptional generosity to the *saṅgha*. By publicly recognizing the eminent qualities and spiritual attainments of outstanding women, the Buddha began challenging centuries-old views about women as objects for subjugation and neglect.

The sincerity and stature of these women stand in sharp contrast to the story of the Buddha's alleged reluctance to admit women to his order. If the women who surrounded him were so competent and well-intentioned, how could it be possible that the Buddha needed to have his arm twisted to accept them? Was his reluctance simply a test of their sincerity? Mahāpajāpatī and her resolute band of women exemplified solidarity and sincerity, giving lie to the banal myth that women are characterless and unable to cooperate and work harmoniously together. The spiritual determination they represented is unmatched by any other group in the Buddhist texts, and their march heralded immeasurable waves of spiritual attainment. The story of these women's valor has withstood twenty-five hundred years of telling and has provided significant meaning and encouragement to millions of the women in the generations that have followed.

Liberating Women to Speak in Their Own Voices

This collection of essays documents the quietly extraordinary lives of women from a diverse range of Buddhist cultures. These exemplary women have emerged from cultures that often dispossess, devalue, and marginalize women, and their stories easily could have been lost to history. Beginning in India and traversing the heartlands of Asia in all the directions in which Buddhism spread, weaving together threads of religion, art, culture, and custom, these orally transmitted legends are treasures of our shared human legacy. These stories belong to a new genre of literature on women in Buddhism that has emerged globally. In giving at long last a voice to Buddhist women, these narratives teach us about the strategies they used to realize their own spiritual liberation even when confined or ignored by society at large. In them, we hear about women who have broken through the stereotype of the undemonstrative Asian woman and have achieved greatness in ways that challenge our own preconceived notions and complacencies.

Recovering lost histories is an ongoing process through which we learn, among other things, the importance of recording our own lives and experiences. Never before, because of the rapid advances that have been made in modern education and technology, has the documentary potential of women been greater. Yet we must never lose sight of the fact that these new elements are still the domain of the privileged, and access to them remains a mere dream to countless millions of people, both women and men, in many parts of the world. A hidden agenda in this collection of stories is to give voice to some of the women who have until now been silenced, and by their example to provide strength for disempowered women everywhere. These narratives are focused on a few of the special jewels of humanity, each of whom has a story that will energize and empower the struggle of women everywhere for equality, justice, and acknowledgment in a world that has been conceptualized primarily only through the work of men.

The genesis of this collection is from within the international Buddhist women's movement that began in 1987 with the advent of Sakyadhita International Association of Buddhist Women and its initiatives to reclaim and revalue the roles of Buddhist women within the multiplicity of Buddhist texts and traditions.[1] Many of the chapters are based on papers presented at the 11th Sakyadhita International Conference on Buddhist Women held in Ho Chi Minh City, Vietnam, in early 2010. That conference was but one of the numerous national and international gatherings that have been convened thus far to celebrate and encourage millions of Buddhist women worldwide in the recovery of their rightful heritage.

The considerable variation in these stories reflects the vast and varied range of experience in the lives of Buddhist women.[2] Rather than homogenize these women's stories and experiences into some preconceived generic template or superimpose successive waves of feminist analysis, I have chosen to respect and retain, as much as possible, the narrative choices of those who tell the stories. Footnotes and prescribed page lengths do not necessarily deem stories to be authentic. Who decrees that footnotes are necessary for telling women's stories? Who demands uniform page lengths for legitimacy? Perhaps it is time to liberate women from these artificial constraints. I have chosen to allow the authors to tell the stories as they wish.

Chapter 1 begins in ancient India, with a female *bodhisattva* who has become a Buddha. The story is significant. It documents a woman's awakening and sets it into writing, providing a historical account of one woman's attainment of the highest achievement. It is stories like these that document the remarkable attainments that women have realized, beginning with the Buddha's foster mother and continuing with other laywomen who were also renowned for their remarkable spiritual accomplishments. The next chapter documents the lives of two distinct generations of twentieth-century Nepalese nuns who faced unimaginable challenges yet quietly triumphed in socially transformative ways.

The geographical focus then shifts to Southeast Asia, with stories that challenge the myth that Buddhist women in Burma, Thailand, and Vietnam are all content with their unequal and subservient status to men. Although these women may give priority to devotional practices, mental cultivation, and the accumulation of merit rather than to more visible external social advancements, it is demeaning to assume that these women lack awareness of the colossal disadvantages they face. Everyone wishes to be free, and no one wishes to be relegated to the fringes. The changes currently under way in these countries are nothing short of miraculous, and they are continually gaining momentum in expanding the inclusion of women at all levels of Buddhist culture. For example, it is significant that when a small group of young monks objected to the theme of the 11th Sakyadhita International Conference on Buddhist Women in Vietnam in 2009—"Eminent Buddhist Women"—on the grounds that women do not deserve this acclaim, they were overruled by the senior leadership of the Vietnam Buddhist Saṅgha.

The focus of the book then moves to East Asia, highlighting the hard-won successes of Buddhist women in Korea and Taiwan. Beginning in the fourth century, nuns took the initiative to transmit the *bhikṣuṇī* lineage from Sri Lanka to China, where, despite political, economic, and social turmoil, successive generations have protected it ever since. Because of the courage and vision of the nuns of Korea and Taiwan, the lineage that was lost for nearly a thousand years in South and Southeast Asia is now being revived. This achievement has been a lifeline to the revitalization of women's spiritual awareness in those countries and the spread of Buddhism to the West. With

the advantages of universal education and higher ordination, many women
are now emerging as Buddhist teachers, moral exemplars, and respected
leaders in their communities, sometimes attracting large followings—accomplishments that were previously rare for women in other Asian countries, or
unacknowledged.

Women in the Tibetan cultural sphere have followed their own unique
trajectory, specializing in solitary retreats that have produced many exceptional women practitioners, but the isolation has also rendered most of them
invisible to the public eye. Many of the highly eminent and dedicated women
practitioners in Tibet, Sikkim, and Mongolia are not seen in historical records
at all because their achievements have rarely been recognized in the exclusively male Buddhist hierarchy. Flying beneath the radar, their presence is
usually recorded only in oral narratives. The stories of how these women have
overcome the extensive disadvantages of a female rebirth have been inspirational to many successive generations of women. Considering the vitality and
impact of the Tibetan tradition globally, one cannot help but wonder how
much more effective it could be if women held leadership roles in Tibetan
Buddhist institutions!

The book concludes with stories of several distinguished women who
have been influential in transmitting Dharma to the West. For example, Bhiksuni Karma Khechog Palmo was instrumental in educating young Tibetan
monks at the Young Lamas' Home in Dalhousie, India, and Bhiksuni Ruimiao brought people together across cultures from many countries despite
differences of language and religion. Bhiksuni Hiuwan similarly transcended
language barriers by speaking the universal language of compassion. Other
teachers, such as Orgyen Chökyi, have reached across time and space to
encourage women seekers and to share their realizations of things "as they
are." When we research, remember, and transmit the inspiring contributions
of these outstanding women to future generations, we help to preserve their
precious Dharma lineages and ensure that women will no longer be quite so
invisible in the history of Buddhism.

Awakening from the Myth of Impossibility

Although some women receive encouragement along the Buddhist path,
many others do not. Stories of ordinary and extraordinary Buddhist women
practitioners, teachers, artists, community activists, and good-hearted human
beings therefore encourage others to tackle retreats, Buddhist studies, and
compassionate social-service activities that they might not otherwise attempt.
But, perhaps most inspiring of all, these stories encourage strength and motivation for women who face hardships, obstacles, and uncertainties in their

everyday lives. The insights and accomplishments of women who are just like them can be the source of their greatest encouragement. For if other women successfully live by the Buddhist teachings in their relationships with partners, children, employers, and friends, then so can they. It is no secret that women suffer like all sentient beings, but they often suffer more because of the subservient status historically accorded to them. One is reminded of the sentiments of Lama Govinda: "Only those who have experienced great suffering are capable of great things in the realm of the spirit." This is not to assert that women must suffer in order to achieve eminence, but to recognize that human suffering need not be debilitating. Given inspiration and encouragement, it can become a catalyst for awakening. Only by acknowledging the pervasiveness of suffering is it possible to move beyond the illusion of self, and self-cherishing, and generate great compassion for others and the suffering of all beings.

A revolution is currently under way in Buddhist societies to upset the myth of women's inherent inferiority and to rescind the restrictions placed on women as a consequence of their imposed second-rate status. There is nothing in the Buddhist scriptures to prevent such a revolution and much to support it. After all, women's equal potential for liberation was reportedly recognized and supported by the Buddha himself in his revolutionary creation of the *bhikṣuṇī saṅgha*. Today's revolution is in the same spirit as the Buddha's. This is not an adversarial or aggressive revolution, but a quiet and natural turn of events in the direction of inclusiveness, justice, and enlightenment for all. Tensions always arise around the fear of change, but Buddhist women are meeting these challenges with clarity and compassion. Many women have gained allies for their just and honorable cause and have revitalized important and lasting conversations with sympathetic male allies that have been beneficial and strengthening to all. This Buddhist feminist revolution is concerned with optimizing the precious human opportunity—a widespread awakening that is transplanting itself deeply into the hearts of millions of women around the world today. To move this awakening forward, Buddhist women need greater opportunities in the real world to realize their potential. At present, for example, despite their numbers and accomplishments, Buddhist women have little representation at the United Nations and many other global forums. This lacuna stems in part from the fact that Buddhist women's capabilities and potential have not been fully recognized, even within their own communities. Another reason is that, until very recently, few Buddhist women have had access to the higher education and community leadership experience that is required to effectively take an active role in international discourse. Unfortunately, many Buddhists continue to believe their own propaganda—that Buddhist egalitarianism already extends to women—even while evidence of women's subordination is before their very eyes.

Today, Buddhist women around the world are struggling for gender equity and the same opportunities as men in their traditions to gain access to education and ordination. There are historical precedents of similar struggles, beginning with Mahāpajāpatī's charismatic leadership and valiant activism that initially won women admission to the *sangha* and continuing with the courageous actions of women, such as the Japanese nuns who reinvigorated the *bhikṣuṇī* lineage at Hokkeji in the thirteenth century. Despite resistance from men to accept that women are as eligible as they are to equal opportunities for ordination within entrenched Buddhist hierarchies, there is full justification for this struggle available in the Buddhist canon itself. In the traditional story of the beginnings of the *bhikṣuṇī sangha*, the Buddha risked social condemnation and exclusion from the religious body politic by admitting women to the *sangha*. The story of Buddha Śākyamuni rationally and magnanimously admitting his stepmother and her disciples to the order is told and retold with pride in Buddhist societies and is currently available on library bookshelves around the world. To deny this precedent and the Buddha's legendary acknowledgment of women's equal potential to attain liberation is folly.

Yet what might set the stage for gender justice in Buddhist institutions is marred by another, parallel narrative in which, oddly, the Enlightened One is represented as needing convincing before he allowed women to join the *sangha*. Over time, the legend of the Buddha's hesitation to admit women to the order worked to subvert his own ideal of a harmonious Buddhist society balanced among laywomen, laymen, nuns, and monks. Instead of this harmonious balance, the ritual and institutional subordination of nuns became canonized through the imposition of the "eight weighty rules," alleged by others to have been decreed by the Buddha, which has had a deleterious effect not only on the social and religious status of women in Buddhism, but also on the psychological, physical, and intellectual development of women up to the present day. Why, when the Buddha taught a path that was equally accessible for all human beings, has discrimination against women in Buddhist societies and institutions been allowed to continue for hundreds of years? Why would anyone think that it is justifiable for any tradition to abandon the Buddha's own vision and deny women equal access to his teachings? One can only imagine that it is a lapse into ignorance—the defilement that propels the wheel of *samsāra*—and is still deeply entrenched in the world and periodically triumphs even over the wisdom and truth of the Buddha's teachings.

Even with the recent spate of books, conferences, and research regarding women and Buddhism, a thorough feminist analysis of gender identity and power relations in the Buddhist context has yet to appear. The enormity of the task is daunting, because no two Buddhist traditions are alike. In each unique tradition, history, language, religion, and culture all intersect with gender to create complex relationships, all of which are currently in the process of monumental changes. Now, after twenty years of publications and gatherings, there is a widespread recognition of the disconnect between egalitarian gender rhetoric and the reality of unequal opportunity for women. This struggle is ongoing and will be resolved as women continue to assert themselves in new and challenging ways. Even in socially advanced countries like Taiwan and Korea, where women stand confidently, teach articulately, and resourcefully manage internationally renowned charitable institutions, it remains common for women to devote themselves to men's projects, often at the expense of their own health and personal development. The independent identity of women is often hampered by antiquated gender expectations and presuppositions that collude to produce unequal, unhealthy power relations with men. I share the widespread assumption that Buddhist wisdom and practice are keys to redressing these problems, but specific solutions need to be wisely and sensitively crafted for each tradition.

The *bhikṣuṇī* ordination issue serves as a litmus test for attitudes toward gender in Buddhist societies. The questions that are being debated among conservative Buddhist scholars in the Theravāda and Tibetan Buddhist traditions today—about whether women should be allowed to take full ordination and, if they are, how it should be conducted—are questions that the Buddha has already answered in full. The mystery is not what the Buddha would have said in such a situation but rather why so many Buddhist scholars and religious leaders are not listening to what the Buddha said. The frequently echoed assertion that *bhikṣuṇī* ordination must wait until the next Buddha appears ignores the fact that Buddha Śākyamuni himself has already answered the question. The powerful established hierarchies hold change at bay, based on antiquated views of women's inferiority. Unwilling to relinquish these unreasonable and self-defeating views, some even manipulate the Buddhist teachings and the monastic codes to justify their dominance. Many monks are willing to ordain women as novices, although this is the right and duty of *bhikṣuṇī*s, yet refuse to allow women access to full ordination.

Access to full ordination for women both improves women's status and signals women's greater inclusion in Buddhist institutions, yet some Theravāda nuns argue against *bhikṣuṇī* ordination on the grounds that it could work to keep women under the institutional thumb of the male elite. This line of argument assumes that institutional subordination is a Buddhist nun's only option, which is certainly not the case. Current efforts to restore the *bhikṣuṇī* order around the world enable Buddhist women to affirm their own legitimacy. This is especially significant for women who are fully qualified and prepared to take their place within Buddhist institutional lines of authority, often for the first time. Renewal and invigoration of the *bhikṣuṇī* order will help to usher in a welcome spiritual revolution that will benefit not only Buddhist nuns and laywomen, but also practicing Buddhists everywhere.

Denying access to religious education and blocking the full participation of women in religious structures might have gone unnoticed in earlier social contexts, when even institutions such as slavery were widely condoned by religious practitioners. But now it is relatively easy to gain knowledge about how race, gender, color, religion, and hegemony have coalesced over millennia to sanction discriminatory power over millions of marginalized people and to endorse their exploitation through sex trafficking, debt slavery, torture, sadistic gratification, and myriad other human rights abuses. Although these offenses are widely deplored as inhuman and criminal, they still rage covertly and in full view, often at the expense of women. In certain Buddhist societies, hiding in broad daylight and justified by the rhetoric of maintaining "the purity of the tradition," gender injustices continue to thrive. Bringing to light the stories of some of the unsung heroes among women who have challenged these clandestine codes and worked for social transformation, skillfully but without compromise, transports us closer to the enlightened society of the Buddha's vision.

Notes

1. Sakyadhita International Association of Buddhist Women, founded in 1987 in Bodhgaya, has initiated major changes for women in the world's Buddhist traditions, especially changing perceptions of women's potential for social and spiritual transformation. http://www.sakyadhita.org.

2. In recent decades, a number of studies about gender identity and power relations in Buddhism have appeared, including Alice Collette, "Buddhism and Gender: Reframing and Refocusing the Debate," *Journal of Feminist Studies in Religion* 22:2(2006): 55–84; Nancy Auer Falk, "The Case of the Vanishing Nuns: The Fruits of Ambivalence in Ancient Buddhism," in *Unspoken Worlds: Women's Religious Lives in Non-western Cultures*, ed. Nancy Auer Falk and Rita Gross (New York: Harper and Row, 1980); Rita M. Gross, *Buddhism after Patriarchy: A Feminist History, Analysis, and Reconstruction of Buddhism* (Albany: State University of New York Press, 1993); and Karma Lekshe Tsomo, "Buddhist Feminist Reflections," in *Buddhist Philosophy: Selected Primary Texts*, ed. Jay Garfield and William Edelglass (New York: Oxford University Press, 2009).

BUDDHIST WOMEN IN
SOUTH ASIAN TRADITIONS

"My Sister's Future Buddhahood"

A Jātaka of the Buddha's Lifetime as a Woman

Karen Derris

The Buddha affirmed that women could attain awakening as *arahants*, just as men could. However, according to orthodox Theravādin tradition, women could not become Buddhas in their female bodies. But what of the many lifetimes that comprise the *bodhisatta* (Sanskrit: *bodhisattva*) path leading to Buddhahood? Could a woman in her female body be a *bodhisatta*? Could a woman advance upon the *bodhisatta* path by attaining the conditions leading to Buddhahood? These questions are explored in a medieval Theravādin *jātaka* that tells the story of an eminent woman who was indeed a female *bodhisatta*. Not only was she on the *bodhisatta* path, but it had been foretold that, in a future lifetime, she would become a Buddha, the Buddha Gotama, the Buddha of our time.

This *jātaka* is found in several medieval Pāli texts.[1] The translation of the story in this chapter is the longest and most elaborate version of the story titled "The Princess Who Gave the White Mustard Oil" ("Princess *Jātaka*") from the *Sotaṭṭhakīmahānidāna* (*Sotaṭṭhakī*), a biography of the Buddha written (or, more accurately, compiled) by a monk named Culabuddhaghosa, of unknown date and provenance, but known throughout the Theravādin medieval world. While the *Sotaṭṭhakī* and the post-canonical *jātaka* stories it narrates were once very popular, these stories have been largely forgotten.

The *Sotaṭṭhakī* narrates the lives of Bodhisatta Gotama from the moment of the first thought for Buddhahood, some twenty incalculable time periods and 100,000 world eons before he attains that goal. Over these trillions of years, the *bodhisatta* meets hundreds of thousands of Buddhas during hundreds of thousands of lifetimes in which he makes the continuous aspiration for his own buddhahood.

In this *jātaka* lifetime, the Buddha was born as a princess and a half-sister of the Buddha of that time, Buddha Former Dīpankara. While we may look to the protagonist's social status as royalty or to her role as a generous donor to the *sangha* as evidence of her eminence, the even more compelling case is her sibling relationship to the living Buddha. And yet, as a woman of high birth, she is kept sequestered in her palace, and it is from this private locale that she negotiates her contact with the *sangha* and her brother, Buddha Former Dīpankara. Her significance as a character in the story is dramatically established by the revelation of who she will become in a far-distant future life—the Buddha Gotama.

Like other *jātakas*, this story narrates common themes of the *bodhisatta*'s development of the conditions of Buddhahood; however, it is remarkable and unique in describing the Buddha as a woman in a previous lifetime. To my knowledge, this is the only Theravādin narrative of the Bodhisatta Gotama's hundreds of human, animal, and celestial lifetimes that depicts a female lifetime of the Buddha. The story focuses upon one of the conditions for attaining Buddhahood: receiving a prediction of Buddhahood from a living Buddha. Revealed by a Buddha's omniscience, a prediction describes a certain future outcome. While this narrative remains technically within the bounds of the Pāli orthodox rules governing who may receive a prediction, notably that the recipient of a prediction of Buddhahood must be male, it pushes as hard as possible against this by introducing a new category of prediction, that is, a prediction of a prediction. The climactic moment of this story is when the Buddha of that time, Buddha Former Dīpankara, makes a prediction that his sister will, in a future lifetime, receive a prediction of Buddhahood from a future Buddha. Just as the traditional prediction announces a certain future outcome, the prediction of a prediction introduced by this narrative also has the same power. By predicting that this woman will receive a prediction in a future lifetime, the Buddha makes her future Buddhahood a known and celebrated certainty. While the orthodox gender rule governing who can receive a prediction is technically not broken, it is substantially subverted.

The "Princess *Jātaka*" as told in *Sotaṭṭhakī* actually includes two distinct versions of the story, one directly following the other. Both versions give the same basic outline of events occurring between three people: the princess, her brother, the Buddha Former Dīpankara, and a monk who aspires to become a Buddha with the same name and is thus called the Bodhisatta Later

Dīpankara. Both versions describe the princess's aspiration for Buddhahood and the foreknowledge of her Buddhahood in a distant future. The second version of the story—given as a quote from an unnamed author and source text—not only serves to authenticate the story given by the *Sotatthakī*'s narrator (a common commentarial device), but also adds important and distinct elaborations to the first telling of the narrative. As the reader will see, this second telling of the story gives an even more affirmative appraisal of the princess's virtues and her capacity to shape her own progress on the *bodhisatta* path. This second narrator places the female *bodhisatta* directly at the center of the story; it is at the time of her gift of oil to the elderly monk, who then offers it to the Buddha Former Dīpankara to make his own aspiration for Buddhahood, that she makes the same aspiration for herself. And while the princess in this second story dedicates her merit to being reborn in a male body in order to attain one of the necessary conditions that would enable her to receive a prediction of Buddhahood, it is in her female body that her brother, the Buddha Former Dīpankara, makes the certainty of her future Buddhahood known. While the necessity of a male birth is acknowledged, it becomes irrelevant from the perspective of a condition for knowing the future. By inventing an entirely new category of prediction, the narrative establishes that this woman is indeed a *bodhisatta* and capable of progress and attainment on that path.

As a biography of the Buddha, the *Sotatthakī* builds upon and extends the narrative frame of the *Buddhavamsa*, the canonical Pāli biography of Buddha Gotama. The *Buddhavamsa* narrates the biography of the Buddha, beginning with his famous lifetime as the ascetic Sumedha when he receives his first prediction of Buddhahood from the Buddha Dīpankara, that is, the Bodhisattva Later Dīpankara in his lifetime when he attains Buddhahood. Like other medieval biographies, the *Sotatthakī* extends the Buddha's biography into even more distant eons of previous lives. It claims to narrate the entirety of lives of the *bodhisatta* Gotama from the moment of his first thought for Buddhahood, some twenty incalculable time periods and 100,000 world eons before he attains that goal. Over these trillions of years, the *bodhisatta* meets hundreds of thousands of Buddhas during hundreds of thousands of lifetimes in which he makes the continuous aspiration for his own Buddhahood. In the *Sotatthakī*, the "Princess *Jātaka*" is the third of all the Buddha's previous lifetimes. This is an important point; by its placement as one of the very first *jātakas*, the events in the Bodhisatta's lifetime as the princess lay the foundation for the development of the *bodhisatta* path and, ultimately, Buddhahood. During the Bodhisatta's lifetime as the princess, she receives the prediction of a prediction, foretelling the lifetime when she will be born as the ascetic Sumedha, the traditional beginning of the Pāli Buddha biography as told in the *Buddhavamsa*.

The story of the Princess *Jātaka* skillfully interweaves its narrative with the *Buddhavamsa*, recasting both the beginning and end of the traditional biography. Buddha Gotama's previous lifetime as Sumedha not only is foretold in this story's prediction of a prediction, but all the events in that famous canonical story are shown to have been shaped by the *bodhisatta's* lifetime as a woman. The actions of the princess set in motion the *bodhisatta's* lifetime as Sumedha, the starting point of the canonical biography when he first received the prediction of Buddhahood from the Buddha Dīpankara. Likewise, this *jātaka* lays claim on Buddha Dīpankara as well, for it also tells of his previous lifetime when he was the *bodhisatta* Former Dīpankara who made his aspiration and received the prediction of his own Buddhahood from Buddha Former Dīpankara. He made his lamp offering to the Buddha on the occasion of receiving his own prediction, a gift signaled by his name, "the lamp maker." This offering of oil lamps was, in turn, enabled by the princess's gift of oil.

Significantly, the princess does not just make her own aspiration for Buddhahood; she defines her future identity as a Buddha, making the etymological claim that when she takes her final lifetime, her name will be Siddhartha, the prince who goes on to become the Buddha Gotama. Diverging from the traditional biography in which the name Siddhartha is given the meaning of "accomplished aim," in this medieval *jātaka* the princess explains that this will be her future name because of the *siddhatthaka tela* (white mustard oil) that she gave as an act of generosity to the monk. With this reenvisioned etymology, the princess's presence is inserted into the traditional biography of the Buddha, insisting that the *bodhisatta* Gotama's lifetime as a princess cannot be forgotten. Indeed, it was the princess's meritorious actions and aspirations that began the entire *bodhisatta* process that enabled Prince Siddhartha to accomplish his aim of Buddhahood in his final lifetime.

By reintroducing this story into present-day conversations, we not only deepen our awareness of the multiple historical Theravadin interpretations of sex and gender, but we potentially also gain useful resources to further the agendas of women who seek to define their roles and broaden their opportunities in Buddhist institutions and communities today. This is not to say that this medieval story offers a completely positive representation of the female sex; it is a complex and internally contradictory appraisal that both highlights the virtues of a particular woman and her spiritual capabilities and describes the limitations she faces because of her female gender. However, as I have argued elsewhere in my interpretation of this *jātaka*,[2] this story is valuable not only because of the arguments it makes for women's soteriological potential, but also because it reveals that the issues of gender politics and sexual identities, as determining factors for spiritual development, were debated and negotiated in early Theravadin literature. As the story below reveals, different views and strategies were voiced, sometimes side by side, in popular Pāli texts. This story provides a model, indigenous to the Theravāda tradition, of reworking and challenging traditional sources. In this instance, medieval writers—most reasonably assumed to be monastic men—challenged the gendered identity of the *bodhisatta* as being only male and altered the traditional vision of the Buddha's biography. Today, women can and should reclaim or write the stories that will enable them to live full lives as Buddhists in whatever way this is meaningfully determined by them in relation to their tradition.

Translation: "The Princess Who Gave a Gift of White Mustard Oil"[3]

Bodhisatta Gotama lived through many hundreds of lifetimes both as a god and as a human being. At one time, when one of his lives among the gods had come to an end, he fell from the world of the gods as a consequence of the bad actions committed in his previous lives and was reborn in this world, but into a royal family. He became the half-sister of the Buddha of that time, the fully enlightened Former Dīpankara.

As a *bodhisatta*, Former Dīpankara spent trillions of years (sixteen incalculable time periods and 100,000 world eons) perfecting the virtues of a Buddha. During a world eon called Sara, he was reborn into a royal family in the city of Campavati. When he was ten thousand years old, he saw the four signs: a sick man, an old man, a dead man, and a renunciant. Inspired, he made the great renunciation of his householder life and went forth into the world as a renunciant. He strove for enlightenment, and after one week of great striving he gained omniscience, attaining *nibbāna* (Sanskrit: *nirvāna*).

Then all the people, led by the king, served the monastic community, led by the Buddha. During this time, another *bodhisatta*, Later Dīpankara, was reborn into a wealthy Brahmin family. Seeing the dangers of lust, he abandoned his home and became ordained in Buddha Former Dīpankara's monastic community. He achieved high levels of spiritual attainment: the five supernatural powers and the eight states of meditative realization. One day, Later Dīpankara saw the splendor of the fully enlightened Buddha Former Dīpankara surrounded by his community. He thought, "Just as this fully enlightened Buddha Former Dīpankara shines surrounded by the community of disciples and causes these beings to be freed from the suffering of *samsāra*, so must I become a Buddha in a future time."

Taking his begging bowl, this monk, Bodhisatta Later Dīpankara, went everywhere throughout the city begging for oil. Returning with a great supply, he anointed the Blessed One's entire hut with four different kinds of scents. Throughout the night he made an offering of many hundreds of thousands of lamps for the Blessed One. The lamps blazed through the night. At daybreak, he approached the Blessed One in the midst of his community of monks. Laying his head at the soles of the Blessed One's feet, he made his aspiration: "O Sir, by the fruit of this offering of lamps, just as you have become a Buddha called Dīpankara, just as you cause all beings to be freed, so in a future time, I also will become a Buddha called Dīpankara for the sake of all beings."

The Buddha heard his aspiration and, after directing his perception towards the past and future, saw that Later Dīpankara's service as a *bodhisatta* was complete. Surrounded by the community of monks, the Buddha Former Dīpankara made a prediction about the Buddhahood of this monk, Bodhisatta Later Dīpankara, who had the aspiration to be a Buddha.

From that time on, this monk went about begging for oil and offered lamps to the Blessed One.

One day, he went through the entire city begging for oil but did not receive any. He then entered the royal palace.

At that moment, the princess (Bodhisatta Gotama), who was sitting on the uppermost level of the seven-storied palace, caught sight of the monk entering the palace at an unusual time for begging. She thought, "I think this monk who has entered the palace now has not come for his own gain. He has come for some other reason." She sent her servant woman to approach the monk and ask him his purpose. Hearing that he had come to request oil, she reported this to the princess.

The princess summoned the monk. She seated him on a throne, washed his feet, and saluted him. Taking a large golden cup, she filled it with white mustard oil shining the color of gold. She took the cup of golden-colored oil and placed it on top of her head. She aspired, "Just as my brother Former Dīpankara is a Buddha, for the sake of the benefit of all beings, so I also will be a Buddha in a future time for the sake of the benefit of all beings. In the time when I am a Buddha they will give me the name 'Siddhatthatela.' "[4] She took the cup of oil down from her head and put it into the monk's bowl. She said, "O Sir, here is the oil just as you wished. Offer it to my brother. When you finish the offering, tell this to my brother: 'O Sir! By this gift of shining white mustard oil your sister wishes to become a Buddha in the future.' " She made the aspiration: "In the time when I become a Buddha, my name will resemble this shining white mustard oil (Pāli: *siri siddhatthakatela*)." Having told her aspiration to the monk, she sent him forth.

The monk accepted her command, stood up from the throne, took his bowl, and returned to the monastery. On that day, he made the greatest offering of lamps he had ever made. He again made his own aspiration for Buddhahood according to his wish for his future. Then, saluting the Blessed One, he said: "Today, O Sir, I made this great offering of lamps with oil given by your sister, the princess; with this gift of white mustard oil your sister wishes to be a Buddha. She made her aspiration by saying, 'In the lifetime when I become a Buddha, let my name be like the name of this shining white mustard oil.' Will her aspiration succeed?"

Accepting the monk's question about his own sister's aspiration, the Teacher responded, "O monk! In this lifetime my sister is a woman, thus, she is not able to receive a prediction."

"Why is it, O Sir, that because she is a woman wishing for Buddhahood, she cannot receive a prediction?"

"O monk! The conditions for attaining Buddhahood are very difficult to create. If having fulfilled the perfections for 100,000 world eons, the person with a strong exertion and firm aspiration is able to combine the eight conditions, then they are then able to receive the prediction (of Buddhahood)."

"What are the conditions, O sir?"

The Teacher recited the conditions with this great verse:

Being human, endowed with the male mark,
Possessing the condition (of an *arahant*), seeing a Teacher
    (Buddha),
Renouncing, being endowed with qualities, service, and will:
From the combining the eight conditions,
The aspiration succeeds.

"The aspiration of a being who desires Buddhahood succeeds only for human beings. The aspiration of a *naga* or *garuda* or *yakkha* or *deva* will not succeed. Even though one is a human being, the aspiration succeeds only for males. The aspiration of a woman, or a eunuch, or a neuter, or one with both sex characteristics does not succeed. Even though one is a man in this existence, the aspiration succeeds only for an *arahant*. Not for others. Even though one is an *arahant*, the aspiration succeeds only for the one aspiring in the presence of a living Buddha. The aspiration does not succeed for one aspiring when a Buddha has attained final *nibbana*, or at a Buddha reliquary, or at the root of a *bodhi* tree. Even though one is aspiring in the presence of a Buddha, the aspiration succeeds only for a person who has gone forth, not for a householder. Even for the one who has gone forth, the aspiration succeeds only for the person endowed with the five supernatural powers and the eight attainments, not for one lacking the perfection of these qualities. Even though one is endowed with the perfected qualities, the aspiration succeeds only for one who has performed the service of abandoning his own life for the Buddha, not for others. Even though one is endowed with perfected qualification born from such service, the aspiration succeeds only for that one who has the great will, the great energy, the great effort, the great search for the sake of the conditions for making a Buddha, not for another."

"What compares to the great will for Buddhahood?"

"The will of this person is like a person who solely by the power of his own arms crosses the entire universe that had become a single body of water. The person with this will is able to swim across the watery universe."

"Or it is like a person who going solely by the power of his own feet tramples the entire universe covered with thorns and bamboo thickets. One with such a will attains Buddhahood."

"Or it is like a person who beats down spears covering the entire universe and treads upon swords strewn about; he is able to go across that entire universe. That one attains Buddhahood."

"Or it is like a person who with his own foot crushes the entire universe filled with glowing coals; he is able to go across that fiery universe. That one attains Buddhahood."

"I will go across by foot, having rescued a person who himself does not know even of these difficult things. The aspiration succeeds for one so endowed with the great will, the great energy, the great effort, the great search, not for another."

"Thus, O monk, she is not able to receive a prediction while she is in this lifetime as a woman."

The monk further questioned the Blessed One, "If it is so, how will your sister's wish to become a Buddha be attained?"

The Blessed One sent forth his perception of the past and saw she had aspired for Buddhahood in her three previous births.[5] Again, sending out his perception of the future, the Buddha saw that she would attain the conditions for becoming a Buddha. Having seen this, he said to the monk:

"O Monk! When the future becomes past in sixteen incalculable time periods and 100,000 world eons from now, just as I am now, then you will also be the Buddha called Dīpankara. At that time, you will predict the Buddhahood of my sister. She will receive the prediction face to face with you. "

Hearing this from the Teacher, the monk's mind was very pleased; saluting the Blessed One, he got up from his seat, circumambulated the Buddha, and departed.

In an earlier telling of this same story, it was said:[6]

In a past time, more than twenty incalculable time periods ago, in the Middle Country in the kingdom of Baranasi, the Blessed One called [Former] Dīpankara, the worthy one, the fully enlightened Buddha, arose in the world. In that time, our *bodhisatta* was reborn as a princess, Dīpankara's sister by a different mother.

She was like a celestial maiden: she possessed a golden complexion, great merit, and great resolve. She was endowed with a (beautiful) voice and with beauty. She waited on her mother and father, and she continuously served the Buddha. She lived in a seven-story palace adorned with the seven jewels; it was like a heavenly palace. Five hundred women who resembled divine maidens surrounded her; she played the five-fold music day and night; she was endowed with the six beauties.

What are the six beauties? Beautiful skin, beautiful flesh, beautiful nails, beautiful bones, beautiful voice, beautiful figure. What are the lips of beautiful skin like? The lips are a color like red wool. This is called beautiful skin. What is the tongue of beautiful flesh like? The tongue is like a *bimba* fruit and the color is like red wool. This is called the beautiful flesh. What are beautiful nails like? The nails are like a blood-red color, full, and the color is like the oleander flower. These are what are called beautiful nails. What are the teeth of beautiful bones like? The teeth are white as the color of a white lotus flower; the color is like a conch shell, like milk; they are like a row of diamonds placed in a crystal slab. These are what are called beautiful bones. The beauty of the voice is like the cuckoo's song. When the cuckoo birds are singing, if an animal heard that song while being chased by a tiger, it would think, "If that tiger wants to eat me, let him eat me; today, I will hear that song," and he would stay still. The tiger does not desire to eat that wild animal. The tiger thinks, "Today, I have heard that song." And both beings would remain motionless like posts. Hearing that sound, the beings in the water also remain motionless, and all the birds flying in the sky stop and are motionless. Thus, she is endowed with the song of a cuckoo. This is called the beautiful voice. She is a woman who has a beautiful figure like a round banyan tree. She is neither very tall, nor very short: the length of her arms is the length of her body. Thus, she is endowed with the six beauties.

The one with such beauty, who resembled a divine maiden, experienced much happiness. One day, she stood at an opened window. At that time, when Bodhisatta [Later] Dīpankara was already old, he ordained, in the presence of the Blessed One, the Former Dīpankara. He was an elderly monk. One day he entered the city and having gone about begging for oil, he made an oil lamp offering to the Buddha.

It is said that once, when he was going about in a city begging for oil, the princess saw him standing in the doorway. She summoned her servant girl and said, "Go quickly, salute this one, learn his wishes, and report back to me."

Acknowledging the command, the servant woman quickly descended the palace stairs, went into the presence of the Elder, saluted him, and asked: "O Sir, what do you wish here?"

He replied: "O Sister, I continuously offer oil lamps to the Buddha. For that reason I am going about begging for oil."

Learning his purpose, she returned to tell the princess.

Hearing this, joy filled the princess's heart-mind; her thoughts were clear and intent. She immediately had this thought: "All the former Buddhas and future Buddhas (*bodhisattas*) were ordinary beings in previous lives and they sought *bodhi*. Had they not abandoned the five abandonments, namely, wealth, children, wife, life, and limbs, (then) indeed they would not have become a Buddha. I am also one of those *bodhisattas* who has yet to become a Buddha. Not having given my wealth, not having protected my morality, when will I be freed?"

She took a golden bowl, filled it with oil, descended from the palace, went into the presence of the Elder, saluted him, and put [the oil] into his bowl. She then made her aspiration: "O sir, by the fruit of the gift of white mustard oil, having been a woman in this birth I will not again be a woman with all its defects. Wherever I am born next I will not again be as before. Becoming a man, let me be able to do the actions made by all the *bodhisattas*. By that merit in a future time just like my brother who is this Former Dīpankara, I, also having become a Buddha, will be called by the name "Siddhattha." Then she requested, "O sir! Tell my brother my aspiration. Having heard the success or non-success of my aspiration in the presence of the Blessed One, please come and tell me, O Sir!"

Hearing her aspiration, the monk agreed to her requests and went to the monastic residence. In the evening time the Blessed One entered the perfumed chamber where Bodhisatta Later Dīpankara worshipped the Buddha by burning white mustard oil lamps that he had made himself. By the light of the lamps, he saw the golden-colored body of the Blessed One; his heart filled with happiness. Wishing the aspiration, he said thus, "O Sir, by the fruit of this gift of lamps, just as you are called the Former Dīpankara, the best in the world together with the gods, the best of men, the golden-colored one, honored by gods and men, I too, in a future time, will be a Buddha called Dīpankara."

After he made his own aspiration, he told the Buddha about the aspiration made by the princess. "O Sir, your sister gave me this white mustard oil. She made an aspiration in this way: 'By the fruit of giving this oil, becoming a man, in a future time I will become a Buddha just like my brother.'" And so he recounted her aspiration. "Will the aspiration succeed?" he asked.

The Blessed One, having known the existence of success, sent forth a divine voice that said, "O monk! In a future time, like me, you will be a Buddha. At that time you will be called Dīpankara; my sister, by giving this oil and by other good actions, will become a man, in that time she will be an ascetic called Sumedha. At that time, when you enter the Ramma city, you will predict my sister's future Buddhahood in the midst (of the assembly) of gods and men."[7]

Hearing this, Later Dīpankara saluted Buddha Former Dīpankara and went to the princess and told her, and she felt great joy and mental ease arise within her. Performing good actions and protecting her morality, she passed from that life and was reborn in heaven.

She was reborn many times among men and gods as a *cakkavatti* king, as the Lord of the gods, as a very rich Brahmin, as a lord who gave many halls, and in the twenty incalculable time periods, having perfected the perfection of giving, and then became a Buddha.

Because of that, [this *jātaka*] is called "The Princess Who Gave White Mustard Oil."

Notes

1. Banjop Bannaruji, ed., *Sotaṭṭhakīmahānidāna* (Bangkok: Privately printed, 2526/1983); *Mahāsampindanidāna*, unpublished transcription by Venerable Nanavasa (I am grateful to Peter Skilling, who generously provided me with a copy of this transcription); S. P. Buddhadatta, ed., *Jinakālamālī* (London: Pali Text Society, 1962); *The Sheaf Garland of the Epochs of the Conqueror*, trans. N. A. Jayawickrama (London: Pali Text Society, 1968); P. S. Jaini, ed., *Paññasa*, 2 vols. (Oxford: Pali Text Society, 1981–1983), and P. S. Jaini, trans., *Apocryphal Birth Stories*, vol. 2 (London: Pali Text Society, 1986), pp. 396–402.

2. For my own historical study of the Princess Jātaka in the context of the Buddha biographical tradition and analysis of this narrative for present-day implications for Buddhist communities, please see Karen Derris, "When the Buddha Was a Woman: Reimagining Tradition in the Theravāda," *Journal of Feminist Studies in Religion* 24:2(2008): 29–44.

3. In this translation I prioritize a readable narrative over a translation that makes the underlying Pāli transparent.

4. By taking the name "Siddhatthakatela," the princess connects the name she will have as a Buddha to the mustard oil she gives to the monk, Bodhisatta Later Dīpankara; at the same time, a pun is being made with one of the names of the Buddha Gotama (whom the princess will become in the future), Siddhartha, often translated as the one who has completed his aim. This story gives another layer of meaning to the Buddha Gotama's name and suggests that when the Buddha has that name in his final lifetime, these events from his much earlier lifetime as the princess are to be recalled. Also at work in this story is the play on the name of the Buddha Dīpankara that is shared with the Former and Later Buddhas. It is significant because, although he is a Buddha unknown to the *Buddhavamsa*, the Buddha Former Dīpankara is the first Buddha to appear in the narratives of the *Sotaṭṭhakī* and thus is presented as the source of the name and the giver of the prediction to Buddha Later Dīpankara, the first Buddha to appear in the *Buddhavamsa* (but known in that text simply as Buddha Dīpankara). One possible translation of the name Dīpankara as the wick of a lamp also suggests (like the name Siddhatthakatela) that the names of Buddhas originate from their donative acts.

5. These three birth stories of a youth who carries his mother across an ocean, a king who loved elephants, and a brahmin who gave his life for a tigress are told earlier in the *Sotaṭṭhakī*.

6. This phrase begins the second section of the story that retells the narrative in a different form; it signifies a commentarial style of quoting another source in order

to strengthen and elaborate the version the narrator just completed. Like many other places in the *Sotatthaki*, the author of this quote is not given, nor is the source from which it comes named. Note that the narrative temporal frame shifts in this version of the story, placing the life of the princess in the past rather than in the narrative present that frames the first telling.

      7. In this prediction of the future prediction, the Buddha continues to reference the *bodhisatta* as a woman, using both a feminine pronoun and describing her as his sister in tension with the emphasis that she has become a man.

2

Two Generations of Eminent Nepalese Nuns

Punyawati Guruma

Nepal, the legendary land of the Buddha's birth, was also the birthplace of two generations of eminent Nepalese Buddhist nuns. Dhammachari Guruma, born in 1898 in Kathmandu, represents the first generation of exceptional nuns in Nepal. Dhammawati, born in 1934 in Patan, represents the second generation. Both of these exceptional nuns were highly intelligent and learned to read as young girls in their homes, even though education for girls was prohibited and there were no schools for girls at the time. Both of them took an interest in Buddhism at a young age and were pioneers of the Theravāda *sāsana* in the Newari community of the Kathmandu Valley. Both of these nuns faced significant obstacles in times when Buddhism was suppressed in Nepal, and both struggled to overcome these obstacles.

These two nuns, against all odds, gathered large followings of devoted Buddhist disciples. Both established *vihāras* (monasteries) for women at a time when almost no *vihāras* for nuns existed in Nepal. As practitioners, they were devoted to public education and social welfare, selflessly sharing their knowledge and helping the needy. Both of them were outspoken advocates of women's ability to practice the Dhamma and their potential to achieve the fruits of the path, including liberation. Both were detained by the authorities: Dhammachari by the Nepalese authorities for starting a literacy program and Dhammawati for traveling to Burma without proper travel documents. And, finally, both encountered opposition from the Nepalese *bhikkhu saṅgha* (community of monks).

For all their similarities, there were also many differences in the life experiences of these two nuns. Between the time of Dhammachari Guruma's birth in 1898 and Bhikkhunī Dhammawati's birth in 1934, vast changes had swept through Nepali society, politics, and religion, especially for women. For example, Dhammachari was obligated to marry, whereas Dhammawati was able to resist marriage. Dhammachari observed the eight precepts of an *anagārikā*, whereas Dhammawati took the unprecedented step of receiving the 348 precepts of a *bhikkhunī* (fully ordained nun).[1] Furthermore, Dhammachari received her Buddhist education privately in Nepal, whereas Dhammawati was able to receive fourteen years of systematic Buddhist education in Burma, culminating in the Dhammachariya degree.

Dhammachari was able to establish one *vihāra* for nuns in Nepal, which was a major breakthrough at the time. Although she had hundreds of lay disciples, she had no direct nun disciples. Comparatively, Dhammawati and her direct disciples have been able to establish ten *vihāra*s for women, as well as to educate and guide thousands of lay disciples and almost fifty direct nun disciples, twenty-eight of whom are *bhikkhunī*s. To understand the similarities and differences between these two remarkable women and the significant contributions they both have made to advance Buddhist education and promulgate the Dhamma, we need to learn more about their unique lives.

Dhammachari Guruma: Obstacles and Determination

Dhammachari Guruma was born Laxmi Nani in 1898 in Kathmandu.[2] From a young age, she took a keen interest in learning and, encouraged by her mother, she learned to read and write. When she was just ten years old, as custom imposed, she was given in marriage to Ketu Kaji Banu, the son of an herbalist. She gave birth to two children, but her son died after vomiting when he was just fifteen months old and her daughter died of fever when she was eight. Her husband also died, which also caused her great sorrow, because she was pregnant at the time. After so much worldly loss, Dhammachari turned to religious practice for consolation. She first learned the *nyungne* fasting practice of Avalokiteśvara[3] from Tibetan lamas and then the eight-precept practice (*astami brata pūjā*) from the Nepalese Vajrayāna tradition.[4]

In 1932, a Nepalese monk by the name of Bhikkhu Pragyananda Mahasthavir, who had been ordained in Kushinagar by Bhikkhu Chandramani Mahasthavir, returned to Nepal from India and began to propagate Theravāda Buddhism, emphasizing the five precepts and the basic teachings of the Buddha rather than ritual practices.[5] Dhammachari Guruma was attracted to the Theravāda teachings and learned as much as she could from this monk, but the next year he left for Burma. In 1934, Dhammacari traveled by foot to

Birganj, near the Indian border, with her friends Shilprabha, Sanunani, and Gyanadevi. There they met up with Bhikkhu Pragyananda Mahasthavir and together they traveled to Kushinagar in India, where Dhammacari received ordination as an eight-precept nun.[6]

When she returned to Nepal, because there were no separate *vihāras* for women at the time, Dhammachari stayed at Kimdol Bahal, a small monastery that housed monks, nuns, and widows. After laypeople began circulating baseless rumors alleging that the nuns were involved in improper relations with the monks, Dhammachari decided to buy a plot of land nearby to establish a *vihāra* just for nuns. Unfortunately, it transpired that a monk named Bhikkhu Dharmalok had also hoped to buy this very piece of land. This led to a disagreement between Dhammachari Guruma and Bhikkhu Dhammalok.[7] He criticized her for leading the recitation of the five precepts, for teaching the Dhamma, and for using an alms bowl for receiving alms, all activities that he deemed to be the purview of monks and inappropriate for a nun. Dhammachari Guruma was not intimidated by his accusations of wrongdoing, however, and challenged him to announce his allegations publicly. After this, her lay followers began to avoid Bhikkhu Dhammalok, and after some years he established a separate monastery for monks at Swayambhu called Anandakuti Vihar. The disagreement between Dhammachari Guruma and Bhikkhu Dhammalok was eventually resolved through the skillful mediation of a talented monk named Amritananda who later lived at Anadakuti Vihar and served as the secretary of the Buddhist Society of Nepal.[8]

Dhammachari Guruma also experienced tremendous obstacles in the form of political repression.[9] In the 1940s, the Rana oligarchy became suspicious of all public gatherings and tried to get Buddhist monastics to sign documents that forbade teaching, performing *pūjās*, and giving ordinations, but the monastics refused to sign. At that point, many *bhikkhus* left the Kathmandu Valley and went to India to avoid arrest. The nuns were also exiled from the Kathmandu Valley but were allowed to stay in Trisuli, to the northwest of Kathmandu.

After being questioned by the authorities, Dhammachari Guruma was eventually permitted to stay in Kathmandu. Despite the harassment and the other difficulties that the nuns faced in getting food and requisites, she was determined and tireless in her efforts to spread Buddhism in Nepal. Over the objections of the *bhikkhus*, as the number of nuns continued to increase, Dhammachari Guruma founded a new monastery for them called Nirvanmurti Vihar near Kimdol Vihar in 1968. Although she lived until the age of seventy-nine, she did not have young nun disciples to continue her legacy. Her successor, Birati Guruma, died just six years later, after which conditions at the *vihāra* slowly deteriorated. One of Dhammachari Guruma's grandnephews filed a petition in the court claiming his right to the property, and, although the case has been taken as far as the Nepalese Supreme Court, it still remains unresolved. In 2005, Kimdol Vihar came under the direction of two nuns, Bhikkhunī Dhamma Vijaya and Molini Guruma, both of whom hold PhDs in Buddhist studies.

Bhikkhunī Dhammawati: "Beloved Daughter"

Dhammawati was born Ganesh Kumari in 1934 in Patan into a family descended from the Sakya clan into which Buddha Sakyamuni was born. Like Dhammachari Guruma, she grew up during a time when the Rana regime forbade women to study. Despite the then-popular belief that women who did study would become witches, she was encouraged by her mother to learn Pāli from Bhikkhu Buddhaghosa at Sumangal Vihara.

As a girl of fourteen and with her mother's blessing, Dhammawati ran away from home to avoid marriage and become a nun. While her father was out one day, she bade her mother a tearful farewell and traveled by foot across the mountains to India together with a monk named Bhikkhu Sugandah from the local temple. In Kushinagara, the place where the Buddha breathed his last, she met Bhikkhu Chandramani, a Burmese monk who had settled there decades before, and chopped off her lustrous long braids with a kitchen knife. In 1950, with Bhikkhu Dhammawudha as her guide, she traveled by foot to Burma. On the way, she experienced many difficulties, which are described in her biography.[10] One of her most exciting exploits was trekking through the jungles of Assam with a party of elephant traders.

When Dhammawati finally arrived in Rangoon, she was detained by the police for two days because she had no passport or visa, documents it would have been impossible for her to get without permission from her father. Eventually, the Burmese authorities, who were pious Buddhists, were so impressed by her striking devotion to the Dhamma that they released her to the care of U Salwin, a leading accountant. While she was living with U Salwin's family, she quickly learned Burmese and began searching for a nunnery.

In 1952, she began her Dhamma studies at Khemarama Nuns' Study Center under the guidance of a nun called Pannyachari. Although she initially experienced some financial difficulties, she managed to earn scholarships as a result of her keen intelligence and diligence. She sailed through even the most difficult of exams, eventually earning the highest degree of Dhammachariya based on exams in the *vinaya*, *sutta*s, and *abhidhamma*. She was awarded the title Sasanadhaja Dhammachariya in Rangoon in 1962.[11]

In 1963, Dhammawati returned to Nepal and began to teach Buddhism to large gatherings of devotees. In 1965, she established Dharmakirti Vihar at Shreegha, Naghal Tole, in Kathmandu. She dedicated herself to teaching Dhamma, publishing more than fifty books on Buddhism in Newari and

Nepalese. In addition, she undertook various social service projects, one of which was establishing a free medical clinic for the public in Kathmandu. She was assisted in her work by Gunawati ("Excellent Conduct") Guruma, a Burmese nun who is recognized for her kindness and patience in helping others, and Ratnamanjari ("Jewel of Wisdom") Guruma, a nun from Tanchin who is skilled in meditation and adept at teaching others. In 1995, the government of Myanmar awarded her the title Aggamahaganthanwachaka Pandit. Dhammawati continues to be highly regarded to the present day, especially by Theravāda Buddhists in Nepal, for her knowledge and for her kind and principled leadership.

Dhammawati has been highly successful in gathering large groups of devoted followers, both nuns and laypeople, and has passed on her lineage to future generations through her disciples. Her first disciples were Bhikkhunī Dhammadina and Kamala Guruma. With her disciples, she established many *vihāras* for nuns, such as Dharmakirti Vihara and Kimdol Vihara. She participated in many international conferences. She empowered her disciples to establish their own monasteries, for example, Bhikkhunī Anoja at Sulaksanakirti Vihar in Chobahal, Bhikkhunī Dhamma Vijaya and Molini Guruma at Nirvanamurti Vihar in Kimdol, Bhikkhunī Kusuma at Bassundara Vihar, Bhikkhunī Sujata and Kamesi Guruma at Gautami Bhikkhunī Vihar in Lumbini, Bhikkhunī Kusum at Vishwashanti Dharmakirti Vihar in Basundhara, Bhikkhunī Kesawati at Nagadesa Buddha Vihara in Nagadesa, and Kamala Guruma at Padmakirti Vihar. Four of her disciples—Bhikkhunīs Daanwati, Tyaagwati, Metawati, and myself—have been encouraged to establish Sakyamunikirti Vihar at Satyapur, Satungal, near Kathmandu. Bhikkhunī Dhammawati laid the cornerstone for the monastery foundation in 2009.

Dhammawati was very unusual among Nepalese nuns of her time, for she traveled abroad and also took an active role in international Buddhist circles.[12] She attended numerous international conferences in Cambodia, India, Japan, Laos, Thailand, and other countries. She was a pioneer in taking *bhikkhunī* ordination against the objections of the Nepalese *bhikkhu saṅgha*. In 1988, she traveled to Hsi Lai Temple in Hacienda Heights, California, along with three of her disciples, and received the full *bhikkhunī* ordination in the Chinese Dharmagupta lineage, becoming the first Nepalese *bhikkhunī* in recent history.[13] Dhammawati sent a number of her disciples to receive an education in Nepal or abroad to places such as Burma, China, India, Sri Lanka, Taiwan, and Thailand. In 2000, she was the host and co-coordinator of the 6th Sakyadhita International Conference on Buddhist Women, held in Lumbini, the birthplace of the Buddha. Just in time for the occasion, she constructed a new Buddha hall at Gautami Bhikkhunī Vihar in Lumbini that could hold all three hundred participants.

In one way, Dhammachari Guruma set the stage for Bhikkhunī Dhammawati's achievements by being the first to courageously face and eventually overcome the many obstacles that Buddhists, and especially nuns, faced during her generation. However, Bhikkhunī Dhammawati was able to surpass Dhammachari's accomplishments in many ways, particularly because she was fortunate enough to have been born at a time when women had greater opportunities for education. These educational opportunities enabled her to provide teachings to a much wider audience and to develop writing skills to publish her many Buddhist books, as well as to create a curriculum for Dhamma classes for children, young people, and adults.[14] Through her teaching activities, she gathered a large number of students and devoted disciples who were financially able to sponsor her Buddhist activities. With the support of these students and disciples, Dhammawati has inspired many young women to become nuns and has established many *vihāra*s throughout the Kathmandu Valley and beyond.

Bhikkhunī Dhammawati has demonstrated outstanding leadership abilities that have set her apart from the earlier generations of nuns in Nepal. She has taken the initiative to travel internationally, and in the process of learning about different cultures and ideas she has become encouraged to bring her invaluable experience home to the nuns of Nepal. Her keen intellect, scholarship, and good sense of humor have earned her respect from people far beyond the ethnic Newar Buddhist community. Every year on her birthday, she assembles more than two hundred nuns and monks to recite the *abhidhamma*, an event that is attended by countless lay adherents. Her tireless effort to spread the Dhamma in Nepal continues to this day. Because of her exemplary leadership and encouragement, a wide circle of students, both lay and ordained, has created a harmonious Dhamma community that is certain to continue her legacy for generations to come.

Notes

1. The ordination that Bhikkhunī Dhammawati attended at Hsi Lai Temple was conducted according to the Dharmagupta school of *vinaya*, which is prevalent in the Chinese, Korean, and Vietnamese traditions. There are 348 *bhikkhunī* precepts in the *prātimokṣa* of the Dharmagupta school, 311 in the Theravāda school, and 365 in the Mūlasarvāstivāda school. These numbers include seven methods of resolving disputes, which, technically speaking, are not precepts.

2. Lochantara Tuladhar, *Dharmacari Guruma: Kindobahaanisen Nirwanmrtitakka* (in Newari) (Kimdol, Swayambhu: Nirvanmurti Vihar, 2007), p. 65.

3. For further information about *nyung ne* (*smyung gnas*) fasting ritual, see Ivette Vargas-O'Bryan, "The Life of dGe slong ma dPal mo: The Experiences of a Leper, Founder of a Fasting Ritual, and Transmitter of Buddhist Teachings on Suffering and Renunciation in Tibetan Religious History," *Journal for the International Association of Buddhist Studies* 24:2(2001): 157–85.

4. At this time, Buddhist practice was severely restricted by the Hindu Rana rulers. Therefore, Nepalese Buddhists were forced to disguise their Buddhist practices to make them appear similar to Hindu practices. See Sarah LeVine and David N. Gellner, *Rebuilding Buddhism: The Theravada Movement in Twentieth Century Nepal* (Cambridge: Harvard University Press, 2005), especially Chapter 2.

5. Tuladhar, *Dharmacari Guruma*, p. 70. In this publication, Dhammachari is mistakenly identified as a *bhikkhunī*, a term that was used for eight-precept nuns at the time.

6. Ibid.

7. Ibid., pp. 71–72.

8. Bhikkhu Chandramani was the president of the Buddhist Society of Nepal, but he lived at Kushinagar and rarely came to Kathmandu. As a result, Bhikkhu Amritananda took the leadership and dominated the Nepalese *bhikkhu saṅgha* until his death in 1990. I am grateful to Sarah LeVine for this clarification.

9. Ibid., pp. 73–75. The Nepalese government's oppression of Buddhism is also described in LeVine and Gellner, *Rebuilding Buddhism*.

10. Re We Thon, *Tami Chet* (Beloved Daughter) (1963). The Newari edition, *Yamha Mhyaaya*, was translated by Bhikkhu Nyanapunnika; the Nepali edition, *Snehi Chhori*, was translated by Mot Kaji Shakya.

11. Soviet Ratna Tuladhar and Reena Tuladhar, *Dhamma and Dharmmawati* (Dharmakirti Buddhist Study Circle, Dharmakirti Vihar, 1999), p. 35.

12. A narrative account of an English scholar's pilgrimage with Bhikkhunī Dhammawati is found in Sarah LeVine, *The Saint of Kathmandu and Other Tales of the Sacred in Distant Lands* (Boston: Beacon Press, 2008), pp. 129–65.

13. For the story of Bhikkhunī Dhammawati's leadership in the Buddhist modernist movement in Nepal, particularly her role in inspiring generations of women to become Buddhist nuns, see Sarah LeVine, "At the Cutting Edge: Theravāda Nuns in the Kathmandu Valley," in Karma Lekshe Tsomo, *Innovative Buddhist Women: Swimming Against the Stream* (Surrey, UK: Curzon Press, 2000), pp. 13–29.

14. More detailed descriptions of Bhikkhunī Dhammawati's educational endeavors are included in Sarah LeVine, "Dharma Educations for Women in the Theravāda Buddhist Community of Nepal," in *Buddhist Women and Social Justice: Ideals, Challenges, and Achievements*, ed. Karma Lekshe Tsomo (Albany: State University of New York Press, 2004), pp. 137–54.

BUDDHIST WOMEN IN
SOUTHEAST ASIAN TRADITIONS

3

Brave Daughters of the Buddha

The Feminisms of the Burmese Buddhist Nuns

Cristina Bonnet-Acosta

"Usually, the nuns in this country have to accept anything that the monks do or say, but I don't accept."

—Sayalay Dipankara

"Nuns are trying hard to reach a certain level and a certain status. All the nuns have many problems, the same problems, so we must insist, with patience."

—Reverend Saccavadi

Burmese Buddhists nuns are now acting in a variety of ways to improve the conditions of their lives.[1] Scholarship about Burmese nuns has tended to characterize them as passive victims of a male patriarchy or as nonconfrontational ameliorants of their status in Burmese society. The studies that portray the nuns as compliant have focused on the injustices inflicted on these women by the monks and the lay community. These studies have offered insightful information regarding the social conditions of the nuns but have neglected to explore the types of agency retained by them.[2] The studies that portray Burmese nuns as practitioners have described the socioreligious status of

Burmese nuns, with particular attention paid to the daily actions that the
nuns undertake to improve their status within the established monastic system without confronting it or trying to change it.³ And these studies, because
they offer a critical reflection of the context within which the nuns actually
live, more successfully portray Burmese nuns as agents of their own lives. My
research has benefited enormously from all of these studies; however, I engage
critically with these portrayals, as they have overlooked the heterogeneity
within the community of nuns, and they do not adequately open a space
to discuss the methods of confrontation and resistance that some groups of
Burmese nuns have developed in order to improve their situation. The picture
I present in this chapter remains fragmented and partial; however, I argue
that this additional perspective can be valuable for a clearer understanding
of the Burmese nuns' situation and the kinds of struggles in which they are
presently engaged.

My research took place in Sri Lanka and Burma from January to July
2006, with follow-up visits in 2007. During the course of this fieldwork, I
came across a wide variety of feminist practices that had been produced
and deployed by these nuns. For the purpose of this chapter, I focus my
observations and analysis on two of the most established movements: first,
the group of nuns who strive to attain full ordination and recognition of this
status in the official Burmese religious institutions; and second, the endeavors
and practices of perhaps the most internationally recognized nun in Burma,
Sayalay Dipankara, both to improve her opportunities as a female monastic
and to gradually extend those possibilities to other nuns.

Burmese Nuns and Transnational Feminist Studies

Literature about Buddhist nuns has proliferated in the last several years. The
controversies over the reinstatement of full ordination have formed the subject
of many articles, books, and conferences around the world.⁴ Burma is home
to the largest number of nuns in any Theravāda Buddhist country and has
one of the highest concentrations of female monastics in any given country.⁵
Yet information about this community is hard to find because of the military
regime that has been ruling Burma since 1962, which has made it very difficult
for outsiders to undertake research there. I therefore include a brief account of
the general situation of the Burmese nuns as well as some basic information
about the history and context of the restrictions they are confronting before
I move on to engage with and describe their feminist strategies.

A recurrent theme during the process of completing this research has
been the issue of applying the Western term "feminism" to the movements
of the nuns who are not associated with any official "feminist organization."

Although I appreciate this valid concern, I have chosen to continue using the term. I agree with Inderpal Grewal and Caren Kaplan when they write, "The issue of who counts as a feminist is much less important than creating coalitions based on the practices that different women use in various locations to counter the scattered hegemonies that affect their lives."[6] The term "feminism" not only allows for an engagement with wider discussions and analyses about counter-hegemonic movements around the world, but it also offers the chance to appreciate the methods of resistance developed by these nuns in the broader context of various practices that share similar concerns and agendas. A broad context ultimately offers a higher possibility of solidarity and collaboration among groups with common interests, which is likely to contribute to their success in improving their conditions.

From the outset, this project has benefited from the theoretical and political approaches offered under the rubric of "transnational feminist theories." Chandra Talpade Mohanty, one of the leading proponents of transnational feminism, describes the project as follows: "Third World feminism" must address itself to two simultaneous projects: the internal critique of hegemonic "Western" feminism and the formulation of autonomous feminist concerns and strategies that are geographically, historically, and culturally grounded. The first project is one of deconstructing and dismantling ideas that disenfranchise women; the second is one of building and constructing empowerment for women. While these projects appear to be contradictory, they must be addressed simultaneously if they are to avoid the risk of marginalization or ghettoization from both mainstream and Western feminist discourses.[7] While these forms of feminism develop strategies to improve the conditions of women in different parts of the world, they do so without resorting to an imitation of the Western ideals for women, and, as Mohanty explains, they are also often involved in critical examinations of the Eurocentric and colonial legacies that Western feminism carries with it.

Another relevant point made by these women from diverse cultures is that the political contestations and demands for transformation that arise in the Third World are not imitations of Western movements, because they take place within different contexts that reflect local struggles and circumstances. In the words of Uma Narayan:

> Feminist movements in various parts of the world develop when historical and political circumstances encourage public recognition that many of the norms, institutions, and traditions that structure women's personal and social lives, as well as the impact of new developments and social change, are detrimental to women's well being, and enable political contestations in which the status quo is criticized and alternatives envisioned.[8]

These discussions about women's movements outside Western feminism are extremely important for our topic because the nuns in Burma to whom I refer in this chapter are involved in issues and struggles that have to do mainly with their gender and with the disadvantages that their womanhood poses in their society. Yet these are women who are neither associated with any official feminist organization nor interested in the egalitarian ideals of mainstream liberal feminism. When I asked about what was most important for these nuns in their desire for change, they all agreed that they aim for the appropriate conditions to develop spiritually. In the words of Sayalay Dipankara: "My goal is to be an *arahant*, and women can also be *arahant*."[9] Similarly, Bhikkhunī Sucinti said to me: "To be able to practice to become an *arahant* is enough for me; I don't care about quarreling, or fighting. I just want the appropriate conditions to practice to become an *arahant*."

As we shall see below, the current conditions of nuns in Burma often are not favorable enough to allow them time for study, prayer, and meditation—the different ways in which one is expected to practice to become an *arahant*. This is particularly true for many nuns, whose daily routine consists of cooking, cleaning, and looking after the monks. Apart from these physical and concrete impediments, nuns are regularly encouraged by the monks to pray so that they can become men in their future existences, and, as Sayalay Dipankara and Bhikkhunī Saccavadi explained to me, this creates a psychological feeling of inferiority in many of the nuns, who feel that the highest goals of their religion are not available to them.

Traditional liberal feminism has often been involved in struggling to achieve the equal rights that men have in Western society. This ideal of egalitarianism is sometimes portrayed as a universal principle but is in fact a product of the European Enlightenment.[10] The benefit of relying on understandings of feminism that do not advocate the same Eurocentric ideals to discuss the strategies of these Burmese nuns is that it allows us to see their strategies more closely in their own contexts and in relation to their interests rather than as an inferior form of feminism that has not yet realized the egalitarian ideal. Otherwise, we risk perpetuating a way of representation that describes the *other* only in comparison to an idealized *self* and, more specifically, one that classifies Asia only in relation to the West. The nuns in this chapter are concerned with autonomy, independence, and respect, but not necessarily with sameness. These nuns have clearly expressed that their most urgent task is to demand the appropriate conditions to enable them to develop spiritually. This does not always involve a request for conditions equal to or even similar to those that the monks experience. An account that overlooks the different ways of engaging with variations among types of inequalities not only would fail to notice the subtleties of the nuns' experience, but also would reinforce the colonial tendency toward female subjugation and the old-fashioned binary oppositions of "us–them" and "self–other."

Before we turn to the specific strategies and ways of contestation that have been deployed by various Buddhist nuns, we need to first briefly examine the general status and conditions of nuns in present-day Burma.

Historical Background and Present Situation

Most Burmese would probably agree that, in the secular life, Burmese women have enjoyed more benefits and rights than women in many other countries. Each Burmese I asked about the status of women in Burma was greatly pleased to let me know about the progressive rights that women have enjoyed in their country throughout history. In the words of Konmari, a Burmese student in exile, "When comparing the situation of Burmese women with that of women from other countries in Asia, I am always proud with the knowledge that Burmese women have been accorded higher status."[11] Similarly, the Moustache Brothers, brave comedians and political activists from Mandalay, speak with a tone of irony in their nightly shows to inform the public about the privileged status of women in Burma: "I don't like the Burmese system for women, is *very* bad. . . . I prefer the Hindu system. If I die, my wife goes to the funeral pyre. . . . Yes! Very good! Then, I could die in peace. But here, here no, if I die, my wife gets all the money, she can marry again, do whatever she likes. . . . I don't like it!"[12] The American anthropologist Melford Spiro takes the point even further when he says: "Burmese women probably occupy a higher social status than any other women in Asia. Indeed, until the dramatic changes in the status of women in the West in the past fifty years, Burmese women enjoyed a degree of economic, legal, and social equality that arguably was unsurpassable either in Asia, or in Europe and North America."[13] And one should not forget that one of the most beloved political figures of contemporary Burma is the revered Aung San Suu Kyi, "The Lady" (as she is referred to in Burma), who has set a propitious example of womanhood not only in her country but also around the world.

Yet this view about the superior status of Burmese women shares the stage with a conflicting view that women are spiritually inferior to men. As a woman in Burma, it is common to be banned access to sacred places because of the "impurity" of the female body. This includes not being able to visit one of the most sacred pilgrimage sites in the country, the top of the Shwedagon Pagoda. Apart from that, it is said in Burma that men are endowed with *hpoung*, an innate glory or charisma that only men possess.

This *hpoung* means that men are superior to women in aspects of the intellect and the spirit.[14]

When I asked various Burmese men and women (including several nuns), they all responded by saying that in the Buddhist sphere, men have higher status than women, but that in secular life, women and men enjoy virtual equality. The Burmese author Mi Mi Khaing explains this by recalling that because the Buddha was a man, and because he was able to achieve the highest spiritual goal of enlightenment, only a man can hope to achieve a similar aim.[15] Whatever the reason might be, women do appear to be seen as ostensibly inferior to men in aspects of spiritual development.

In the case of female Burmese monastics, the situation becomes more interesting because they are not recognized as nuns but rather as pious laywomen. Although they renounce the householder's life and immerse themselves in a religious routine, these nuns are not officially considered to be "inside" the religion, but rather only "related" to it.[16] In fact, the term "nun" is only an English rendering of the Burmese term *thilashin,* the denomination used in Burma. *Thila* is a derivation from the Pāli term *sīla,* which means morality and right conduct. In Buddhism, *sīla* is also used to refer to the precepts that are the foundation of the Buddhist life. *Shin* means "one who possesses or holds." Therefore, *thilashin* literally means "one who holds the precepts" or the *sīla.*

This designation is significant because it differentiates the nuns from their male counterparts, who are called *bhikkhus,* which means "mendicant" or "almsman." While *bhikkhus* are seen as exemplary holders of the ideals of the traditional Buddhist monastic life, *thilashins* are only considered to uphold a minimum aspect of this ideal, which consists of eight or ten rules of conduct.[17]

The term *thilashin* itself is a relatively recent Burmese word. The Burmese scholar and monk Rawe Htun explains that the first recorded use of the term *thilashin* appears in the *Ratana Kyemon Court Drama* (ca. 1752–1885 during the Konbaung period).[18] Previous to this, the story goes a long way back in history to the time of the Buddha (ca. 2500 BC). The Buddhist scriptures state that Mahāpajāpatī, the Buddha's aunt and stepmother, asked the Buddha to accept her and her companions as nuns. After some hesitation, he agreed that women could be part of the monastic community because they too had the capacity to become fully enlightened.[19] These nuns were called *bhikkhunīs.* Texts also state that at the time of the Emperor Ashoka of India (273–232 BC), two monks, Sona and Uttara, were sent to Suvannabhūmi ("the golden land," which Burmese identify with today's Lower Burma) to spread the teachings of the Buddha. It is said that 3,500 men and 1,500 women entered the Buddhist order at that time.[20] Subsequently, the events are somewhat blurred. During the Pyu period (ca. 1000 BC–832 CE), there are Chinese sources that refer to *bhikkhunīs* in Burma. The renowned scholar of Burma, Gordon H. Luce, has translated and quoted from these texts: "When they come to the age of seven, both boys and girls drop their hair and stop in the monastery where they take refuge in the Saṅgha. On reaching the age of twenty, if they have not awaked to the principles of the Buddha, they let their hair grow again and become ordinary townsfolk."[21]

This quote shows that women at that time could go forth and remain in the monastic life if they so desired, suggesting that full ordination was possible. Later on, during the Pagan period of the eleventh to the thirteenth centuries, there are inscriptions that refer to female religious mendicants. According to Pe Maung Thin and Than Thun, they were fully ordained *bhikkhunīs*.[22] It is not clear how this order of nuns died out; Pagan was sacked by the Mongol emperor of China in 1298 CE, and after this, Burma was in a state of political turmoil for several centuries. It is known that there were very influential *thilashins* during the reign of King Mindon (1825–1878) and that their lineage has survived until the present day.[23] Textual Theravādin tradition of the Vinaya argues that the order of *bhikkhunīs* cannot be reinstated once the lineage has been broken, as was the case in Burma's history.

Because they are not considered fully ordained *bhikkhunīs*, *thilashins* are given considerably less respect, veneration, and support than monks. *Thilashins* always sit behind the monks, and monks are the only ones allowed to conduct the ceremonies and to preach. As Bhikkhu Nagasena, a Theravādin monk who studied in Burma for several years, explained: "Monks are more favored and come first when both nuns and monks come together in a particular social and religious event." Karma Lekshe Tsomo has also noticed the difference in the conditions between *thilashins* and monks:

> . . . [*Thilashins*] who do not receive support from family members must go to neighboring villages for alms twice a week or travel long distances twice a year to their home villages to collect donations of rice, which they carry in huge bundles on their heads. Most telling of all, when monetary donations are distributed, nuns generally receive only a fraction of what the monks are offered. . . .[24]

In the official religious organization of Burma, the Ministry of Religious Affairs is ruled by the State Sangha Maha Nayaka Council of Myanmar, which consists of approximately forty-seven monks who have the legal right to decide and foresee the regulations of the monastic community. Therefore, the nuns have very little say in the decisions made for the religion in general. Nevertheless, their services are crucial to the preservation of the community of monks. Nuns are often in charge of cooking, cleaning, and managing the monasteries where monks live. In addition, one of the rules that monks have to follow is that of not touching money. Therefore, it is often the duty of the nuns to administer the money on behalf of the monks. While the monks depend on the nuns for their conservation, they also undermine the image of the nuns by demeaning them for having to handle the money, an activity seen as worldly and polluting.[25]

I have been told by several Burmese nuns that monks often give sermons to the nuns in which they encourage them to pray to become men in their next lives so that they can then attain a higher level of spirituality that is not available for them as women. In the course of my fieldwork, two nuns, citing this as the reason, acknowledged that they pray to become men in their future lives.[26]

With these often discouraging conditions, it is outstanding that many *thilashins* persevere in their determination to live a dedicated Buddhist monastic life. It is important to remember that these women do not necessarily experience these differences as oppressive. Many of them are also endowed with immense reverence for the male community of monks. Hiroko Kawanami, an anthropologist who has been working with the community of Burmese nuns for almost twenty years, points out that their identity is often closely linked to the services they provide to the monks.[27]

From within the complex web of relationships between the institutionalized views about nuns and the actual lives of the nuns themselves, as well as between the apparently oppressive conditions in which they dwell and their compliance with it, different views on the topic can be heard that voice some of the ways that nuns cope with the religious institutions to which they belong. Several studies, most notably by Kawanami, address the kinds of power to which nuns are entitled and how they make use of their daily conditions to attain their desired ends.[28] Throughout her work, Kawanami emphasizes the ways in which the Burmese nuns exert power and achieve their ends within the religious community while supporting and accepting the general monastic institutions.[29] Her work has shed much light on the social status of Burmese nuns, their daily routines, their aspirations, and many other aspects of their lives. However, the nuns who have found that their interests and aims cannot be met within the Burmese monastic institutions and have dared to confront the establishments to try and induce transformation and reform have not yet found a voice in the work of Kawanami or in any other concise study, as far as I know. While most of the nuns have understandably remained submissive within a political environment that harshly punishes dissent toward the establishment, there are others who have bravely challenged its regulations and demanded better conditions to grow spiritually. It is therefore to these nuns and their practices that the rest of this chapter is devoted.

Toward a Burmese *Bhikkhunī* Lineage:
Burmese Nuns in Sri Lanka

Historians and archaeologists hold that the official order of female nuns, or *bhikkhunīs*, disappeared from Burma sometime after the thirteenth century. In Sri Lanka, the *bhikkhunī saṅgha*, or community of nuns, appears to have thrived until the eleventh century.[30] In the fifth century, the lineage of *bhikkhunīs* was taken from Sri Lanka to China and then to Korea and Vietnam. To this day, the order of fully ordained nuns has continued in these countries. In 1996, an effort was started among the Sri Lankan Theravāda nuns to reestablish the order of *bhikkhunīs* to their tradition by relying on the continuing lineages from China, Korea, Taiwan, and Vietnam. In 1998, the first international ordination ceremony took place in Bodhgaya with the support of important Buddhist leaders such as His Holiness the Dalai Lama, Thich Nhat Hanh, and others. Since then, the option of full ordination is offered yearly to Theravāda nuns in Sri Lanka.

According to generally accepted lines of interpretation of the traditional Theravāda Buddhist scriptures, the order of nuns can be initiated only after certain conditions have been met. One of these conditions is that there should be at least five *bhikkhunīs* to ordain the aspiring novice.[31] Because the order of Theravāda nuns has gradually disappeared from all countries, aspiring Theravāda nuns are currently relying on Mahāyāna nuns, whose lineage started from the Sri Lankan nuns. Because Mahāyāna Buddhism is deemed inauthentic and often inferior by most Theravāda Buddhists, this ordination process has been controversial and unacceptable to most monks in Sri Lanka, Thailand, and Burma. Nevertheless, several fully ordained nuns have established nunneries in Sri Lanka and Thailand and are able to follow their religious practices with a relatively low degree of opposition.[32] In Burma, however, a similar movement has not yet started, and the reasons for this are an interesting topic for our discussion.

In her essay "Buddhist Nuns in Transition: The Case of Burmese Thilá-Shin," Kawanami gives an insightful overview of the current status of the nuns in Burma. She argues that the standards of the Buddhist education for nuns are rising and that nuns are increasingly being recognized for their educational achievements. She also sees the contemporary trend for young urban middle-class girls in Burma to become temporary nuns during their vacations as a sign that there is a "new kind of social appreciation and changing attitudes towards Buddhist nuns."[33]

After reviewing the movement for reestablishing the full ordination of nuns in Theravāda countries, she claims that such attempts would not help the nuns in Burma because these ordinations are seen as springing from the Mahāyāna school, which is denigrated in Burma. She also concludes,

"Since their delicate religious position rests entirely in complying with the existent authority of the *Bhikkhu Saṅgha* it is unforeseeable that the Buddhist nuns themselves would be particularly instrumental in the restoration of the *Bhikkhunī Saṅgha*. . . ."[34] Kawanami believes that the identity of the nuns is closely related to the services they provide to the monks, and that "therefore, equality and independence may not be an attractive proposition for them, but rather threatening and confusing to their basic sense of religious identity."[35]

Kawanami is critically attentive to not assuming that the interests of Western Buddhist women in gaining equal religious status are necessarily the same as the interests of the Burmese nuns. However, Kawanami's arguments assume one single identity in the wide and heterogeneous community of Burmese nuns. Furthermore, this "religious identity" is then portrayed as the main reason for their not aspiring to full ordination, and, as we will see, this ignores other crucial political and economic issues in contemporary Burma.

Reverend Saccavadi and Full Ordination in Burma

During my time in Sri Lanka in May 2006, I had the privilege of visiting Sri Sanghamitta Nunnery. There, I met Bhikkhunī Saccavadi, with whom I had been in contact for several months. The story of this nun has intrigued me since I first heard it, because it hints at alternative explanations for the lack of a movement for the restoration of *bhikkhunī*s in Burma. Saccavadi is a Burmese nun who was ordained as a *thilashin* in 1986. She passed the highest Buddhist examinations in Burma, attaining the degree of *dhammacariya* with the highest grade among all the *thilashin*s. In 1998, she moved to Sri Lanka to pursue her graduate studies. In 2002, she joined a group of *bhikkhunī* aspirants in Bodhgaya and received her full ordination. When she went to visit her ill father in Burma in 2005, she was arrested for seventy-six days, charged under Section 295 of the Burmese criminal code, which relates to "abusing religion" and to the "desecration of religious buildings and properties."[36] After what she described as a very traumatic time, which included being beaten and intimidated along with other physical and emotional abuses, she was allowed to leave the jail after being forced to ask for forgiveness for her actions and made to change out of her robes into the robes of a *thilashin*. After this, she was taken immediately to the airport to return to Sri Lanka, where she again wore her *bhikkhunī* robes and where she resided for several years until disrobing in 2008 because of the traumatic experiences she had suffered in jail in 2005. Saccavadi informed me that she knows about several *thilashin*s who would very much like to attain the status of a *bhikkhunī*, but who are greatly discouraged by monks from doing so. Before her visit to Burma, Bhikkhunī Saccavadi wrote to the religious authorities of her country for "supplication for recognition of my *bhikkhunī* ordination in Sri Lanka as a fully ordained Myanmar *bhikkhunī* in the Theravāda tradition."[7] She received a letter back from the Mahanayaka Monastery in Yangon, the official quarters of the highest monks in the country, stating that:

> We, who know the right view from the wrong view as taught by the blessed one [Buddha], submit herewith: That, Ma Saccavadi, who had received *bhikkhunī* ordination in Sri Lanka, has now brought forth a wrong view with the sole malicious intent to destroy the Buddha dispensation that now flourishes in Myanmar.[38]

The religious authorities of Burma were opposed at once to the attempts of any women to become fully ordained nuns. The reason given by the monks in authority was that this action violates the rules passed on since the time of the Buddha. However, Saccavadi and other Burmese in exile who support the *bhikkhunī* ordination explained to me that it can also be seen as a matter of maintaining their status as the sole receivers of the highest donations. Saccavadi described this to me as follows:

> People respect monks more than nuns. So, monks fear that they will lose their fame; they really fear that they will have to share their donations with the nuns. Buddhist clergies only depend on devotees and most of them are afraid of sharing. This egocentric attitude is mainly dependent on craving for own survival, and fear. They need to glorify themselves for survival.

Why a *Bhikkhunī* and Not a *Thilashin*: Aspiring for Higher Ordination

When I asked my friends who are fully ordained Theravāda nuns about the reasons for seeking this status, they voiced their explanations in similar ways. On the one hand, fully ordained nuns receive more support than *thilashins* because ordination represents a higher status, and on the other, this also gives them the confidence in their spiritual capacities to strive for the highest Buddhist goals. As Karma Lekshe Tsomo explains the former:

> The status of nuns within the Buddhist traditions seems to correlate with ordination status. Coincidentally or not, where full ordination as a *bhiksunī* is available, the nuns' level of education and status within the society also tend to be high. Where novice ordination as a *srāmanerikā* is available to nuns, women are

recognized members of the Saṅgha . . . even though they are not
afforded equal treatment. Without access to full ordination or even
novice ordination, women in such Theravāda countries . . . are in
secondary and often subservient roles, relative to the monks, in
the religious sphere.[39]

During my fieldwork, *thilashin*s explained to me that they are often reminded
by the monks of their inferior status, and this creates an inferiority complex
that discourages them from striving in their studies and their meditation.
They are often told that the highest goals of the Buddhist path are not accessible to them as *thilashin*s.

Charges of Westernization against the *Bhikkhunī* Movement

In one of her essays, Kawanami argues that the reinstatement of the order of
nuns may be seen as a "Westernizing" trend and that is likely to be rejected:
"It is unforeseeable that the Buddhist nuns themselves would be particularly
instrumental in the restoration of the *Bhikkhunī Saṅgha*, the movement of
which may only be seen as an imposition of 'Western,' thus foreign, ideas."[40]
Elizabeth Nissan has also seen this movement for the restoration of the order
of nuns as a mimicking of Western ideals of equality and freedom.[41] Wei-yi
Cheng has argued that these ideals of equality and freedom are not applicable
to Buddhist nuns and that, therefore, the Western feminist movement is not
an appropriate model for the struggles of the nuns.[42] While these claims
should be kept in mind in any critical study that tries to distance itself from
orientalist representation,[43] as we have seen, there are several *thilashin*s who
are interested in full ordination because it gives them greater possibilities for
development. Additionally, it is now clear that historically efforts have been
made within Buddhist cultures to reinstate the order of nuns.[44] Not only
that, but it is clear from Saccavadi's story that nuns are facing great difficulties in trying to reclaim this status.[45] These obstacles are not their identity
or their confinement to tradition, as others have argued, but rather a very
direct opposition from the male monastic community that is supported by
the military government under which Burma is ruled today.

Uma Narayan, an Indian feminist scholar, wrote *Dislocating Cultures:
Identities, Traditions, and Third World Feminism* precisely to offer an alternative explanation to these charges of Westernization. While her focus is mostly
on the Indian context, her claims are also relevant to other developing countries in which political movements of and for women are deemed ineffective
under the charge of being Western replicas of feminism. She suggests that

the movements of the so-called Third World feminisms are not imitations of Western agendas, but arise in response to local issues in particular cultures:

> Those in Third-World contexts who dismiss the politics of feminists in their midst as a symptom of "Westernization" not only fail to consider how these feminists' experiences within their Third-Contexts have shaped and informed their politics, but also fail to acknowledge that their feminist analyses are results of political organizing and political mobilization, initiated and sustained by women *within* these Third World contexts.[46]

Narayan's work offers what I think is a more appropriate way of seeing the struggle of the Burmese nuns for full ordination. While the issue of full ordination is slightly more complicated because it was initially an effort made mostly by Western Buddhist practitioners, we have seen that the conditions for nuns in Burma provoke reactions and demands for change that they themselves are undertaking not in order to imitate Western women, but so that they can have a more appropriate situation to practice their religion to its fullest. There are, however, other feminist practices among Burmese nuns that have nothing to do with aiming at equal status with men. What follows is one of the most successful examples of this in contemporary Burma.

Dipankara and a Unique Subversive Model

A few minutes away from the former British hill station of Pyin Oo Lwin, one finds the beautiful meditation retreat center Brahma Vihari May Myo Meditation Center run by Sayalay Dipankara. Sayalay, as her students refer to her with affection, has been a nun for seventeen years. She ordained when she was twenty-two years old and has stayed in the monastic robes ever since. Her story is another provocative example of the nonconforming ways in which Burmese nuns have challenged the monastic institutions of their country to achieve their ends and desires and to combat what they understand are inadequate conditions for their lives as nuns.

The first thing one notices when meeting Sayalay Dipankara is that her robes are brown instead of the usual pink and orange. I was curious about the reasons for this, and she explained:

> Because this is the forest tradition, we wear brown. Long time ago some nuns wore pink, but the forest tradition wore brown, then the government decided to change all the nuns to look the

same: pink. For me, pink is not my color . . . it is too attractive. I feel better wearing brown, it is more peaceful, is a more calm color. . . . I told them: "What does the robe color matter? What matters is my mind." So, I just didn't change the color. At first the government said that I have to change the color to pink or that I would get in trouble, but I still haven't changed it. Only very few nuns wear brown in Burma; most nuns wear pink.[47]

This had been one of her first confrontations with the monastic authorities of Burma. She describes herself as a very stubborn woman who is determined to attain her purposes. The way in which she has successfully bypassed the system and at the same time achieved the respect of the Burmese religious community is evidence again of Narayan's argument: women's politics structure themselves around various local issues rather than imitating a Western model of feminism. Sayalay had not come directly in contact with Western ideas when she decided to stray from the typical roles of a nun. She was very unhappy with her daily activities of having to cook and look after the monks. As she says: "I was crying all the time because there were many difficulties and misunderstandings; also, not only the monks, but some lay men also wanted to come and control the nuns, so there was a lot of tension. Nuns are happy, they don't get tired of serving the monks, but I thought, 'I want freedom.' "

Soon after all these struggles that were taking place within her, she told her teacher that she wished to go overseas to learn more about Buddhism. It is very uncommon for nuns to travel outside Burma. In fact, Sayalay explained to me that as a monk, it is very easy to get a Burmese passport and a visa to visit most foreign countries, but as a nun, it is almost impossible to get permission to travel outside the country. She was determined and insistent, and after much bureaucratic interference, many refusals, and numerous threats, she obtained a passport to travel outside Burma. She started traveling to Singapore and is now an established meditation teacher who travels every year to teach in places like the United States, Canada, Taiwan, England, Australia, Hong Kong, Japan, Malaysia, Sri Lanka, and Singapore, among others.

Nuns are not commonly seen as teachers of the Dhamma. Burmese people usually have more respect for the monks than for the nuns and therefore accept teachings mainly from the monks. This is still the case with Sayalay; although she has achieved an international reputation as a highly developed meditation master, most of her students are foreigners and not Burmese. Burmese people respect her and are proud of her, but they do not often attend her meditation retreats or her Dhamma talks. Although it is possible that her international reputation is partly due to the fact that Western practitioners probably identify and agree with Sayalay's ideals of women's freedom, it should be noted that the majority of her followers are from other Asian countries like Korea, Indonesia, and Malaysia, where gender structures similar to those in Burma operate.

Since she was very young, she believed that she had something to contribute to the Buddhist community by spreading the meditation teachings of the Buddha. She says:

> I think women can also be teachers; they can also teach the Dhamma and practice the Dhamma. That is why I am very stubborn. If I was not that stubborn, then I have to do everything that the monks tell me. At first, my teacher was very upset with me, but I didn't care. I still wanted to do what I wanted to do . . . , so I did it.

The strategy of Sayalay is very different from that of Saccavadi and the other Burmese nuns who are striving for both full ordination as well as equal status with men. Sayalay is not interested in becoming a fully ordained *bhikkhunī*, but she has resolved to live a monastic life in which she can dedicate herself to her main aim, meditation, and in which she does not need to resort to being subservient to the monks to receive support. She thinks that through her actions, other nuns will be inspired and realize that they have the potential to be respected Dhamma teachers and to serve others in this way: "I hope that other nuns will see this example and they will also start teaching the Dhamma."

An important reason why the case of Sayalay Dipankara adds interest to the discussion about the strategies that Burmese nuns use to bring about favorable changes for themselves in the monastic institutions is that she has resorted to meditation rather than study to establish a higher status for herself and her disciples. In traditional Buddhist practices, monks and nuns are supposed to develop both in intellectual understanding of the doctrines (*pariyatti*) and in meditation practices to realize the doctrines (*patipatti*). Kawanami has indicated that in the field of Buddhist education, nuns have found a way to improve their status by attaining academic qualifications similar to those of the monks:

> It seems to me that the most plausible direction for the strengthening of the nuns' religious position is in the area of Buddhist education. . . . Education for them has become their "symbolic capital." The rising academic standards of the nuns may allow them to secure a higher and more equal position in the religious domain without becoming marginalized or treated as "anomalies."[48]

Indeed, in Burma there are hardly any nuns who serve as teachers, and it is even rarer to attain respect from Burmese society without relying on academic Buddhist education. Sayalay Dipankara is an interesting case because her high status in society comes from her credentials as a meditation teacher and not as a Buddhist scholar. In her own words, "I don't have any studies degrees. I don't like to study, I haven't studied anything, I just like to purify my heart and to practice meditation and the Dhamma." Although Sayalay is perhaps one of the few nuns in Burma who can secure enough support through just the teaching of meditation, as Kawanami noted, and education remains the main way in which Burmese nuns strengthen their status in society, Sayalay's story points toward a different alternative for the nuns.

Burma is often referred to as the land of pure *patipatti*, or meditation practice, in contrast to Sri Lanka, which is famous among Buddhists for its high standards of *pariyatti*, or intellectual learning. There are several very successful meditation teachers in Burma, but all of them, with the exception of Sayalay, are monks.[49] Therefore, the fact that Sayalay Dipankara has established herself as a respected meditation teacher is likely to open doors for these positions to be available to other women as well.

It is important to note that the position of a meditation teacher carries with it a high degree of social respect and, therefore, financial support. However, this is not the only reason why teaching meditation would be desirable. It is also conceivable that, over time, nuns will gain more confidence in their spiritual capacities and as a result be more prepared to confront the derogatory statements that are often made about them.[50] Sayalay explained to me how nuns are usually seen by the monks:

> The nuns are seen as very, very low, very inferior. It is very difficult for them to get support. Even if they get some support, say, one day they go for alms and they get 1,000 *kyats* [less than a dollar], then they have to go back and give 500 *kyats* to the monks. It is very difficult. Also they have to spend their whole lives cooking for the monks. There is still the belief that nuns are inferior.

As mentioned before, many times nuns, and other women as well, pray to become men in their future lives. As Sayalay recounted:

> Women pray to become men because they don't want to be so inferior any more. Also, my teacher [Pa-Auk Sayadaw] at first told me that I have to pray to become a monk. He said that, in that way, I can progress and teach and all that. . . . I said: "*No!*" Women can also teach and meditate. My goal is to be an *arahant* and women can also become *arahant*. Next life, I don't care if I am a man or a woman, my goal is to be an *arahant*.

To have a female role model who can teach without encouraging other women to pray for a future existence as a man could have a profound effect by helping women to acknowledge that their female bodies are plausible vehicles for spiritual development.

The case of Sayalay Dipankara is also important for the broader discussions about feminism outside Western conventions. Liberal feminism, which has stood at the core of Western feminism, has argued for more than three centuries about the rights of women to have a similar status to men.[51] However, Dipankara has never resorted to a struggle for gaining equal status with men. Her interest lies in cultivating the appropriate conditions to develop her religious and spiritual practices while at the same time reassuring herself and other women about the capacities of females to reach enlightenment and teach the Dhamma. She has never set the high position of the monks as her ideal; instead, she has developed a suitable lifestyle for herself (and hopefully for other nuns) that is not hampered by the political and religious power of the monks. In this way, she is another important voice in the chorus of women across cultures who have developed their own strategies to circumnavigate the social institutions in which they live in ways that make their experience more fulfilling and satisfying.

Notes

1. A different version of this paper was initially published in *Orientalia Parthenopea* 8(2008): 201–22.

2. See Thameechit, "Burmese Sisterhood: Unacknowledged Piety," *The Irrawaddy* 8:9(2000), http://www.irrawaddy.org/database/2000/vol8.9/culturearts.html; Friedgard Lottermoser, "Buddhist Nuns in Burma," *Sakyadhita Newsletter* 2:2(1991); Martin H. Petrich, "Buddhist Women in Burma: The Rocky Path Towards Liberation," in *Netzwerk Engagierter Buddhisten* (1998), http://www.buddhanetz.org/projekte/women.htm.

3. See Hiroko Kawanami, "The Position and Role of Women in Burmese Buddhism: A Case Study of Buddhist Nuns in Burma," PhD diss., London School of Economics, 1991. Kawanami has also written various articles dealing with the topic of Burmese nuns; I refer to her other articles further on in this paper.

4. Because of space constraints, the copious literature that has been published recently about Buddhist nuns cannot be reviewed here. However, partial but comprehensive bibliographies of such works can be found on the Sakyadhita website: http://www.sakyadhita.org, and on the online *Journal of Buddhist Ethics* under Women in Buddhism: http://blogs.dickinson.edu/buddhistethics. Some of the most influential texts are Tessa Bartholomeusz, *Women under the Bo Tree: Buddhist Nuns in Sri Lanka* (New York: Cambridge University Press, 1994); Karma Lekshe Tsomo, ed., *Sakyadhita: Daughters of the Buddha* (Ithaca, NY: Snow Lion Publications, 1989); Chatsumarn Kabilsingh, *Thai Women in Buddhism* (Berkeley, CA: Parallax Press, 1991); and Elisabeth Nissan, "Recovering Practice: Buddhist Nuns in Sri Lanka," *South Asia Research* 4:1(1984): 32–49.

5. Hiroko Kawanami, "Patterns of Renunciation: The Changing World of Burmese Nuns," in *Women's Buddhism, Buddhism's Women: Tradition, Revision, Renewal,* ed. Ellison Banks Findly (Somerville, MA: Wisdom Publications, 2000), pp. 159–71.

6. Inderpal Grewal and Caren Kaplan, eds., *Scattered Hegemonies: Postmodernity and Transnational Feminist Practices* (Minneapolis: University of Minnesota Press, 2002), p. 18.

7. Chandra Talpade Mohanty, *Feminism without Borders: Decolonizing Theory, Practicing Solidarity* (Durham: Duke University Press, 2003), p. 17.

8. Uma Narayan, *Dislocating Cultures: Identities, Traditions, and Third World Feminism* (New York: Routledge, 1997), p. 13.

9. The word *arahant* comes from the present active participle of the verb *arahati* (Pāli), "to be worthy." In Theravāda Buddhism, it refers to one who has destroyed all greed, hatred, and delusion and attained *nibbāna* (liberation).

10. John Higham, "Multiculturalism and Universalism: A History and Critique," *American Quarterly* 45(1993): 195–219.

11. Konmari, "The Status of Burmese Women: A Comparative Essay," in *Burma: Voices of Women in the Struggle,* ed. The Thanakha Team (Bangkok: Alternative Asean Network on Burma, 1998), p. 69.

12. Broadcast June 21, 2006. It is also interesting to see the way that Indians are represented in this statement as more oppressive to women than Burmese; they function as the "others" for this Burmese portrayal of "Burmese culture," a topic that deserves greater study.

13. Melford Spiro, *Gender, Ideology and Psychological Reality* (New Haven, CT: Yale University Press, 1997), p. 11.

14. Ibid., p. 21.

15. Mi Mi Khaing, *The World of Burmese Women* (London: Zed Books, 1984), p. 16.

16. Kawanami explains: "The position of the Burmese government (the Ministry of Home and Religious Affairs) reflects an official view that only the monks and novices are classified as "inside the religion" (*thathana win*), implying that they are "officially acknowledged members of the religious community." In comparison, Buddhist nuns are referred to as "descendants of the religion" (*thathana anwe*) or "related to the lineage" (*rhathana nwe-win*)." Kawanami, "The Position and Role of Women," p. 93. As we shall see, this classification has inopportune consequences for Burmese nuns, because they have considerably less official authority than monks do.

17. While normally fully ordained *bhikkhunīs,* or nuns, would be expected to abide by 311 precepts, *thilashins* follow only eight or ten of those rules. For a fuller explanation, see Kawanami, "The Position and Role of Women," p. 85.

18. Rawe Htun, *The Modern Buddhist Nun,* trans. San Lwin (Yangon: Parami Bookshop, 2001), p. 47.

19. For a detailed examination of the founding of the *bhikkhunī saṅgha* (community of nuns), see I. B. Horner, *Women Under Primitive Buddhism* (Delhi: Motilal Banarsidas, 1990), pp. 95–161; and Ute Hüsken, "The Legend of the Establishment of the Buddhist Order of Nuns in the Theravāda Vinaya-Pitaka," *Journal of the Pali Text Society* XXVI(2000): 43–69.

20. N. A. Jayawickrama, trans., *The Inception of Discipline and the Vinaya Nadana: Bahiranidana of Buddhaghosa's Samantapasadika, Sacred Books of the Buddhists* XXI (London: Luzac & Co., 1962), p. 61.

21. G. H. Luce, "The Ancient Pyu," *Journal of the Burma Research Society* 27–28(1937): 251.

22. Pe Maung Tin, "Women in the Inscriptions of Pagan," *Journal of the Burma Research Society* XXV–III(1935): 151; Than Tun, "Social Life in Burma in the 13th Century," *Journal of the Burma Research Society* XLI(1958): 45. There is some controversy about whether or not they were fully ordained nuns. Rawe Htun argues that although they had renounced the householder's life, "they could not be descendants of the *bhikkhunī* lineage and by what term they had been known cannot be traced." Rawe Htun, *The Modern Buddhist Nun* (Yangon: Parami Bookshop, 2001), p. 40.

23. For the stories of these nuns, especially Saya Kin and Saya Mai Nat Pay, see Kawanami, "The Position and Role of Women in Burmese Buddhism," pp. 72–76.

24. Karma Lekshe Tsomo, ed., *Buddhist Women across Cultures: Realizations* (Albany: State University of New York Press, 1999), pp. 10–11.

25. Kawanami, "The Position and Role of Women in Burmese Buddhism," p. 264.

26. Descriptions of each of these studies can be found in Hiroko Kawanami, "Buddhist Nuns in Transition: The Case of Burmese Thilá-Shin," in *Indian Insights: Buddhism, Brahmanism, and Bhakti*, ed. P. Connolly and S. Hamilton (London: Luzac Oriental, 1997), p. 214; Spiro, *Gender, Ideology and Psychological Reality*, p. 40; W. C. B. Purser and Kenneth J. Saunders, eds., *Modern Buddhism in Burma* (Burma: The Christian Literature Society, 1914), p. 65.

27. Kawanami, "Buddhist Nuns in Transition," p. 220.

28. In addition to articles by Kawanami mentioned earlier, there are a few other brief papers dealing with the topic. See, for example, Ingrid Jordt, "Bhikkhunī, Thilashin, Mae-Chii: Women Who Renounce The World in Burma, Thailand and the Classical Pali Buddhist Texts," *Crossroads: An Interdisciplinary Journal of Southeast Asian Studies* 4:1(1988): 31–39.

29. Kawanami, "The Position and Role of Women in Burmese Buddhism," pp. 10–11.

30. See Nancy Auer Falk, "The Case of Vanishing Nuns: The Fruits of Ambivalence in Ancient Indian Buddhism," in *Unspoken Worlds: Women's Religious Lives in Non-Western Culture*, ed. N. Falk and R. Gross (San Francisco: Harper & Row, 1979), pp. 207–24.

31. For more information regarding the controversy over the restoration of the *bhikkhunī* order to the Theravāda tradition, see Karma Lekshe Tsomo, "Mahāprajāpatī's Legacy," in *Buddhist Women across Cultures: Realizations*, ed. Karma Lekshe Tsomo (Albany: State University of New York Press, 1999), pp. 1–48; Senarat Wijayasundara, "Restoring the Order of Nuns to the Theravādin Tradition," in *Buddhist Women across Cultures*, pp. 79–90. In his book *The Revival of the Bhikkhunī Ordination in the Theravāda Tradition* (Penang, Malasia: Inward Path Publisher, 2011), Bhikkhu Bodhi thoroughly describes the traditional Theravāda scriptures regarding *bhikkhunī* ordination and also includes and translates a Pāli text from Mingun Jetavan

Sayadaw from Burma that argues that the *bhikkhunī* order has never actually been extinct.

32. Until recently in Thailand, women could be arrested for "impersonating a monk," which was considered a crime. Now the nuns have won a legal argument through the Thai Constitution that states that both men and women have similar rights. For more information about the order of nuns in Thailand, see Vishvapani, "Bold Steps for Nuns," *Dharma Life Magazine* 19(2002), http://www.dharmalife.com/issue19/asianbikkhunis.html.

33. Kawanami, "Buddhist Nuns in Transition," p. 210.

34. Ibid., p. 211.

35. Ibid., p. 221.

36. Tin Aung Khine, "Burma Arrests Buddhist Activist Nun," *Radio Free Asia*, July 7, 2005.

37. A copy of this unpublished letter was provided to me by Bhikkhunī Saccavadi.

38. A copy of this letter was translated by Maung Paw, who provided it to me.

39. Tsomo, *Buddhist Women Across Cultures*, p. 9.

40. Kawanami, "Buddhist Nuns in Transition," p. 211.

41. Nissan, "Recovering Practice," pp. 32–49.

42. See Wei-yi Cheng, *Buddhist Nuns in Taiwan and Sri Lanka: An Assessment of Feminist Approach*, PhD diss., University of London, 2004.

43. Edward W. Said, *Orientalism* (London: Routledge and Kegan Paul, 1978). I am using the word "orientalist" in the sense that Said made known in his famous book to refer to representations and depictions of the Oriental as inferior and untrustworthy, always contrasted to the superior and reliable Western *man*.

44. See Bhikkhu Bodhi, *The Revival of the Bhikkhunī Ordination in the Theravāda Tradition*, especially pp. 57–66.

45. There are other Burmese nuns in exile who have obtained full ordination. While there is not enough space in this chapter for me to recount the stories of other nuns, they were all eager to tell me about the difficulties they faced from within the Burmese male monastic community when they were trying to become *bhikkhunī*s.

46. Narayan, *Dislocating Cultures*, p. 13.

47. This and all the other citations of Sayalay Dipankara's words are from a personal meeting in Pyin Oo Lwin on June 29, 2006.

48. Kawanami, "Buddhist Nuns in Transition," p. 221.

49. There have been some exceptional lay meditation teachers in Burma—most of them men—such as Saya Thet Gyi (1873-1945) and Sayagyi U Ba Khin (1899-1971). One of the latter's successors is a Burmese woman reverentially called *sayamagyi*, or venerable lady, an interesting example of the way conditions are changing for women in Burma.

50. There is even a common Burmese saying: "The death of a son or spouse, a loss in business, indebtedness, and lack of fulfillment, all lead women to become nuns." This is a popular depiction of nuns in Burma.

51. Rosemarie Tong, *Feminist Thought: A More Comprehensive Introduction* (Boulder: Westview Press, 1998), p. 15.

4

Pioneering *Bhikkhunīs* in Contemporary Sri Lanka and Thailand

Tomomi Ito

Historically, one of the most significant events in contemporary Theravāda Buddhism has been the reintroduction of the *bhikkhunī saṅgha*, which had been lost for several hundred years. After a period of debate and controversy, the number of *bhikkhunīs* and *sāmaṇerīs* in Sri Lanka has dramatically increased. At the same time, in Thailand, more than ten women have received *bhikkhunī* ordination from foreign Buddhist *saṅghas*, and they are now striving to consolidate their own monastic community.[1] The development of Theravāda *bhikkhunī saṅghas* in these two countries, each with a rich Buddhist tradition, is a ray of hope for many Buddhist women around the world who await formal sanction of their *bhikkhunī* ordination by traditional Buddhist orders. This chapter highlights both the achievements of a group of Sri Lankan ten-precept nuns who have worked toward the establishment and expansion of *bhikkhunī* ordination in Sri Lanka as well as the achievements of a group of Thai *bhikkhunīs* who enjoy the support of their surrounding communities of monks and laypeople. Through an examination of these two cases, the chapter identifies significant factors in the success of newly launched *bhikkhunī saṅghas* taking root in their traditional Buddhist societies.

Motives for the Development of a Sri Lankan *Bhikkhunī Saṅgha*

The cornerstone of the recent development of a Sri Lankan *bhikkhunī saṅgha* was the group of ten women who were ordained by the Korean *saṅgha* in December 1996 in Sarnath, India.[2] A subsequent key development was the ordination of a group of twenty women by Taiwan's Foguangshan order in February 1998 in Bodhgaya, India. At the 1996 ordination ceremony, there were some Sri Lankan *silmātā* (ten-precept nuns) who later became *bhikkhunī*s in February 1998 after observing a *bhikkhunī* ordination ceremony during their pilgrimage in India. One of them said that for a long time she had been thinking that *bhikkhunī* ordination was no longer possible, but, looking at the concrete example of the ceremony held by the dual *saṅgha* of *bhikkhu*s and *bhikkhunī*s from East Asia, she was inspired to conceive for herself a realistic plan regarding *bhikkhunī* ordination.

As soon as they returned to their home temples in Sri Lanka, the two nuns, Siri Sumeda and Sugunapali, visited all the *bhikkhu* temples in their home district of Kurunegala and asked the senior *bhikkhu*s for their opinion about taking *bhikkhunī* ordination. Then all the *bhikkhu* abbots unanimously said, "We bless you wholeheartedly; we welcome the implementation of the *bhikkhunī* order." One *bhikkhu* named Punnasara Thera even offered immediate support for the ordination of nuns as *bhikkhunī*s. Encouraged by the positive response, Siri Sumeda and Sugunapali wrote a letter calling on all ten-precept nuns in Sri Lanka to attend a meeting to discuss *bhikkhunī* ordination. In response, sixty nuns came to a meeting held at the Kurunegala Red Cross. Of the sixty, twenty-six senior nuns were selected through interviews to establish the Sri Lankan Bhikkhunī Association. These twenty-six nuns received support from the elder *bhikkhu*s Punnasara Thera and Sumangara Thera. Sumangala Thera offered his meditation center, and the nuns developed it as the Kalundewa Bhikkhunī Education Academy, where they received nine months of lectures and training from highly educated *bhikkhu*s.

After the training, ten of the nuns along with another ten from Horana District were nominated by Somanlankara Thera, a close friend of Sumangala Thera, to attend the February 1998 ordination ceremony in Bodhgaya, India. Upon their return to Sri Lanka as fully ordained *bhikkhunī*s, three more groups of nuns were ordained in the same year in Sri Lanka, increasing the number of *bhikkhunī*s to one hundred within one year. The *bhikkhunī* ordination coordinators did not send all the nuns who received training at Kalundewa to Bodhgaya, in order to reserve some of them for a group that was to follow the first group and expand the movement of *bhikkhunī* ordination in Sri Lanka. Although these ordinations did not escape harsh criticism from various quarters, after several years *bhikkhunī* ordination became quite common. According to Bhikkhuni Siri Sumeda, every year approximately thirty nuns apply for the *bhikkhunī* ordination qualification exam at the Bhikkhunī Education Academy in Dambulla.

The key question is: How did the *bhikkhunī saṅgha* materialize so smoothly in Sri Lanka after so many years of rejecting the possibility? Here

I would like to raise at least three points. First, the momentum was fostered over several decades, particularly through organizing and improving the education of ten-precept nuns in the mid-1980s. The Ministry of Buddha Sasana offered an opportunity for ten-precept nuns to attend classes on Buddhism taught by educated *bhikkhu* teachers. The Ministry also called for the establishment of the Sri Lankan Silmata Association with branches in all districts, except for the politically unstable areas controlled by the LTTE (Liberation Tigers of Tamir Eelam).

One *bhikkhunī* from Horana District said that the Silmata Association did not discuss much about the *bhikkhunī* issue; there were just a few who said, "If we had a *bhikkhunī* order, that would be good, but the *bhikkhus* would not like it, so they won't help us." However, the same *bhikkhunī* said that when she took classes in Buddhism as a young *silmātā* in the late 1980s, her *bhikkhu* teacher always told her, "You must be clever, study hard, and be qualified, so that you can be a *bhikkhunī* someday in the future." Therefore, she always wanted to become a *bhikkhunī* so that she would be able to do higher Buddhist practice, which *silmātās* do not do. In 1997, when she found a letter from Siri Sumeda about the plan for a *bhikkhunī* ordination in Bodhgaya, she was very happy.[3] A review of recent history clearly reveals that empowering ten-precept nuns through the establishment of their own association and education has been an essential step. It should be noted that these reforms were proposed by an enthusiastic petition drafted and submitted to the Ministry of Buddha Sasana by Kusuma Devendra, who later, in December 1996, courageously risked social controversy by becoming the first Sri Lankan *bhikkhunī* in recent history.

The second factor that helps to explain the rapid expansion of *bhikkhunī* ordination in Sri Lanka is the fact that through the initiatives taken by the senior ten-precept nuns, the senior members of the existing nuns' order were transformed into leaders of the new *bhikkhunī* order, and consequently a large group of junior nuns was able to take the same step forward. Siri Sumeda and Sugunapali, the two nuns who organized the letter for the nuns' meeting after observing the December 1996 Sarnath ordination, were then serving as the secretary and the president, respectively, of Silmata Association in Kurunegala District. The twenty *bhikkhunīs* ordained in February 1998 were all abbesses of their own independent nunneries and were considered to be sufficiently senior in terms of length of time of ten-precept ordination and social status. The three most senior of the twenty *bhikkhunīs* were appointed as preceptors (*upājjhāyas*) for the next cohort of *bhikkhunī* candidates, and the eight next most senior *bhikkhunīs* were appointed as reciters (*kammavagacariyas*). Well before their *bhikkhunī* ordination, these nuns had known of each other's social and educational statuses and administrative positions through such occasions as chanting and almsgiving ceremonies, which brought together dozens of nuns invited from different places. Because high-status nuns took the lead in ordaining as *bhikkhunīs*, nuns who were junior to them followed their example and also became *bhikkhunīs*; thus, many groups of ten-precept nuns from different nunneries and ordination lineages together made the shift to become *bhikkhunīs*.[4] In other words, despite the democratic ideals of the modern world, contemporary Buddhist nuns are not equal among themselves and are not free from the constraints of authority and seniority, but when the whole hierarchy was well preserved and unchallenged, the ten-precept renunciants could smoothly change their religious status from *silmātā* to fully ordained *bhikkhunī*.

At the same time, it is important to note that a subtle sense of seniority does upset the nuns' world when nuns assume the status of fully ordained *bhikkhunīs*. Some groups of nuns were unwilling to be ordained by *bhikkhunīs* who were senior in terms of full ordination but who had been ordained as ten-precept nuns for a shorter period. In such cases, nuns were able to contact a foreign *saṅgha* through their own channels and arrange their own *bhikkhunī* ordination ceremony.[5] This allowed them to assume the most senior position in their own group, independent of other groups of *bhikkhunīs* who had already been ordained before them. *Bhikkhunīs* ordained through different channels rarely hold monastic ceremonies together. Because of the many alternative channels for receiving ordination, plural orders of *bhikkhunīs* are now coming into being. As a result, the plural orders do not fit into a single, unified *saṅgha*.

The third indispensable factor that explains the rapid transition of Sri Lankan nuns to *bhikkhunīs* was the support of senior *bhikkhus*. In every case of implementation of a new *bhikkhunī* order, there were several *bhikkhus* who offered support for nuns to become *bhikkhunīs*; such *bhikkhus* did exist in many places. The grand project of restoring the *bhikkhunī saṅgha* was a reasonable objective and could even be seen as a way to enhance the reputations of those who significantly contributed to its achievement. There appears to be one important condition: the authority of the *bhikkhus* needs to be well respected and unchallenged; otherwise those *bhikkhus* in positions of authority could ignore or even disrupt attempts to reform the status quo.

Social Acceptance of a Thai *Bhikkhunī* Community

The same three factors that underpinned the restoration of *bhikkhunī* ordination in Sri Lanka can be found in the case of Nirotharam Women's Dhamma Practice Center, a *bhikkhunī* community located in northern Thailand.[6] The center was founded in 1995 as a community of *mae chīs* who strictly kept the rules of one vegetarian meal a day and minimized their expenses in addition to observing the regular eight precepts. The founder of the community, formerly known as Mae Chī Rungduan, now Bhikkhunī Nandanani, imposed this strict discipline on herself when she entered the renunciant life because her devotion to Dhamma practice was serious and she was ready to confront the difficulties that arise from becoming a young eight-precept *mae chī*. Her intense devotion surprised senior monks and others, and her effective preaching at group retreats and on local radio broadcasts became popular. Mae Chī Rungduan and her *mae chī* disciples formed a consolidated community of highly disciplined female practitioners.

The group of *mae chī*s at Nirotharam already observed the rule of refraining from the use of money, which is one of the precepts that is added to the lay practitioner's eight precepts to create the ten precepts of ordained novices. For these nuns to assume the form and status of a *sāmaṇerī* was regarded as merely confirming the religious practice that they had already undertaken. Hearing reports of the group's decision to become *sāmaṇerī*s in Sri Lanka, Luang Pu Thong, the monk teacher of the abbess and a highly respected elder *bhikkhu* in the region, commented that the *sāmaṇerī* form requires a visible adherence to even stricter disciplines. In 2006, the group of *mae chī*s materialized their aspiration for *sāmaṇerī* ordination in Sri Lanka through the help of a Thai *bhikkhu*'s contact with Sri Lankan *bhikkhunī*s. Two years later, in 2008, five *sāmaṇerī*s responded to the urging of a Sri Lankan *bhikkhu* and became fully ordained *bhikkhunī*s.

For a period of time, a Thai *bhikkhu* living near the nuns' center offered his help by ordaining Nirotharam female disciples as *sāmaṇerī*s despite the risk of possible controversy. The abbess later removed this risk from the Thai *bhikkhu* by ordaining her disciples as *sāmaṇerī*s herself because her Sri Lankan *bhikkhunī* preceptor authorized her to do so. At the time of my visit in September 2009, the Nirotharam *bhikkhunī*s were receiving intellectual support from a Thai *bhikkhu* in the form of Pāli instruction, and stories have circulated about the popularity of the center's retreat. So far, the nuns' ordination and act of taking up of the yellow robes—traditionally monopolized by *bhikkhu*s—has not isolated them from their local communities of *bhikkhu*s and laypeople; instead, they have received ongoing respect from them.

The harmonious establishment of the Nirotharam *bhikkhunī* order was based on the public confidence that nuns obtained through their rigorous observance of precepts and their contributions in terms of Dhamma teaching over the past fifteen years. One Nirotharam *bhikkhunī* mentioned that her teacher never created problems with people and never came into conflict with monks. Instead, she humbly respected monks and seized every opportunity to meet them to update them about her group's activities.[7] The abbess, Bhikkhunī Nandanani, said that the principle of respecting monks is clearly stated in the *garudhamma*s, the eight weighty rules that the Buddha is said to have given Mahapajapati when she first requested *bhikkhunī* ordination. It was the Buddha's wisdom that peacefully launched a new female monastic order, supported by the already well-established *bhikkhunī saṅgha*.[8]

Launching a New Female Monastic Order

While I was studying the issue of *bhikkhunī* ordination among Theravāda Buddhist nuns, I encountered many people who expressed doubts about a seemingly feminist or Western bias in the movement. These people seemed to assume a simple dichotomy between the English-speaking, elite feminist women who are associated with a group of international Buddhist women promoting *bhikkhunī* ordination, and other women practitioners, who are happy to remain in their current status and have little interest in promoting their status in the secular world. The reality is never so simple. This ethnographic study, conducted among various groups of Thai and Sri Lankan *sāmaṇerīs* and *bhikkhunīs* who were previously eight-precept or ten-precept nuns, suggests that among local women practitioners there had been unspoken hopes of becoming fully ordained *bhikkhunīs* that had not been expressed publicly. Many of these women seized the right moment of opportunity for ordination and then applied all of their social skills, cultivated in the tradition of their own society, to carefully handle the risks. Although rarely as outspoken or explicitly feminist as the elite, English-speaking *bhikkhunī* opinion leaders, they are nonetheless forging a revolutionary movement within their otherwise patriarchal and conventionally structured Buddhist worlds.

Notes

1. Tomomi Ito, "Questions of Ordination Legitimacy for Newly Ordained Bhikkhunī in Thailand," *Journal of Southeast Asian Studies* 43:1(2012): 55–76.
2. The following story is based on my interview with Bhikkhunī Siri Sumeda at her temple in Kurunegala on February 17, 2008.
3. Bhikkhunī Badra Dharmarakshmi, interview by the author, February 18, 2008.
4. Siri Sumedha Bhikkhunī, interview by the author, February 17, 2008.
5. Ibid.
6. The following story is based on my interviews with Nandanani Bhikkhunī and Pannabhari Bhikkhunī on September 25, 2009.
7. Pannabhari Bhikkhunī, interview by the author, September 25, 2009.
8. Nandanani Bhikkhunī, interview by the author, September 25, 2009.

5

Bhikkhunī Ta Tao

Paving the Way for Future Generations

Bhikkhunī Dhammananda (Chatsumarn Kabilisingh)

Thailand has been a Buddhist country for more than seven hundred years. In spite of the fact that it has the highest percentage of Buddhists of any country in the world,[1] Thailand cannot claim to be a *majjhimadesh* (central land) in the true, Buddhist sense of the word. As H.H. the Dalai Lama has often said, for a country to be a central land, it must have a complete fourfold Buddhist society as established by the Buddha. Unfortunately, Thailand lacks a recognized *bhikkhunī saṅgha*.[2]

In the previous century, there have been at least two attempts to introduce the *bhikkhunī saṅgha* to Thailand. The first attempt was by Narin Bhasit, who arranged ordination for his two daughters, Sara and Chongdi.[3] But because of Bhasit's political involvement, the ordination was considered a conspiracy against the *saṅgha,* and was rejected soon after the attempt was made. This resulted in an order promulgated by Somdet Kromma Luang Jinavorn Sirivaddhana,[4] the Sangharaja (Supreme Patriarch), on June 18, 1928, forbidding Thai monks to give any level of ordination to women.[5]

The next attempt, or what I called the second wave, came with the ordination of Voramai Kabilsingh in 1956, who became fully ordained in Taiwan in 1971 and thus became the first Thai *bhikkhunī* in history. This chapter documents the life of Bhikkhunī Voramai Kabilsingh (1908–2003) and her work to pave the way for the third wave of *bhikkhunīs* in Thai history. As years pass by, a person's life may easily become mystified or glamorized. This is an attempt to record her life and work as objectively as possible. I have continually postponed this venture, because it is not easy to be objective in writing about one's own mother. Still, in trying to understand the history and development of *bhikkhunīs* in different countries, it has become inevitable for me to record the story of her life, not only as a historian of Buddhism, but also as a dutiful daughter.

The Family Background

Bhikkhunī Ta Tao was born Lamai Kabilsingh in a family of six siblings in 1908 in Rajburi, a province some hundred kilometers west of Bangkok. Her father, a Chinese merchant, only wanted sons, but in this family, there was only one son and five daughters. When Lamai was born as the youngest daughter in the family, her father was not happy. Never once did I hear his name mentioned by her. Soon after her birth, he left for China with the only son and left his wife to care for the family—a young mother thirty-six years old with five daughters. The fact that her father wanted only sons became reflected in Lamai's own deep-rooted need to have a son.

As a young widow, Lamai's mother, Somcheen, could not defend herself against the powerful local landlord who tried to claim her land, and so she settled in Bangkok with her five daughters. Her closest sister, Chalam, married a Chinese merchant who owned a store selling foreign food. Lamai helped with the work in the store in the evening and went to Assumption Girls' College during the day. Her experience in the store exposed her to English, which turned out to be very useful in the latter part of her life. As a businesswoman, her sister Chalam became very successful financially.

Lamai wanted to pursue higher education. Since early childhood, she had been interested in literature. Her first story was published when she was seventeen. Her interest in journalism and writing continued until she was in her eighties. She started her career as a schoolteacher working for the government. During the day she taught at school, and in the evening she enrolled for a certificate in physical education. In this way, she pursued her own interests and also advanced her teaching career. During her training in physical education, she became the first Thai woman to excel in sword fighting and jujitsu. At the physical education college, she met Korkiat Shatsena, who later became her husband.

In 1932, while she was teaching, Lamai joined a group of Thai boy scouts who were traveling to Singapore by bicycle. The ride took twenty-nine days, and when she returned she had many stories to tell. She wanted to write down these stories because she was teaching both boys and girls and wanted to show her students that women were capable of the same things as men. She was a feminist, even though she had never heard the word. The story of her travels by bicycle to Singapore was published many years later.

Her Marriage

Because of her own unhappy family experiences and the attitude of her father, Lamai did not have a positive view of marriage. She never intended to get married, even though she was courted by Korkiat Shatsena, the son of a well-to-do family from the south of Thailand. At the beginning of World War II, the Japanese army was winning the war, and there was a rumor that the Japanese government had approached the Thai government hoping to marry strong, brave Japanese soldiers to educated Thai women. As a teacher, she was on the list of possible candidates.

With this imminent threat, she made a decision and informed the authorities that she had a boyfriend whom she expected to marry. Her intention was only to avoid being married off to a Japanese man, but her supervisor took her seriously and arranged for her marriage at the palace of a respected prince in April 1942. She followed her new husband to the south, where she continued to work as a schoolteacher. During this time of war, I, her only child and a daughter, was born on October 6, 1944. She had always wanted a son—a deep-rooted desire ingrained in her by her father—so the birth of a daughter was something of a disappointment.

A Shift in Life

After her marriage to this son of an affluent family in the south, she changed her name to Voramai by adding part of her husband's name to her own. Her husband, Korkiat Shatsena, was deeply involved in politics. He was the first person to establish the Democratic Party on a solid basis in Trang Province.

Voramai did not see any future in the south for me and another daughter she had adopted, so to give us better educational opportunities, she moved back to Bangkok. There, as a single parent, she worked for some years to support her family by writing and producing jewelry as a sideline. She sent me to the best school in Bangkok, Rajini Bon, founded by a Thai princess.

Meanwhile, her husband continued to be involved in politics and the Democratic Party. While he was working in parliament, Voramai sat in the section designated for journalists who were responsible for reporting on the crisis among the Muslim population in the south. Voramai was the only reporter trusted by Muslims to do fact finding for the government. She submitted a proposal to the government that included twelve points to be addressed in resolving the crisis. Now, half a century later, the same problems persist, so her work has been republished. Her adventurous and daring spirit encouraged her in her later work, and she continued to write even after she decided to become ordained as a Buddhist nun.

Working side by side to support her politician husband, Voramai was exposed to various social problems. Sometimes she traveled with her husband by foot to faraway villages. After seeing so many poor children and realizing that they would eventually be the future of the country, she developed a heartfelt commitment to education. Later, after receiving higher ordination, she founded a school for orphans, which has continued for three decades.

The Spiritual Path

The turning point in Voramai's life came in approximately 1954, when a highly respected doctor found that she had a tumor that needed to be operated on. The date was fixed and she was hospitalized to prepare her for the operation to remove the tumor. Her sister came to visit her, accompanied by a white-robed *mae chī* named Maechee Thongsuk. She was one of the leading disciples of Luangpo Sod, a famous monk at the time. He was particularly well known for healing by meditation. Being hospitalized, Voramai could make only a small donation. The next day, Mae chī Thongsuk returned carrying a message from Luangpo Sod that she need not go through with the operation.

Voramai was too modern to listen to the respected monk. She decided to go through with the operation, but, to the surprise of the team of the medical doctors, no tumor could be found! That left a big question mark in her mind. Could it be that the respected monk had truly cured her by removing the tumor?

She decided to pursue the issue for herself, which meant that she had to visit the monk Luangpo Sod and learn to practice meditation. As soon as she was strong enough, she went to see Luangpo Sod at Wat Paknam. In those days the temple was not accessible by land, so she had to cross the canal by boat. When he saw her, he laughed and commented, "Didn't I tell you that you did not need the operation?"

Voramai was deeply impressed and put aside all her work and other engagements to pursue the meditation technique he had taught her. In addition to the respected monk Luangpo Sod, Maechee Thongsuk also became her teacher. She applied herself earnestly to the practice and soon received the title Dhammakaya, which meant that she was qualified to teach others. Her life had completely changed, and she now focused her attention only on the Dhamma and the practice of meditation in which she had been initiated by the master Luangpo Sod.

In 1955, she began publishing a monthly magazine called *Vipassana Bantherngsarn* to educate people about the Buddhist teachings and the practice of meditation that she had received from Luangpo Sod. She continued to publish this monthly magazine for the next thirty-two years. It was an effective tool for educating the public, and it also helped her create a network for her activities. Through intensive study and practice of the Buddha's teachings, she became increasingly dedicated to the monastic life. In May 1956, she was ordained.

Ordained Life

At that time in Thailand, women could only be ordained as *mae chīs*, who wear white robes and have shaved heads. Some *mae chīs* live at home, some live together in a nunnery, and some live in one corner of a monks' temple. The lifestyle is informal, and the *mae chīs* have no official status. In the annual report of the *sangha*, *mae chīs* are mentioned only as a group of women who take up residence in some temples. In other temples, the abbots make it clear that *mae chīs* are not to take up residence in their temples. Today, the Institute of Thai Mae chī has its offices at Wat Bavornnives. The Foundation keeps a register of the *mae chīs* in the country and records a number of less than five thousand. In fact, there are many more *mae chīs* who do not see any benefit in registering with the Foundation. Altogether, it is estimated that there are no more than ten thousand *mae chīs* in Thailand.

When Voramai Kabilsingh initially made inquiries and sought ordination as a *bhikkhunī*, all the doors were closed. The answer she received from all the monks she approached was the same: "It is not possible. The *bhikkhunī* lineage has died out." The difficulty was that Thailand has never had a *bhikkhunī* lineage, so the monks were not familiar with the idea. For Thai monks, the existence of *bhikkhunī*s is only something recorded in the Buddhist texts some 2,500 years ago. The monks had no information about any living *bhikkhunī*s in modern times.

Voramai went to the esteemed *bhikkhu* Chao Khun Pra Prommuni, who was the deputy abbot of Wat Bavornnives in Bangkok, and on May 2, 1956, she received ordination from him. Technically, she took eight precepts and, to protect her ordination master, she wore white on the day of ordination. But she indicated to him that she intended to wear light yellow robes thereafter.

Clash with the Government Authorities

The district chief was very unhappy with Voramai's decision to wear light yellow robes, even though they were not the color of the monk's robes, and he summoned her to his office in Muang District in Nakhonpathom. He banged the table in front of her, wanting to know the reason for her activities, and asked her to conform to the expected white robes of a nun, but she refused. The mayor of Nakhonpathom Province could not decide the matter and requested the *sangha* to consider whether what she was doing was blasphemous. The highest committee of the Thai *sangha*, called the Council of Elders, met with the *sangharāja*, who sits as the president of the council. Interestingly, her teacher and preceptor, Chao Khun Pra Prommuni, was one of the members of this supreme Council of Elders. When her case came to the table, he simply told the committee, "I was the one who gave her ordination."

Chao Khun Pra Prommuni was a man of few words, but everyone respected him for his clarity in the Dhamma and Vinaya. He had been one of two teachers presiding when the present king was ordained. The fact that the newly ordained nun was wearing light yellow, the color of a gourd blossom, was the issue at hand, and the question was whether she was impersonating a monk. Chao Khun Pra Prommuni asked the committee of most senior monks, "Can we use this color?" Everyone, in unison, answered, "No, it is against the Vinaya. Monks cannot wear this color." He then asked a very sensible question, "Then why are we forbidding it?" The result of the incident was that the Council of Elders simply certified the case as: "Do not see any harm to the *sangha*," and that was the end of the inquisition.

Building a Nuns' Community

In the Thai tradition, renunciant Buddhist women wore only white. To wear yellow was unheard of. The newly ordained nun became the talk of the town, but she persisted and many young women joined her. She trained them well, both in Dhamma and in Vinaya. She also taught them handicrafts, so that they could be self-sufficient.

The nuns who stayed with her were involved in many activities. Voramai was far ahead of her time, and some of her activities were quite daring for those times. For example, she started a stone factory, which was one of the very earliest. The nuns set to work chiseling soapstone to make various utensils to sell to support themselves. When the community grew larger, she opened a publishing house, and the nuns worked to bring out a monthly magazine.

This self-sufficient attitude might have been a result of Voramai's upbringing. In her early years, she had seen the model of the Catholic nuns, who were quite self-reliant and engaged in various social activities. She told us the story of Sister Rose, a Catholic sister at Assumption Convent, who observed what a good student Voramai was and offered to take her to France for higher studies. Of course, this offer came with a string attached: she must convert to Catholicism. Voramai confessed that she had been tempted, as she always had a great aspiration for higher learning, but her pride in being a Buddhist got the better of her. When she went to school the next day, she intentionally wore a big Buddha amulet around her neck, outside her uniform. Sister Rose took the hint and never made her offer again. Much of the training in handicrafts, discipline, and etiquette that Voramai had learned from the Catholic sisters was retained and passed down to her daughters and students.

Building a Temple

The idea of building a temple for *bhikkhunī*s had been with Voramai since the beginning. She realized that in order to start a temple, at least six *rai*[6] of land were required by law. So she moved to Bangkok and bought a piece of land exactly six *rai* in size in Nakhonpathom, about forty minutes outside the city. This is where Songdhammakalyani Monastery has always been located.

She began by building an *uposatha* hall in the 1960s, and the project took ten years to complete.[7] She offered the whole piece of land to the Buddha by marking the *sima* boundaries at the four corners of the land.[8]

Ordination as a *Bhikkhunī*

During this time I, Voramai's only daughter, went for further studies in Canada and came back with information to help actualize my mother's dream of becoming fully ordained as a *bhikkhunī*. In 1971, we went to Taiwan, where Voramai sought *bhikkhunī* ordination. Bhikkhu Ming San came forward to help her make connections and arranged to organize an ordination for her.[9] In Taiwan, ordination was only given annually, so a special ordination had to be arranged. Her preceptor, the respected *bhikkhu* Tao An Fashih of Sung San Temple in Taipei, who published a monthly Buddhist magazine in Chinese called *The Lion's Roar*, took a strong liking to Voramai.

The *bhikkhunī* ordination was conferred by the *bhikkhu saṅgha* only, and her preceptor, along with twelve other *bhikkhu*s, conferred the ordination.[10]

She was given the ordained name Ta Tao, which can be translated into Thai as Maha Bodhi Dhammacarya. However, upon her return to Thailand, people still called her by her lay name. Bhikkhu Tao An visited Songdhammakalyani Monastery to see how his disciple was doing. Of course, he was happy to see that Bhikkhunī Ta Tao was well established, despite the fact that she had support from neither the government nor the *sangha*. It had taken her fifteen years to realize her aspiration of receiving full ordination.

Her Activities

Because she was alone, Bhikkhunī Ta Tao could not perform any of the *sangha-kamma*s, because they require a specific number of *sangha* members. Still, she continued her temple activities, which included teaching Dhamma and practicing meditation. From her first master, she had learned to help people with her healing abilities and had become quite well known for that. When she was in her prime, between the ages of fifty and eight-four, people flocked to the temple to seek her help to heal their illnesses and obtain advice on how to become successful in life. At times, she did not get sufficient food, and her mealtimes became irregular because she had so many visitors. This became a constant problem, and she developed chronic gastric trouble.

Bhikkhunī Ta Tao did not emphasize chanting and was not strong on rituals; the *vinaya* requires a minimum of five nuns to perform a house blessing and similar rituals, which she could not perform alone. Her role was as a Dhamma teacher. Writing was at the forefront of her activities, as she published Dhamma messages for her readers and temple members. When she traveled around the country, she found many departed spirits who were suffering, mostly from war. For many years, she gave Dhamma teachings for the departed and guided them to forgiveness, which helped heal and nurture both the living and the dead.

When the 2nd Sakyadhita International Conference was held in Thailand in October 1991, Bhikkhunī Ta Tao was unable to walk. However, she received the Sakyadhita conference participants at Songdhammakalyani Monastery and handed each one of them a wooden rosary as a gift. The eminent Buddhist women teachers gathered there were Bhikkhunī Ta Tao, the host and abbess of Songdhammakalyani Monastery; Bhikkhunī Hiuwan;[11] Bhikkhunī Hyechun;[12] and Ayya Khema.[13] It was a meeting of some of the greatest female masters of our time. I stayed in the background with Ranjani de Silva, who later helped organize an important ordination for *bhikkhunī*s in Sri Lanka. In the audience were many members of Sakyadhita International, including Bhikkhunī Karma Lekshe Tsomo and numerous others.

Passing the Candle to the Next Generation

Bhikkhunī Ta Tao lived a very full life, engaging in Dhamma activities and receiving visitors from around the world. In 2001, I gave up my career as an academic and received the *sāmaṇerī* (novice) precepts in Sri Lanka, where I became known as Dhammananda.[14] One day when Bhikkhunī Ta Tao was ninety-four years old, when I was still a *sāmaṇerī*, she called me to her side and said, "I am leaving." Jokingly, I teased her, saying, "Oh, you cannot leave now. This is a temple for *bhikkhunīs* and I am only a *sāmaṇerī*. If you leave now, then there will be no *bhikkhunī* here." Bhikkhunī Ta Tao nodded her head, indicating that she could not leave yet.

Two years later, in February 2003, I received the full ordination of a *bhikkhunī*, also in Sri Lanka, and returned to Songdhammakalyani Monastery to lay the groundwork for a *bhikkhunī saṅgha* in Thailand. In one casual conversation, I asked Bhikkhunī Ta Tao how many *bhikkhunīs* she would like to see in her temple. Without hesitation, Bhikkhunī Ta Tao replied, "One hundred." Suddenly, she became very practical and asked me, "Could you afford to feed them?" I reassured her that I could. The great master Bhikkhunī Ta Tao passed away very peacefully on June 24, 2003, at the age of ninety-five years, two months, and eighteen days.

Songdhammakalyani Monastery has had *bhikkhunīs* in residence since 1971. Just one week after Bhikkhunī Ta Tao passed away, *bhikkhunīs* arrived from Sri Lanka, Indonesia, and Vietnam. Although one *bhikkhunī* (Bhikkhunī Ta Tao) has departed, six more *bhikkhunīs* have arrived. The *bhikkhunī saṅgha* spent the *vassa* in the temple and trained together for three months under Bhikkhunī Rahatungoda Saddha Sumana, a preceptor from Sri Lanka. The *bhikkhunī patimokkha* was recited for the first time in Thai history during the *vassas* of 2003 and 2004.

The candle has now passed to the third generation of *bhikkhunīs* with the hope that they will fully enjoy the conditions that the great master Bhikkhunī Ta Tao offered her life to prepare.

Sabbe sankhara anicca
Everything is impermanent.

Appamadena sampadetha
May all of us practice earnestly.

Notes

1. Thailand is said to be 95 percent Buddhist. Myanmar is second, with 87 percent.

2. Although there are an estimated twenty thousand *mae chi*s in Thailand who live as nuns, they are not officially recognized as members of the *saṅgha*. See Chatsumarn Kabilsingh, "The Future of the *Bhikkhunī Saṅgha* in Thailand," in *Speaking of Faith: Global Perspectives on Women, Religion, and Social Change*, ed. Diana L. Eck and Devaki Jain (Philadelphia: New Society Publishers, 1987); and Chatsumarn Kabilsingh, *Thai Women in Buddhism* (Berkeley: Parallax Press, 1991).

3. He was also known locally by his nickname, Narin Klueng Klueng.

4. The former Prince Bhujong Jombhunuj.

5. The full details of this incident have been recorded in my article "Three Waves of Bhikkhunīs in Thailand," *Yasodhara: Newsletter of International Buddhist Women's Activities*, July 2003.

6. An area of 2.2 *rai* is equal to one acre.

7. The *uposatha* hall is the main shrine room where proper *saṅghakamma* (actions or procedures of the *saṅgha*) are held.

8. This was reconstructed in 2001 to make it suitable for the performance of *saṅghakammas*.

9. Bhikkhu Ming San is now based in Indonesia.

10. For further information on *bhikkhunī* ordination from a Thai perspective, see Monica Lindberg Falk, *Making Fields of Merit: Buddhist Female Ascetics and Gendered Orders in Thailand* (Seattle: University of Washington Press, 2007), especially pp. 81–101.

11. An old friend, she founded Hua Fan University outside of Taipei.

12. The late president of the Korean National Bhikkhunī Association.

13. She was later ordained as a *bhikkhunī* at Hsi Lai Temple in Hacienda, California, in 1988 and was a co-founder of Sakyadhita International Association of Buddhist Women.

14. My previous name was Chatsumarn Kabilsingh, and I taught as an associate professor at Thammasat University in Bangkok.

6

Eminent Nuns in Hue, Vietnam

Elise Anne DeVido

Vietnam has a long tradition of *bhikkhunī*s dating from the twelfth century. However, opportunities for nuns to obtain education and training remained scarce until the early twentieth century, when Buddhist reformers in Vietnam, China, and other Asian nations advocated for the education and systematic training of nuns, encouraging them to teach, write, and publish. Throughout the twentieth century, both nuns and laywomen have played crucial roles in Vietnamese Buddhism. Yet to date, no book akin to Bhikkhu Dong Bon's *Biographies of Twentieth-Century Eminent Monks* has been published,[1] not even for the modern period.

Some published work on nuns has recently become available. For example, Bhikkhu Hai An and Ha Xuan Liem's *Lich su Phat Giao Hue* (History of Buddhism in Hue) has eighteen very useful biographical sketches of nuns from Hue.[2] Ha Liem Ha also has some informative pages on Hue's eminent nuns during the nineteenth and twentieth centuries.[3] There is also the biography of Su Ba by Le and Ho, *Duong thien sen no* (The Lotus Flower Blooms on the Chan Path), and Bhikkhu Dong Bon of Xa Loi Temple is currently working on a book of biographies of prominent nuns of the twentieth century. Additionally, in recent years, Vietnamese nuns have undertaken research on their own history and have presented papers in places such as the conferences of Sakyadhita, which encourages research about Buddhist women whose contributions to Buddhist history have been minimized or ignored by male historians.

As a contribution to this field, this chapter discusses in some detail the life of Bhikkhunī Dieu Khong (1905–1997), also known as Su Ba, one of Vietnam's most eminent twentieth-century nuns and a disciple of the pioneer Bhikkhunī Dien Truong (1863–1925). The chapter also gives a brief history of Dieu Khong's outstanding disciple, Bhikkhunī Tri Hai (1928–2003), a prolific scholar, teacher, ordination master, and translator who undertook many charitable works. These three women were all linked to the imperial household of the last Vietnamese dynasty, the Nguyen (1802–1945), based in Hue, and they also became students and patrons of Buddhism. Dien Truong was a great-granddaughter of the Minh Mang emperor; Dieu Khong's father was an imperial minister; and Tri Hai belonged to the royal family, too, though she was just seven years old when the dynasty ended.[4]

A Biography of Su Ba

Thich Nu Dien Truong (1863–1925) was the first fully ordained nun in the modern history of Vietnam.[5] Born Ho Thi Nhan, she was the daughter of a princess in the imperial family, a granddaughter of the royal prince and poet Tung Thien Vuong and a great-granddaughter of the Minh Mang emperor (reigned 1820–1840).

Dien Truong had a niece named Ho Thi Hanh who later became Bhikkhunī Dieu Khong, known as Su Ba by her disciples.[6] Ho Thi Hanh was born in Hue in 1905, the youngest in her family of four sisters and six brothers. Her mother was Chau Thi Luong (1865–1941). Her father, Ho Dac Trung (1861–1941), served as a high official under three emperors, Duy Tan, Khai Dinh, and Bao Dai.[7] Growing up in the early twentieth century, Su Ba was influenced by the interchange among cultures at that time—between old and new, East and West. She studied hard at school and was gifted in both Chinese and French. At fifteen years of age, she finished high school and continued to study at home as well as to take part in social action. She wanted to study politics and read about Gandhi, the French and Russian Revolutions, and about Phan Chu Trinh and Pham Boi Chau, Vietnam's famous anticolonial nationalists.[8]

As a young woman, Su Ba participated in charitable associations founded by Lady Dam Phuong (a teacher of women in the Royal Household). In 1926, she founded the Women Workers' Union (WWU). In her poem that follows, we can see a type of feminism that blends Western ideas about women's rights and workers' rights (unions), traditional Confucian ideals for women, and the paradigm of Vietnam's Trung-Trieu, the patriotic heroines who fought against Chinese invaders early in Vietnamese history[9] but who, in the early twentieth century, in a Vietnam under French colonial rule, were symbols of anti-French resistance:

"A Poem for the Women Workers' Union" (1926)

The Women Workers' Union is established in Hue. . . .
Economics enhances women's rights.
Vietnamese women can shoulder the country
To maintain the race of the dragon and the deities
Exemplifying women's [traditional Confucian] values of work-
    ing hard, exhibiting appropriate demeanor, appropriate
    speech and behavior, being modest and virtuous.
All women should be hard-working.
Follow the symbol of the Trung-Trieu heroines,
Passed down from generation to generation.[10]

At first, the WWU existed only in Hue, but it then spread all over Central Vietnam. To raise funds for it, Su Ba held auctions of the handmade fine arts made by WWU members. She became very successful at this and opened a famous shop called Nam Hoa[11] where many foreigners came to purchase items. She then founded another relief association, the Lac Thien Association, which had both Vietnamese and French members. This association helped women and the poor, but also helped the anticolonial movement, for example, the 1930–31 Nghe-Tinh Soviet movement.[12] When some of the participants were arrested, Su Ba went to the French authorities to negotiate for their release.[13]

At about this time, Su Ba often went to Truc Lam Temple and consulted with Bhikkhu Giac Tien, the abbot there. One day, the abbot asked her, "What are you doing now?" She answered, "I'm continuing my charity work and the Women Workers' Union." Bhikkhu Giac Tien said, "It's like a big tree, with many branches and fruits. The tree looks like it's flourishing, but what about the roots? What if the roots are rotten? In the end, the tree will fall down. Likewise, you will fail." Su Ba was very surprised and asked, "What is the root?" Bhikkhu Giac Tien answered, "You must cure the root. That's most important. People are distracted with the 'outer worldly appearances,' so they cannot discern their inner mind. If you don't improve the inner mind, it will be like a tree with rotten roots and the tree will soon fall down."

The master told Su Ba, "If you have a good mind, you should study Buddhism to improve your mind and teach the people. That way, there will be many people with hope for future generations who will struggle for an independent country." After hearing these words, Su Ba was surprised and

wondered: " 'Why are there are so many high-minded people in the temple?' "
She had thought that monastics merely chanted and never thought about
life, the welfare of society, or the nation. The words affected her deeply, and,
having decided to become a nun,[14] she went to live with her sister, Ho Thi
Chi (1902–1985),[15] at Khai An Temple. Every day for three years, she went
to study at Truc Lam Temple.

In 1932, at the age of twenty-seven, she took the three refugees with
Bhikkhu Giac Tien at Truc Lam Temple. Her Dharma name was the Respected Trung Hao (Lam Te lineage, forty-second generation). Her Dharma name
after she became a *sāmaṇerī* was Dieu Khong and her style name was Nhat
Diem Thanh (*Yi dian qing*, lit., "one-dot clear").

That same year, Dieu Khong bought land and had a temple built with
donations from other laywomen. Dieu Khong asked Dieu Huong to be the
abbess, and Phuoc Hue named the temple Dieu Duc Nunnery. Dieu Huong,
who had the position of supervising the nuns there, was known for her
high level of Dharma cultivation. Many people therefore came to Dieu Duc
Nunnery to study with her, and the temple produced many outstanding and
famous nuns.[16] In the fall of 1944, Su Ba was fully ordained at Thuyen Ton
Temple under Thich Giac Nhien. In 1971, at the age of eighty-eight, Dieu
Huong passed away and was buried at Dieu Duc. The following three sections
discuss highlights of her extraordinary life.

Su Ba and the Buddhist Revival in Vietnam

From the 1920s through the 1940s, many Buddhists from all three regions
of Vietnam—north, central, and south—sought to reform and revitalize Buddhist institutions through the Buddhist Restoration Movement (Chan Hung
Phat Giao), part of a transnational Buddhist modernization movement.[17] Buddhists throughout Asia were promoting reforms in temple administration
and systematic education and training for both monks and nuns. Buddhist
associations were founded, modern publishing established, and social welfare
work expanded. Roles and responsibilities in teaching and administration also
increased for laypeople.

Although not mentioned in the general Buddhist histories of Vietnam,
Su Ba contributed greatly to the Chan Hung Phat Giao in Central Vietnam
and should figure prominently in historical accounts of the Vietnamese Buddhist revival. Aided by her fluent French and the fact that her father worked
at court, Su Ba played a crucial role in founding the Annam (Central Vietnam) Buddhist Association. In 1932, she sent the application form for this
association directly to Emperor Bao Dai and he accepted it. Together with

Bhikkhu Giac Tien, Bhikkhunī Phuoc Hue, Dr. Le Dinh Tham, and others, she established the association in Hue, with branches in other areas of Central Vietnam.[18] After two years, every district throughout Central Vietnam, from Thanh Hoa to Phan Thiet, had provincial and branch associations with teachers and lecturers propagating Buddhism.

After Su Ba became a *sāmaṇerī*, she sold her jewelry and requested donations from other people to build nunneries. In addition to the Dieu Duc, Dieu Vien, and Khai An Temples mentioned above, she also founded eleven other temples in Vietnam[19] as well as many schools for nuns.[20]

Su Ba was a major force in Buddhist education. She founded Buddhist institutes such as the one at Tay Thien Temple in Hue, the first primary school at Truc Lam Temple, and a school for nuns at Tu Dam Temple (moved to Dieu Duc Temple in 1934) where she taught the *Huayen Sūtra* and the *Jingce*.

Su Ba was also a prolific poet and Buddhist scholar. She translated many Buddhist works from Chinese to Vietnamese (*quoc ngu*).[21] As an ordination master, she lectured to nuns on Buddhist doctrine and the *Diamond Sūtra*; she also gave Dharma talks to laypeople. She contributed to the founding of orphanages all over Central Vietnam.[22] Each of Su Ba's contributions to the revitalization of Buddhism in Central Vietnam deserves a full and in-depth study; however, thus far these have been sorely lacking in the available historiography.

Su Ba and the 1960's Buddhist Struggle Movement

All her life, Su Ba took action to protect Buddhists and Buddhism, not only during the French colonial period, but also during Vietnam's Buddhist Struggle Movement. Again, existing narratives unfortunately do not acknowledge Su Ba's activities during this time.[23]

As is well known, the series of regimes established by the United States in South Vietnam, beginning with Ngo Dinh Diem's, had disastrous consequences for Buddhists. With petitions, demonstrations, and hunger strikes, Buddhists all over the country rose up to fight to save Buddhism in Vietnam, but it all was to no avail. In Hue, Su Ba volunteered to immolate herself to protest against the Diem regime and went with her sister Dieu Hue to Saigon. There, while many monks and nuns participated in a hunger strike, Su Ba chanted the *Thuy Sam Sūtra* continuously while awaiting her death. But the Buddhist leaders refused her request, telling her that Bhikkhu Thich Quang Duc would shoulder the responsibility and that Su Ba, who was still young, should continue to work for Buddhism.

The self-immolation of Thich Quang Duc on June 11, 1963, and the subsequent self-immolation of many other monks, nuns, laymen, and laywomen shocked people all over the world and propelled the Buddhist Struggle Movement to receive international attention. After Thich Quang Duc's self-destruction by fire, Su Ba wrote this poem:

> The fire is roaring all around, but his body didn't move;
> The gasoline is spread all over the ground but his mind is not stirred;
> Thich Quang Duc now resides happily in the Pure Land and follows the Buddha;
> I am suffering in this world; I miss Thay (Master/Teacher).[24]

When she returned to Hue, Su Ba asked some nuns to disguise themselves in order to go out to each district and distribute a letter she had written encouraging people to continue to support Buddhism and not give up hope. After the fall of the Diem regime on November 1, 1963, imprisoned monks and nuns were released from jail. In 1964, the United Buddhist Church was established with headquarters at An Quang Temple, but Buddhists continued to be oppressed under successive regimes in South Vietnam. Despite state oppression and under horrific wartime conditions, Vietnamese Buddhists helped with wartime relief and established not only orphanages, but also more than two hundred Bodhi Schools, which ranged from primary to high school levels. During the 1960s, Su Ba, with Bhikkhus Tri Thu and Minh Chau, the layman Ngo Trong Anh, and others, established Van Hanh University in Saigon, the first Buddhist university in Vietnam.[25]

Su Ba and the Post-Reunification Period

After 1975, Su Ba held the position of the leading nun of South/Central Vietnam and made many contributions to help unify Buddhism in South and North Vietnam. She was an ordination master and a committee member of both the Hue and the National-level Buddhist Congregations. In 1983, as part of her lifelong emphasis on Buddhist education, Su Ba helped to establish two Buddhist universities, one in Ho Chi Minh City and one in Hanoi. She supported the Buddhist magazine *Giac Ngo* in Ho Chi Minh City and continued her translation work and poetry. In 1985, when she was eighty years old, Su Ba began to translate the hundred volumes of the *Mahāprajñāpāramitāśāstra* by Nāgārjuna, finishing the last volume in 1997, the year she passed away. She lived in a frugal and simple way, freely helping others and always adhering to the Dharma for all her monastic life. On September 23, 1997, at the age of ninety-three, she passed away at Hong An Temple in Hue. Su Ba had spent fifty-three years in the *sangha*. Her *stūpa* is located near the temple.[26]

Tinh An and Tinh Nhu, disciples of Su Ba, consider her to be a great being (*da zhangfu*): strong in will, free in thought, and independent in every way. From my brief visit to the temples associated with Su Ba in Hue and from speaking with her disciples and students, it is clear that she was and remains a powerful inspiration to many people in the world. Her disciples and students, among whom are temple abbesses, live and practice all over Vietnam and abroad in places such as Taiwan, China, England, India, the United States, Canada, Australia, and Germany.[27] One inspiring example is Su Ba's former personal attendant, Bhikkhunī Hue An, who built Phuoc Son Temple in the hills near Hue. For many years, Hue An has been of remarkable help to the poor in the region, especially students and flood victims.[28] The 2009 biography of Su Ba by Le Nghan and Ho Dac Hoai includes many heretofore unknown details about her life and accomplishments, but if we are to understand the full range of her achievements and contributions to Buddhism and to Vietnamese history, there is much more work to be done.

Su Ba's Disciple: Ni Truong Tri Hai

Bhikkhunī Tri Hai (Tam Hy), one of Su Ba's outstanding disciples, was born Nguyen Phuoc Cong Tang Ton Nu Phung Khanh in Hue on March 9, 1938, to an aristocratic family of devout Buddhists who were descendants of the Minh Mang emperor (reigned 1820–40).[29] Phung Khanh excelled in her studies. After she graduated from high school at the age of seventeen, she wanted to renounce the household life, but first she became a high school teacher in Da Nang. After that, she went to the United States where, from 1962 to 1963, she took graduate courses in the English Department at Indiana University, Bloomington.[30] After completing her studies in late 1963, she returned to Vietnam. In 1964, she finally renounced the household life and became a nun under Bhikkhunī Dieu Khong at Hong An Temple in Hue. As a novice nun, she was chosen to become an assistant to Bhikkhu Minh Chau at Van Hanh University, the first Buddhist university in Vietnam. In 1968, she took the *sikkhamana* precepts in Nha Trang. She was selected to be the librarian at Van Hanh University and the manager of the School of Youth for Social Service. In 1970, she became fully ordained in Da Nang and was given the monastic name Tri Hai. At Van Hanh University, she lectured to both monastics and laypeople, translated, and also undertook many charitable activities. For example, the humanitarian organization Oxfam asked her to head the Vietnam Oxfam Association, which she directed from 1965 to 1975. She also taught Levels III to V of the Majjhima Nikāya in English at the Vietnam Buddhist Academy and Van Hanh Temple.

When in Hue, Bhikkhunī Tri Hai lectured on the *Canh Sach* (Guishan's Admonitions) at Dieu Hy and Hong An Temples. During *vassa* each year, she was invited to lecture at Phuoc Hoa Temple in Hoc Mon and Dai Giac Temple in Soc Trang. From 1996 to 1999, she taught the *bhikkhunī vinaya* and the *bodhisattva* precepts at the Intermediate Buddhist School (Thien Phuoc Temple) in Long An Province. At the ordination ceremonies at Thien Phuoc Temple in Long An, she was invited to lecture on the *bhikkhunī vinaya*, where she gave the examinations and was head of the exam group. In 2003, she was the vice-master at the ordination ceremony at Tu Nghiem Temple. At the time of her death, she was the director of finances and vice president of the Vietnam Buddhist University in Ho Chi Minh City.

Bhikkhunī Tri Hai was a Dharma master, teacher, translator, poet, editor, and publisher. She knew English, French, Chinese, Pāli, and some German. She has more than one hundred published works, including introductory works for Buddhist students, a Pāli-English-Vietnamese dictionary, works introducing Tibetan Buddhism, and works on contemporary philosophers such as Gandhi, Krishnamurti, Tagore, and Erich Fromm.[31] For decades, she was involved in charitable works throughout Vietnam. Tragically, on December 7, 2003, while returning from a charitable mission in Phan Thiet Province, she and two other nuns (Sa Di Phuoc Tinh and Bhikkhunī Tue Nha) were killed in a traffic accident. Bhikkhunī Tri Hai was sixty-six years old and had been a nun for thirty-three years.

At the memorial service and afterward, letters, poems, and couplets of praise and remembrance poured in from all over Vietnam and around the world for Bhikkhunī Tri Hai, an eminent nun of Vietnam and a beacon of wisdom and compassion.[32] She is buried at Dieu Khong Temple in Hoc Mon District, outside Ho Chi Minh City. The Dieu Khong Temple that she built in 2003 is now home to six nuns.[33] Two of them, Bhikkhunīs Tue Dung and Tue Nguyen, are currently building a new temple complex and continue Tri Hai's charitable activities: visiting hospitalized cancer patients during the Lunar New Year to give donations ("red envelopes") and giving aid to the elderly, sick, handicapped, and orphaned.

Bhikkhunī Tue Dung became a nun in 1980 after hearing Tri Hai speak in 1979 on the *Diamond Sūtra*. She has completed some translations from English and French into Vietnamese. Each year on the death anniversary of Tri Hai, Tue Dung publishes a manuscript or republishes a work by Tri Hai, for example, the Majjhima Nikāya, translated from Pāli by Thich Minh Chau, abridged and annotated by Tri Hai.

Sustaining the *Bhikkhunī* Legacy

This chapter has documented some of the important contributions made by Buddhist nuns of Hue to the development and maintenance of Buddhism in Vietnam. Through decades of war and political repression, these eminent nuns have given much to the defense, revitalization, and modernization of Buddhism in Hue, and Vietnam as well. Their selfless work continues to serve as a gracious example for people around the world today. I urge Vietnamese nuns and all interested others to research documents, interview elder nuns, and chronicle the accomplishments of Vietnamese Buddhist nuns from all time periods, particularly the twentieth century, before these stories of generosity, intelligence, fortitude, and selflessness become lost to Buddhist history forever.

Notes

1. Thich Dong Bon, ed., *Tieu Su Danh Tang Viet Nam The Ky XX* (Biographies of Eminent Vietnamese Monks of the Twentieth Century), vol. I (Ho Chi Minh City: Thanh Hoi Phat Giao, 1995); vol. 2 (Hanoi: Ban Ton Giao, 2001).

2. Thich Hai An and Ha Xuan Liem, *Lich su Phat Giao Hue* (History of Buddhism in Hue) (Ho Chi Minh City: Van Hoa, 2006), pp. 433, 639–56.

3. Ha Xuan Liem, *Nhung chua thap Phat giao o Hue* (Some Buddhist Pagodas in Hue) (Hanoi: Van Hoa Tong Tin, 2007), pp. 516–26.

4. There is a dearth of "objective" scholarship in any language on the last dynastic house in Vietnam, partly because of a loss of primary historical materials, but more because of this dynasty's complex relations with French colonialists. Some emperors resisted and others, especially the final two, collaborated with the French, thus posing an ideological conundrum for nationalist and revolutionary historians.

5. Thich Hai An and Ha Xuan Liem, *Lich su Phat Giao Hue* (History of Buddhism in Hue) (Ho Chi Minh City: Van Hoa, 2006), pp. 433–34; and Nguyen Lang, *Viet Nam Phat Giao Su Luan* (Essays on the History of Buddhism in Vietnam) (Hanoi: Van Hoc, 1994), pp. 152–55.

6. *Su Ba* is a term of respect for one's master if she is a senior nun. *Su* means teacher and *ba* is a respectful term for an older woman. *Ni Truong* is a term of respect for a senior nun.

7. Le Ngan and Ho Dac Hoai, eds., *Duong thien sen no* (The Lotus Flower Blooms on the Chan Path) (Hanoi: Lao Dong, 2009), pp. 15–23. This is a biography of Su Ba Dieu Khong.

8. Ibid., pp. 30–31.

9. The Trung-Trieu heroines were three oft-extolled patriotic heroines in Vietnamese history. The Trung sisters were noblewomen who led the first major insurrection against the Chinese invaders in 40 CE. They defeated the Chinese and established an independent state that extended from Hue to southern China. In 42 CE, when captured by the Chinese, they committed suicide. In 248 CE, a woman named Trieu An, who was not from an aristocratic background, led a revolt against the Chinese and committed suicide rather than surrender. She is popularly referred to as "Vietnam's Joan of Arc."

10. Le and Ho, eds., *Duong thien sen no*, p. 61.

11. Nam Hoa is a nativist/patriotic term, meaning to Vietnamize and to cast off French and Chinese cultural and political influence. Like Gandhi's idea of *swadeshi*, it is a call to boycott foreign products.

12. In 1930–1931, an uprising against French rule occurred in Nghe An, Ha Tinh, and parts of nearby provinces, after which Soviet-style local regimes were proclaimed. However, the French quickly suppressed this movement.

13. Le and Ho, *Duong thien sen no*, pp. 31–32.

14. Ibid., pp. 79–81.

15. This sister had been the second wife of Emperor Khai Dinh, who reigned from 1916 to 1925. She was well educated and spoke fluent French. The emperor wanted to marry her (his first wife had left him). Although Ho Thi Chi was unwilling to marry, she had no choice, for if she refused, her father and the whole family would be exiled from court. However, Ho Thi Chi never became pregnant; it was presumed that the Emperor was impotent, because he had at least twelve wives and none ever became pregnant. When a royal servant woman gave birth to a son who was proclaimed by the French rulers and Khai Dinh to be the son of the emperor, heir to the throne, and the future Bao Dai Emperor (reigned 1925–45), the Emperor promoted the servant woman to the status of Lady, and, in 1924, she became the Maternal Empress Tu Cung, thus shutting out Ho Thi Chi from the royal household. Su Ba and Ho Thi Chi's parents' donated the land for Khai An Temple, named "Khai" for the Khai Tinh Emperor and "An" from Ho Thi Chi's royal title, An Phi. Ho Thi Chi thereafter took solace in both Buddhism and Catholicism. Nguyen Viet Ke, *Stories of The Nguyen Dynasty's Kings* (Danang: Danang Publishing House, 2008), p. 107; Le and Ho, *Duong thien sen no*, pp. 20, 23, and 25; notes from visit to Khai An Temple, July 7, 2009.

16. Dieu Duc's legacy continues; since 1991, Dieu Duc has operated an Intermediate Level Buddhist Institute for Nuns.

17. For more on the "Buddhist Revival" in Vietnam, see Elise A. DeVido, " 'Buddhism for This World': The Buddhist Revival in Vietnam, 1920–1951, and Its Legacy," in *Modernity and Re-enchantment: Religion in Post-revolutionary Vietnam*, ed. Philip Taylor (Lanham, MD: Lexington Books, 2008), pp. 250–96.

18. The official French name of the Annam Buddhist Association was Société d'Étude et d'Exercice de la Religion du Bouddhisme de l'Annam. Without permission from the French colonial government in Hue, any organization and its members would have been immediately suppressed. Likewise, the Buddhist Associations in the North and the South were established under French auspices.

19. The temples she founded included Hong An, Kieu Dam, Dinh Hue, Dong Thuyen, Hong Duc, Lien Tri, and Lien Hoa in Hue; Bao Thang in Hoi An; Bao Quang in Da Nang; Tinh Nghiem in Quang Ngai; and Dieu Quang in Nha Trang.

20. Schools were established at Giac Linh Temple in Sa Dec; Tu Nghiem, Duoc Su, and Dieu Trang in Ho Chi Minh City; and Dieu Phap in Ho Nai, Long Thanh.

21. For example, *Thanh duy thuc luan* (*On the Doctrine of Consciousness-Only*) (n.p., n.d.); *Du gia su dia luan* (*Yogācārabhumiśāstra*) [this includes the *bodhisattva* precepts manual] (n.p., n.d.); *Lang gia tam an* (Lankāvatāra Sūtra) (n.p., n.d.); *Di Lac ha sanh kinh* (*Maitreya Ascension Sūtra*) (n.p., n.d.); and *Trung quan luan luoc giai* (*On the Madhyamaka*) (n.p., n.d.).

22. Le and Ho, *Duong thien sen no*, pp. 34–35; 82–86.

23. For example, Thich Thien Hoa (1970), who knew her. Thich Thien Hoa, *50 Nam Chan Hung Phat Giao* (Fifty Years of Buddhist Revival in Vietnam) (Saigon: Sen Vang, 1970).

24. Le and Ho, *Duong thien sen no*, p. 36.

25. Ibid., pp. 34–36; 97–108.

26. Ibid., pp. 30–38; 111–17.

27. Noted to me by her disciple Bhikkhunī Tinh An, July 3, 2009.

28. I visited Phuoc Son Temple on July 8, 2009, on a hot summer's day and was impressed by the efforts of the local people, young, old, female, and male, who were engaged in the hard labor of laying a macadam road to facilitate access to the hilltop temple complex.

29. *Nguyen Phuoc* refers to the royal family, the last dynastic house in Vietnam, 1802 to 1945. *Cong Tang* signifies that her great-great-grandfather was the Minh Mang Emperor and *Ton Nu* that she was a female royal family member. Phung Khanh was her given name. Explanation by Bhikkhunī Tue Dung, e-mail correspondence, August 4, 2009. My impression from speaking with Tri Hai's disciples is that she rarely, if ever, mentioned her royal background; in fact, some disciples were not aware of it. Tri Hai was seven years old when the Nguyen Dynasty ended in 1945, and thus her interactions with the imperial household were indirect. After reading the memorial volume, it is obvious to me that Tri Hai studied and worked very hard and lived simply and frugally and for the benefit of others. See, for example, the photographs of Tri Hai laboring barefoot in the mud and pedaling a cart in which one nun and three elderly laypeople are sitting in Vien Nghien Cuu Phat Hoc Viet Nam, comp., *Tuong niem Ni Truong Thich Nu Tri Hai, 1938–2003* (In Remembrance of Venerable Nun Tri Hai, 1938–2003) (Ho Chi Minh City: Tong Hop, 2004), pp. 29 and 390.

30. Information provided by Registrar's Office, University of Indiana, Bloomington, August 14, 2009.

31. Noted to me by her disciple Bhikkhunī Tue Dung, July 1, 2009.

32. *Tuong niem Ni Truong Thich Nu Tri Hai*, pp. 71–227, 255–318.

33. I noticed a White Tara statue inside the main entrance gate. Tri Hai was interested in Tibetan Buddhism and translated a number of English works on the subject into Vietnamese.

7

Bhikṣuṇī Như Thanh

A Polar Star among Vietnamese Nuns

Thích Nữ Như Nguyệt

Against the background of Vietnam's recent Buddhist history and its grow-ing *bhikṣuṇī* order, this chapter introduces the work of Bhikṣuṇī Như Thanh (1911–1999), an exemplary *bhikṣuṇī* who devoted her entire life to the cause of uniting Vietnamese Buddhist nuns and teaching the Dharma in order to help liberate human beings from suffering. Happily, her achievements are being magnified by successive generations. Just as the daughters of the Bud-dha throughout the world have made great strides in many different fields, so too in Vietnam, where the leadership qualities of Bhikṣuṇī Như Thanh helped inspire the Vietnamese *bhikṣuṇī saṅgha* to great achievements, even during extremely difficult times.

There is an irony in praising this eminent *bhikṣuṇī*, because at heart, she was a very humble person. As the respected abbess of one of the first nunneries in Saigon, South Vietnam, Bhikṣuṇī Như Thanh had no desire for wealth or fame. In fact, during her lifetime, she did not approve of us writ-ing her story. I was fortunate enough to have had firsthand experience with her. I was her full-time personal attendant for more than twenty-two years, until her last days, and I knew her as a Buddhist practitioner, a teacher, an educator, a writer, a feminist, and a Dharma friend. It is now time for me to chronicle her achievements.

The Buddhist Revival Movement in
Twentieth-Century Vietnam

Since ancient times, Vietnamese Buddhism has been affected by the political currents of the times. After the golden eras of the Đinh, Lê, Lý, and Tran Dynasties, toward the end of the Nguyen Dynasty, Buddhism began to decline. During the hundred years of French domination (1854–1954), Christianity established a solid position in Vietnamese society, while Buddhism was no longer at the forefront and, in fact, became distorted. Without a proper understanding of the essentials of Buddhism, ordinary people developed a polytheistic approach: the Buddha was taken for an important god and was worshipped together with Confucius and Lao Tzu in a pantheon of gods in temples across the country. Buddhism became mixed with the folk religions of China, and most temples practiced superstitious forms of worship and ritual. By the 1930s, Buddhism had seriously declined, especially in southern Vietnam. Many Buddhist followers, both monastic and lay, felt an urgency to change the situation and build a new form of Vietnamese Buddhism.

In the early twentieth century, following the Buddhist reform movements initiated by Dhammapala in India and the great teacher Bhiksu Taixu (1890–1947) in China, a movement to reform Vietnamese Buddhism arose as the result of a campaign carried out by several senior monks. From 1920 to 1945, this movement spread throughout the country, and several Buddhist institutes and associations for the study of Buddhist doctrine were founded. In southern Vietnam, the Association of Buddhist Studies was established in Saigon in 1931, and a Buddhist Institute of Learning was established in Trà Vinh in 1934. In central Vietnam, a Buddhist Institute of Learning was established at Hue in 1932.[1] In the northern outpost of Hanoi, a Buddhist institute was established in 1934.[2] Buddhist magazines were published to help propagate and update Buddhist teachings—publications such as *The Sound of Dharma, Buddhist Teachings for Youth, The Sound of Compassion, The Sound of Perfection*, and *The Torch of Wisdom*.[3] The new movement tried to replace Chinese characters with Romanized Vietnamese, making Buddhist texts easier to read, interpret, and reproduce, thus aiding a better understanding of Buddhism among the population.

Along with the enthusiastic monks who led the revival movement, there was also a *bhikṣuṇī* from Huệ Tâm in North Vietnam named Diên Trường, who was very active. She constructed the famous Trúc Lâm Temple in Hue and held classes on Buddhism for nuns. Following her example, a *bhikṣuṇī* named Dieu Hương initiated Buddhist studies classes for nuns at Tu Đàm Temple in Hue in 1932. In the south, Buddhist studies for nuns began for the first time at Giác Hoa Nunnery in Bac Liêu Province in 1927. In 1936, classes on Buddhism also began on the outskirts of Saigon under the leadership of

Bhikṣuṇī Dieu Tinh, and at about the same time, classes for nuns were established at Lương Xuyên Buddhist Institute of Learning in Lương Xuyên Province.

Unfortunately, the efforts of the Buddhist revival movement were
interrupted by World War II (1940–1945). After the war, Buddhist organizations were reopened in Hanoi under the leadership of Bhikṣuṇīs Tri Lien
and Trí Hai. This movement spread to Hue, where Buddhist associations
were also reorganized. In Saigon, a new organization called the School of
Buddhist Studies was established in South Vietnam. In 1947, Bhikṣuṇī Như
Thanh established Huê Lâm Temple in Saigon for training *bhikṣuṇī*s to teach
Dharma and to do charity work. This created a firm foundation for the
bhikṣuṇī revival movement and the founding of the Bhikṣuṇī Saṅgha Association of South Vietnam in 1956.[4]

In 1950, the World Buddhist Association was founded as a consortium
of Buddhists from sixty-four member countries to consider ways to keep pace
with changes in contemporary society. At about this time, a movement to
create a unified association of Buddhists from the north, central, and south
of Vietnam arose and spread quickly. After much consultation, the Vietnam
Buddhist Saṅgha was founded at Quán Su Temple in Hanoi under the leadership of Bhikṣu Thích Tinh Khiet. This organization united Buddhists all over
Vietnam and brought an end to the tendency for monastics and temples to
each go their own way, both doctrinally and in practice.[5]

The Eminent Qualities of Bhikṣuṇī Như Thanh, Leader of the Bhikṣuṇī Reform Movement in Vietnam

Bhikṣuṇī Như Thanh was born Nguyen Thi Thao in 1911 in southern Vietnam.
As a young child, she exhibited strong determination and persuasive powers.
Her father was a mandarin in the feudal government of Vietnam, which had
by then fallen under French colonial influence. As the daughter of a well-to-
do family, she was sent to a French school, but after a short time she decided
that modern education was not for her and refused to attend school. Instead,
she asked to be allowed to study at home with her father, who was a learned
man of the old school. Her father acquiesced. He provided his daughter with
a classical Chinese education and, in addition, he taught her about Buddhism.
Both branches of knowledge came to shape her future as a nun.

In the early twentieth century, French-educated Vietnamese intellectuals organized national and communist-nationalist anticolonial movements.
Challenged by these movements, the French colonists lashed out with great
anger; countless lives were shattered overnight and tragedy became common-
place. In 1932, at the age of twenty-two, recognizing the impermanent nature
of life and all existence, Thi Thao requested her parents' permission to ordain.

Although the order of Buddhist nuns began very early in Vietnam, from at least the second century CE with the ordination of Man Nương (ca. 175–255), there is only scattered mention of them in historical documents, and there is not enough information to reach any conclusions about their lives and activities. However, it is safe to say that throughout much of Vietnamese history, Buddhist nuns have played a very modest role and have always been overshadowed by their male counterparts.

Historical sources reveal that prior to the twentieth century, there were clusters of Buddhist nuns in Vietnam whose contributions were mostly directed toward the construction of temples. However, in the early twentieth century, the tide began to turn. A great number of Vietnamese Buddhist nuns became active in spreading Buddhist philosophy, publishing Buddhist books, and other tasks. However, their efforts remained largely scattered for the first half of the twentieth century.

During the 1930s, Bhikṣuṇī Dieu Tinh did her best to activate the *bhikṣuṇī*s,[6] but she was unable to effect substantial changes. It was Bhikṣuṇī Như Thanh, abbess of Huê Lâm Temple, with her persuasive power and vision, who helped galvanize the nuns and initiated the *bhikṣuṇī* revival movement. She said, "If we sisters remain disconnected and do not unite, we are no different than orphans—lonely upon the sea, buffeted by the wind, totally unorganized."

For twenty-nine long years (1927–1956), Bhikṣuṇī Như Thanh silently and patiently went from place to place, from Sài Gòn to the remote villages of My Tho, Cai Ly, Sa Déc, Can Thơ, Rach Giá, Cà Mau, and Châu Đoc, in search of people with a similar mind-set and passion. Wherever she went, she advocated a united future for *bhikṣuṇī*s. Thanks to her unique mobilizing capacity, on October 6, 1956, a council of *bhikṣuṇī*s was organized at Huê Lâm Temple, and the Bhikṣuṇī Saṅgha of South Vietnam was formally established and institutionalized in Articles 13 and 14 of Chapter II of the regulations of the South Vietnam Buddhist Saṅgha, thus fulfilling the dream of generations of Vietnamese *bhikṣuṇī*s.[7] Under the newly institutionalized regulations, Vietnamese Buddhist nuns enjoyed unprecedented independence from the *bhikṣu saṅgha*; though reporting to the *bhikṣu saṅgha* administratively, *bhikṣuṇī*s were now solely in charge of their own internal affairs. Another major change brought about by the new regulations was that all nunneries across the country would now follow uniform standards regarding religious practice, monastic observances, and even architectural design. The improved standards of monastic discipline enabled the *bhikṣuṇī*s to achieve new prominence and respect.

Bhikṣuṇī Như Thanh was given the honor of heading the organization. Her virtues and capabilities were lauded by monks as well as by nuns. In his article about the life and work of Bhikṣuṇī Như Thanh,[8] Bhikṣu Đong Minh used the word "eminent" to describe the respect and admiration he felt for her. Bhikṣu Thích Giác Thien, another eminent monk of the time, agreed: "The abbess is a person who possesses extraordinary self-discipline, an excellent ability to expound the Buddha's teachings, exceptional organizational abilities, and an outstanding ability to mobilize others."

In 1972, the Bhikṣuṇī Saṅgha of South Vietnam was renamed the Mahāyāna Bhikṣuṇī Saṅgha. This change enabled the *bhikṣuṇīs* in southern Vietnam to reach out and embrace their sisters in the northern and central parts of the country, marking another milestone in the history of Vietnam's *bhikṣuṇī* order. As a consequence, today Vietnamese nuns from all parts of the country have established a remarkable degree of solidarity, national cooperation, and mutual support.

Exemplary Organizational Abilities

From the time the *bhikṣuṇī saṅgha* was formally founded, Bhikṣuṇī Như Thanh initiated a number of large-scale organizations throughout the country, thus brilliantly demonstrating her leadership skills. Despite enormous challenges and disruptions during many years of war and suffering, she managed to forge a coalition of nuns from north to south. The unification of *bhikṣuṇīs* not only empowered them to advocate for equal rights for monks and nuns, but also enhanced their capacity to educate others and shine the light of Dharma and to dispel the darkness of ignorance. The twenty-six articles and nine sections of the Bhikṣuṇī Saṅgha Regulations clearly set forth the organization's objectives and the strict discipline that every Vietnamese *bhikṣuṇī* is expected to follow.

Large nunneries such as Tu Nghiêm and Dươc Sư became exemplary institutions for Buddhist education. In line with their objectives, they offered courses in Buddhist studies and monastic discipline and intensive summer retreats. In addition, Bhikṣuṇī Như Thanh served as the head preceptress for fifteen ordination ceremonies between 1946 and 1998 and thus significantly contributed to spreading the essence of Buddhism among Vietnamese women.

Along with the developments occurring in the *bhikṣuṇī saṅgha*, Buddhism in general was being reinvigorated as temples were reorganized, polytheistic and superstitious elements were eliminated, and Dharma classes were initiated to improve standards of Buddhist education. The temples also instituted charitable activities, such as health clinics offering both Asian traditional treatments and Western medicine, orphanages, nursery schools, primary schools, and vocational training, all free of charge, making health care and education accessible to thousands of people at a time when Vietnam had not yet fully recovered from the terrible destruction of war. This strengthening of individual temples helped build the strength of the *bhikṣuṇī saṅgha*, while at the same time the increasing influence of the *bhikṣuṇī saṅgha* empowered the local nunneries and fostered their development, enabling them to better serve society.

Fostering Self-sufficiency

In line with the Zen saying, "A day of no work is a day without food," the nunneries were encouraged to become self-sufficient. Self-sufficiency was important for two reasons: first, to help the nuns understand the hardships entailed in making a living, so that they would be thrifty and grateful to their donors; and second, to help the nuns become independent, so that they would not have to depend on others and could concentrate on the virtuous life. At Huê Lâm Nunnery, self-sufficiency was especially stressed. The many enterprises that the nunnery began—vegetarian restaurants, soy sauce production centers, a Buddhist tailoring shop, a *sūtra* publications center, an incense production center, and so on—are still functioning today and generate sufficient income to support the expenses of the nunnery and its social welfare activities. To foster independence from the *bhikṣuṇī saṅgha*, Bhikṣuṇī Như Thanh tackled the issue of self-sufficiency on two fronts: at the broader level, she set up South Vietnam Bhikṣuṇī Saṅgha Support Board; at the local level, she encouraged nunneries to form Triple Gem Protection Boards, organizations established to preserve Buddhism, to be led and operated by the lay community.

These efforts toward self-sufficiency developed naturally from the insight that dependence on the *bhikṣu saṅgha* weakened the *bhikṣuṇī* community. If the nuns always asked for help from the *bhikṣu saṅgha*, then they might become dependent and lose their capacity to manage their own affairs. Bhikṣuṇī Như Thanh said, "The *bhikṣuṇī*s living the true Buddhadharma have an opportunity to open their minds, propagate the light of Dharma, and make it brighter, which creates infinite merit."[9] It was this very independent spirit that compelled her response to Bhikṣu Trí Thu, who proposed that *bhikṣuṇī*s should take up charity work, such as managing orphanages, and leave the teaching of Dharma to the *bhikṣu*s. Bhikṣuṇī Như Thanh politely but strongly responded that *bhikṣuṇī*s wished to take up both tasks: "Those *bhikṣuṇī*s who have the capacity to teach can teach, and those *bhikṣuṇī*s who have the capacity to do charity work can do charity work."[10]

Today, *bhikṣuṇī*s are invited to teach Dharma at various temples and at many Buddhist schools. They all owe a debt of gratitude to Bhikṣuṇī Như Thanh. Both the temples and their charitable projects are still self-sufficient and autonomous.

Capable of Interpreting the Dharma

Bhikṣuṇī Như Thanh thoroughly understood Prajñāpāramitā philosophy and often transmitted these teachings with the expectation that future generations could grasp the substance of the Buddhadharma and preserve the tradition. Her thorough understanding of the philosophy contained in the *Prajñāpāramitā Sūtra*—that *śūnyatā* (emptiness) inherently has no form and that *prajñā* (wisdom) is infinite—demonstrated her capacity for insightful interpretation of the Buddha's core teachings. Indeed, she seemed to embody its essence. Her philosophical acumen is evident in her writings, including *An Outline of the Prajñāpāramitā Sūtra*,[11] which systematizes the essential teachings of the *Great Prajñāpāramitā Sūtra* composed of six hundred volumes, and *Practicing the Way of Bodhisattva* (1989),[12] which is based on the *Avatamsaka Sūtra*.

Bhikṣuṇī Như Thanh's character is epitomized by the great vow: "Looking up, I seek enlightenment. Looking down, I liberate sentient beings." Those who were fortunate enough to attend her teachings were impressed with both her eloquence and her thorough understanding. Her words came forth naturally and directly from her heart. At Buddhist conferences, she always spoke lucidly and made such clear arguments that she earned the high esteem of all, even from the *bhikṣu*s.

A Bright Mirror of Virtuous Conduct

Buddhism is not just doctrine: it is a religion of practice. Bhikṣuṇī Như Thanh's advice to *bhikṣuṇī*s was in accord with her own practice in daily life. She was well known for her strict discipline—a model of solemnity and virtuous conduct—such that, out of respect, her disciples felt reserved in her presence, afraid of making mistakes. Yet a spirit of equity was also evident in the way she helped all Dharma practitioners and seekers equally, without discrimination. All were impressed by her boundless compassion and concern for the sufferings of the less fortunate. She taught great compassion in sincere and simple words: "Consider the weakness of others as your own. Consider the hunger of others as your own. Look into the hearts of others and realize your humanity is the same."

Once I heard a story about an outbreak of cholera some time ago at Hai Sơn Temple. Everybody in the temple was infected. One nun was so seriously infected that she was in a coma, close to death. Bhikṣuṇī Như Thanh was also infected, but, without concern for herself, she took care of the dangerously ill nun throughout the night, without sleeping. The next day, the nun regained consciousness. The abbess also recovered, perhaps as a result of her selflessness.

Practicing the Bodhisattva Way Continuously

Bhikṣuṇī Như Thanh advised her disciples to have an expansive attitude and not just concentrate on their own liberation. To practice the way of the *bodhisattva*, one must have strong will, take the *bodhisattva* vows, and practice good conduct, which means to practice the six perfections (*pāramitā*s):

> Who knows about the entrance exam to the school of
>   enlightenment?
> It is not based on a capacity to award degrees.
> It is based on wide and deep will.
> By saving human beings, you pass the exam.[13]

Throughout her life, Bhikṣuṇī Như Thanh worked single-mindedly at practicing the way of the *bodhisattva* by cultivating the six perfections of *bodhisattva* behavior: generosity, ethical conduct, patience, joyful effort, concentration, and wisdom. In her practice of generosity, she not only donated alms to charity, but she also gave Dharma teachings; opened Buddhist schools; and wrote, compiled, and translated numerous books and Dharma poems for the sake of future generations.[14] Despite her solemn outward appearance, she offered with a compassionate heart protection to the destitute and the homeless. Her ethical conduct was reflected in her practice of the precepts, both major and minor, as she presided over bimonthly confession ceremonies (*uposatha*) and set an excellent example of moral discipline.

Bhikṣuṇī Như Thanh's practice of patience was also exemplary. Overcoming the eight worldly concerns—gain and loss, attachment and aversion, honor and dishonor, praise and blame—she carefully cultivated Buddhist values. Her capacity for joyful effort was remarkable. She would forget herself completely in her work and read through the night. Sometimes, when overseeing the construction of temples, she would forget to eat or sleep. Although she did not have time to go on retreat, her power of concentration was deep. She practiced profound meditation without distraction or attachment, always appearing peaceful and content. She was an especially talented Dharma teacher as well as a wise decision maker and an effective leader of the *bhikṣuṇī* community. With her great love for and understanding of the *Prajñāpāramitā Sūtra*, it could be said that the abbess had attained the wisdom of listening, contemplating, and cultivating.[15]

Unfulfilled Wishes

Currently, the number of Vietnamese nuns is estimated to be 20,579, roughly ten times higher than the number of monks in the country.[16] These nuns receive education, share the tasks of the *bhikṣu*s, set up monastic centers, teach the Dharma to the public, set up and preside over precept-transmission platforms, and live their lives on an equal footing with the monks in almost every field. Many nuns have the opportunity to study at long-established Buddhist learning centers overseas, and many have earned PhDs. These opportunities and the enhanced stature of Vietnamese nuns would not have been possible without the lifetime devotion of Bhikṣuṇī Nhu' Thanh and the pioneering nuns of her time.

In her work *Practicing the Bodhisattva Way*, Bhikṣuṇī Nhu' Thanh wrote, "Everyone, whether man or woman, who develops insight and wisdom, diligently observes the Buddha's precepts, and works and practices to benefit oneself as well as others, who aims high [for the benefit of all], will definitely succeed on the path." She was in every way a practitioner of her words, which explains her outstanding success.

During her life as a nun, Bhikṣuṇī Nhu' Thanh slept for only two hours a night; the rest of her time was divided between meditation and work. But there was not enough time for this outstanding *bhikṣuṇī* to achieve all of her aspirations. She had hoped to construct a great temple with space for the *bhikṣuṇī saṅgha* to study and practice in a peaceful, natural environment. She selected land at Tao Phùng Mountain in Vũng Tàu, a lovely costal town, and carved her aspiration in stone: "Great Temple of the Bhikṣuṇī Saṅ gha." However, the Buddha Hall of Hai Vân Temple has not yet been built. Bhikṣuṇī Nhu' Thanh was eighty-one years old when the groundbreaking ceremony of the Avalokiteśvara Hall was performed, after which her health began to decline. The stone stele is still there, as if waiting. A center in Vũng Tàu for laypeople to practice Pure Land has yet to be constructed.

The *bodhisattva* way is not a task that lasts for a mere two or three lives. Bhikṣuṇī Nhu' Thanh often consoled us: "Don't worry. I will return to fulfill my aspirations. As I mentioned in *Practicing the Way of the Bodhisattva*, I will give Dharma talks, meditation talks, set up nunneries, build monasteries for monks and nuns, establish a center for laypeople, and help spread the supreme Dharma." Surely, this *bodhisattva* will be reborn to fulfill her expectations!

Notes

1. Nguyen Lang, *Phat Giáo Viet Nam Su Luan* (Critical History of Vietnamese Buddhism), vol. 3 (Paris: Lá Boi, 1985), pp. 51–98.

2. Ian Harris, ed., *Buddhism and Politics in Twentieth Century Asia* (New York: Continuum, 2001), p. 261.

3. Robert E. Buswell, ed., *Encyclopedia of Buddhism*, vol. 2 (New York: Macmillan Reference, 2004), p. 883.

4. Tran Hong Lien, *Sư Trưởng Như Thanh với sự hình thành và phát triển Ni Bộ Nam Việt* (The Abbot Như Thanh and the Formation and Development of the Bhikṣuṇī Saṅgha of South Vietnam) (Ho Chi Minh City, 1999), p. 93.

5. Dương Kinh Thành, *Cay đai thu trong rung thien Ni Bo Bac Tông* (Great Tree in the Meditation Forest of the Mahāyāna Bhikṣuṇī Saṅgha) (Ho Chi Minh City: Religious Publishing House, 1999), p. 107.

6. Bhikṣuṇī Diệu Tịnh, "Từ Bi Âm (The Voice of Compassion)," *Buddhist Magazine* (Sài Gòn) 1933, pp. 70–73.

7. Thich Giac Thien, *Su Truong Như Thanh: Her Life and Work* (1999), p. 75.

8. Bhikṣu Đong Minh, *Some Little Stories about Eminent Bhikṣuṇī Như Thanh: A Biography* (Su Truong Như Thanh: Her Life and Work) (Ho Chi Minh City: Ho Chi Minh Publishing House, 1999), p. 197.

9. Bhikṣuṇī Như Thanh, "Guidelines on the Responsibilities of *Bhikṣuṇīs*," in *Commemorating Bhikṣuṇī Như Thanh* (Ho Chi Minh City: Huê Lâm Monastery, 1999), p. 139.

10. Taken from a talk given by Bhikṣuṇī Như Thanh at the Conference on Dharma Teaching held at Nha Trang Buddhist Institute in 1962. This educational document is now kept at Huê Lâm Monastery.

11. Su Truong Nhu Thanh, *Bat Nha Cuong Yeu* (Ho Chi Minh City: Ho Chi Minh Publishing House, 1983), p. 118.

12. Bhikṣuṇī Nhu Thanh, "Luoc Giai Kinh Hoa Nghiem," in *Pham Nhap Phap Gioi, Hanh Bo Tat Dao* (Ho Chi Minh City: Ho Chi Minh Publishing House, 1989), p. 245.

13. Bhikṣuṇī Như Thanh, *Entrance Exam to the Buddha's School: An Anthology of Đàm Hoa Poetry* (Ho Chi Minh City: Van Nghe Publications, 1999), p. 125.

14. For more Zen and Dharma poetry of Bhikṣuṇī Như Thanh, see Như Hiên and Nguyen Ngoc Hien, *Nu si Viet Nam* (Vietnamese Women Poets) (Ha Noi: Ha Noi Publishing House, 2007), pp. 658–68.

15. Bhikṣu Thich Trí Quang, "Commemorating the Venerable Abbess of Huê Lâm Monastery," p. 188.

16. These statistics are cited in the 2011 annual report of the Department of Bhikṣuṇī Affairs, which operates under the direction of Vietnam Buddhist Saṅgha's Board of Bhikṣu Affairs and can loosely be deemed the current administrative equivalent of the Mahāyāna Bhikṣuṇī Saṅgha that operated during Bhikṣuṇī Như Thanh's time.

8

Bhikṣuṇī Trí Hai

A Scented Lotus Life

Thích Nữ Huong Nhu

In the last two thousand years of Vietnamese Buddhist history, one star shines brightly in the literary sky: Bhikṣuṇī Trí Hai (1938–2003). She was a refined, talented, and enlightened scholar and philosopher who carried herself with a dignity that elevated her like a marvelous pure lotus. Her talents certainly merit her inclusion among eminent Buddhist women.

The Life of Bhikṣuṇī Trí Hai

Bhikṣuṇī Trí Hai (1938–2003) was a gifted and virtuous Vietnamese nun of royal descent. She was born Cong Tang Ton Nu Phung Khanh on March 9, 1938, to a family of six brothers in Vi Da Village, Thua Thien, in Hue, the ancient capital in central Vietnam. She was given the Dharma name Tam Hy by the respected Bhikṣu Thich Tinh Khiet, the head of the Buddhist Saṅgha, at Tuong Van Pagoda, Hue, when she had been just three months in her mother's womb. Her father, Nguyen Phuoc Ung Thieu, was of royal descent from the Nguyen Dynasty, and her mother, Dang Thi Que, was such a wonderful person that she has been eulogized with these words: "Dear Mother! You are as kind as the Buddha and the most thoughtful mother in the world."[1]

Phung Khanh grew up as a gentle and beautiful student who won many hearts. Even as a teen, she was natural, intelligent, dignified, and wise. She realized at a young age that she wanted to escape from the mediocre seductions and passions of everyday life. In 1960, Bhikṣuṇī Trí Hai graduated with a BA in English from the Pedagogical University of Hue. After a few months of teaching at Phan Chu Tring High School in Da Nang Province, she went abroad to study. In 1964, she traveled to the United States, where she graduated from Princeton University with an MA in literature. In the same year, she became a Buddhist nun at Hong An Pagoda under the guidance of the respected Bhikṣuṇī Dieu Khong, a well-known and virtuous Vietnamese nun. In 1970, she received *bhikṣuṇī* ordination at an ordination ceremony held at Hong An Pagoda in Vinh Gia, Da Nang. Her great determination and virtue are remembered by her Dharma companions: "We still remember that in the initial stages of monastic life, Bhikṣuṇī Trí Hai proved to be outstanding and excellent in all respects. She was extremely well loved and respected by her teachers and sisters in Dharma. . . . when she moved to southern Vietnam, she devoted much of her time to research and education. The entire monastic community and laity as well were extremely fond of her. As she became more and more well known, we were all very proud of her."[2]

Bhikṣuṇī Trí Hai was among the first lecturers at Van Hanh Zen Monastery in Ho Chi Minh City and the Vietnam Institute of Advanced Buddhist Studies (now the Vietnam Buddhist Research Institute), founded in 1984. It should be noted that she was the first and only *bhikṣuṇī* who taught at a Buddhist institute in Vietnam at that time. At the Buddhist Institute, she taught *prātimokṣa* (the codes of monastic discipline) and gave many wonderful lectures to monks and nuns on the Middle Length Discourses in English. She taught *prātimokṣa* and served as the *ācārya* and the chief instructor for the board of examiners at many ordination ceremonies. In addition, she was the abbess of three temples in Ho Chi Minh City: Tu Uyen, Dieu Không, and Liên Hoa Nunnery. In early December 2003, she was officially appointed as deputy director of the Vietnam Buddhist Research Institute.

In December 2003, Bhikṣuṇī Trí Hai left the world as a result of a tragic road accident, and Vietnamese Buddhist nuns experienced a heartbreaking loss, especially the younger generation, who lost an extremely talented and virtuous teacher. In Vietnamese Buddhism, Trí Hai's death was like a brilliant star fading. But the eminent Bhikṣu Thich Hien Pháp, remembering the core truths of the Dharma, put Bhikṣuṇī Trí Hai's death into perspective: "Even though the original phenomenon of Bhikṣu Trí Hai has now gone, such a fine past will always be a driving force and strength for succeeding generations of nuns, impelling them to strive in their studies, to improve the high quality of Vietnamese nuns on the path of Dharma propagation, to liberate living beings from ignorance, to serve the Buddhist community and the nation, and to bring happiness and peace to living beings."[3]

Translations and Writings

With her outstanding intelligence and broad knowledge of both Buddhism and secular learning, Bhikṣuṇī Trí Hai became a luminary figure in Vietnam Buddhist literature. Known for her diligence and humility, she produced much valuable literary work. In addition to her outstanding and nuanced writings, she turned to translating the works of others, which brought her great happiness. "By practicing skillful means in everything we do, we can transform our daily life into a source of pleasure, an achievement that is more beautiful than the most beautiful dream of our life."[4] She continued to live a simple, virtuous life even after publishing nearly one hundred valuable written works, including both translations and original compositions. Her ability to produce such a large body of work was the result of her diligence and her spiritual approach to life. She was a unique figure in the history of Vietnamese literature, especially Buddhist literature. As Bhikṣu Thich Thien Nhơn, an eminent monk of the Vietnam Buddhist Saṅgha, commented: "She was an excellent translator and researcher who mastered the doctrines of both Theravāda and Mahāyāna. She was greatly devoted to Buddhist education and research."[5]

Because of her subtle and brilliant intelligence, she selected works for translation from antique Chinese literature, English, French, German, and even modern Chinese. Many scholars recognize that, so far, no other nun has so thoroughly mastered both the Asian and Western literary traditions, working in the fields of Chinese, Pāli, and Sanskrit and in English, French, and German. Her translations of Western literature became especially famous, including works by J. D. Salinger, Gandhi, Herman Hesse, Will Durant, and Erich Fromm. Her translation of Hesse's *Siddhartha*,[6] completed just after her school days, deserves special mention. Her translations of these works are masterpieces. According to one commentator, "Her translations are so beautiful and truthful that people like to read them repeatedly. They get the feeling of reading the original version, but in Vietnamese, with a natural, polished and poetic style."[7] In her preface to *Siddhartha*, Bhikṣuṇī Trí Hai expressed her perception of life while she was still a very young nun: "The entire work of Hermann Hesse is an anthem that encompasses the extreme pangs of life and people's heartfelt expectations in thousands of lives. Though lonely, powerless, and faced with uncertainties, they seek refuge from the limitations of a mediocre and boring life."[8] Her polished translations were indeed infused with the same vitality and elegance as Hesse's work.

Charitable Activities

In addition to her intellectual and literary achievements, Bhikṣuṇī Trí Hai was diligent in her practice, and she was respected as an emanation of Avalokiteśvara because of her compassionate efforts to relieve the miseries of the world. She said: "Charity does not mean simply financial support, but is a means to transform indifference to happiness." Before 1975, when she joined Van Hanh University, she did many things for the poor. After 1975, with a generous and kind heart, her unstinting efforts to disseminate the Buddha's message of compassion and wisdom continued to benefit many kinds of suffering people, including lepers, the aged, orphans, the handicapped, mental patients, ethnic minorities, and people in remote parts of Vietnam. No one who came in contact with her will ever forgot the tears she shed when she mentioned the unfortunate. She especially cared about HIV/AIDS patients. She often talked about the loneliness of the ones who bore the disease and how we could help them to achieve peace before their death. Her *bodhisattva* heart was immeasurably pained when she saw abandoned dogs and cats, to whom she gave loving care. Great compassion is a wonderful medicine to relieve the suffering of living beings. Great compassion was her skillful means to achieve enlightenment. She wrote:

> Great compassion, like a flower,
> Blooms from real wisdom.
> Great compassion, like light,
> Radiates from the lamp of concentration.[9]

She considered cows on their way to slaughter as her close relatives.

Selfless Compassion

Bhikṣuṇī Trí Hai's face radiated the spirit of a genial artist, and her generous smile reflected the diversity of paths that lead to enlightenment. Indeed, Bhikṣuṇī Trí Hai was a bright star, a sweetly scented lotus of compassion and wisdom. Vietnamese Buddhist nuns are proud of Bhikṣuṇī Trí Hai for her compassionate heart and her selfless vow to serve humanity. They find her to be a vital source of spiritual inspiration that endlessly lightens their footsteps.

Notes

1. Nguyen Duc Son, *Memories of Phung Khanh*, unpublished manuscript, September 2009.

2. "Impressions and Feelings of Dharma Relatives," in Thich Thien Nhơn, *The Commemorative Record of Bhiksụnī Trí Hai* (1938–2003) (Ho Chi Minh City: Vietnam Buddhist Research Institute, General Publishing House, 2004), p. 54.

3. Thich Hien Phap, "A Firmament, A Star," in ibid., p. 13.

4. Tarthang Tulku Rinponche, *Skillful Means*, trans. Thich nu Trí Hai (Ho Chi Minh City: Ho Chi Minh City Publishing House, 2000).

5. Nhơn, *The Commemorative Record*, p. 16.

6. Hermann Hesse, *Siddhartha*, trans. Phùng Khánh and Phùng Thăng (Saigon: La Boi Publishing House, 1965). Phùng Khánh was her lay name and the co-translator Phùng Thăng was her brother..

7. Doctor Ngoc Ninh, "In Memoriam," in *The Commemorative Record of Bhiksụnī Trí Hai* (1938–2003), p. 101.

8. *Siddhartha*, p. 4.

9. Poem by Bhikṣuṇī Trí Hai.

BUDDHIST WOMEN IN
EAST ASIAN TRADITIONS

9

Bhikṣuṇī Hiuwan

Enlightening Society by
Institutionalizing Buddhist Education

Yu-chen Li

Bhikṣuṇī Shig Hiuwan[1] (1913–2004) is commemorated in Taiwan for several outstanding accomplishments. She is celebrated as the first Buddhist nun to become a professor, she is honored as a productive and creative painter, and she is memorialized as the founder of the first Buddhist university in Taiwan, where she served as both role model and spiritual mentor for students majoring in science and technology.[2] Her successful endeavors in multiple roles have forever distinguished her as an extraordinary Buddhist female leader.[3] Unlike Buddhist monks whose leadership relies heavily on monastic hierarchy or Buddhist nuns who build their charisma on ascetic practices and philanthropic activities, Hiuwan represents a different set of practices and a unique path of female religiosity. To understand her significance, I first discuss the major events of Bhikṣuṇī Hiuwan's life and the sources and implications of her popularity. Using her work as an example, my purpose is to examine the formation of female religiosity and leadership as Buddhism interacted with society in postwar Taiwan.

From Lady Yunshan You to Buddhist Nun Hiuwan

Bhikṣuṇī Hiuwan was a professor emeritus of Buddhist arts at Chinese Culture University[4] and president of the Lotus Ashram of Buddhist Women when she died on October 15, 2004, at the age of ninety-two. Regarded among Buddhist leaders in China, Hong Kong, Malaysia, and Taiwan as the preeminent heir of the Jianan school of art as well as the Buddhist Tiantai lineage, Bhikṣuṇī Hiuwan produced many famous Chan paintings and wrote numerous books on subjects that ranged from classical Buddhist philosophy and Tientai meditation to what she termed "education of enlightenment."[5] As one of a very small number of Buddhist pioneers, she was instrumental in transforming general college education through Buddhist educational ideals. She effected important changes through her publications, her teaching at various Buddhist institutions, and her founding of Huafan University in 1991.[6]

Bhikṣuṇī Hiuwan was born in Guangzhou in the politically pivotal year of 1912. As a young girl, before starting her education in the Confucian classics at age of five, Yunshan You followed her grandmother in chanting the Buddhist sūtras. She received most of her Chinese education at home from a female tutor, Shaoyi Liang. Later, she left home to attend a Western-style junior high school and, in 1933, graduated from the Lijing Artist College in Hong Kong. It was during her time at Lijing that Yunshan You met her art master, Jianfu Gao (1879–1951), who was also known as a famous revolutionary and pious Buddhist.[7] After graduation, she was selected by St. Paulo Girls High School to teach Chinese literature and Chinese painting. After completing her daily tasks at this Christian school, You used all her leisure time to learn about Buddhism at Chonglan Junior High School, whose president was a pious Buddhist woman, and the Buddhist Bodhi Center, which became her home in Hong Kong.

Lady You received a very privileged education, as was typical for young women of elite families at that time. The goal of this type of education was to protect a daughter's virtue as well as to equip her with modern knowledge as befitted a desirable bride. Faith was not necessarily required. However, the learned young women who emerged from this educational system, for instance, Lady Bicheng Lü (1883–1943) and Lady You, subsequently played important roles in introducing Buddhism in English.[8]

Initially, the Sino-Japanese War, which began in 1937, does not seem to have affected Lady You's life. In 1940, she transferred to Lijing Girls High School, where, having been recognized for her distinguished achievement as an artist, she became known as a star of the Lingnan School of painting. During 1941, You began her extensive travels. Following Gao's emphasis on drawing from nature, she visited Guizhou to paint landscapes. She had originally intended to spend only a few weeks there, but after she left Hong Kong in September, the Japanese military suddenly took over Hong Kong and, in October, closed the border. She therefore continued her travels until 1945, journeying through southeastern China to escape the war. She traveled alone, visiting famous Buddhist monasteries and their abbots, such as the Chan master Xuyun at Nanhua Monastery in Guangdong. She supported herself by selling the paintings she made during the journey. It was so extraordinary for a woman to travel alone at this time in history that she quickly drew the attention of various local newspapers. Because of her established fame as an artist from Hong Kong, her paintings were very popular and usually sold for comparatively high prices. She donated most of the income to local schools. As a woman who dared travel during wartime and exhibited her drawings of local natural scenery in art exhibitions, then generously donated the proceeds to charity, You became a legendary figure from the 1940s until the present day.

At the end of her travels, You learned that her two sisters and father had been killed in the war. It is said that this family tragedy drove her to seek refuge in the Three Jewels in Chengdu with Bhikṣu Changyuan. Bhikṣu Changyuan gave her the Dharma name Longji and predicted she would receive ordination later. You decided not to receive ordination until after fulfilling her dream as an artist. She arrived in Guangzhou in 1945 and took a temporary teaching job at National Third Junior High School for Chinese Immigrants before beginning another great trip in 1948, this time to India, the homeland of Buddhism. She spent one year visiting Buddhist sacred sites in Vietnam and Cambodia, then traveled to India via Singapore. From 1948 to 1951, You taught Chinese painting at the College of Art at Tagore University in Shantiniketan, West Bengal. After going on pilgrimage in India, she went climbing in the Himalayas, where she spent one month painting the mountain scenery.

This great journey did not lead Lady You home again. At the age of thirty-nine, she went to Hong Kong, where she helped educate the children of Chinese refugees. At the same time, she became a teacher at the Buddhist Lotus in the East Institute, the Precious Enlightenment Female High School, and Precious Enlightenment Buddhist Institute. She also founded Cloud's Gate Institute and the Original Spring Publication Company. During this period, Lady You lost her artist master Gao Jianfu but found her Buddhist master Tanxu, the 44th-generation patriarch of Tiantai School.[9] After the war, many eminent Chinese monks fled to Hong Kong, creating a wonderful place to learn Buddhism. Tanxu moved from Shenyang, a provincial capital in northeastern China, to Hong Kong, and You spent five years there studying the *Lotus Sūtra* and Tiantai meditation under him.

Once Lady You decided to receive ordination from Tanxu, she also decided on education as her future "religious practice" and set out on another trip to collect resources. For three years, starting in 1956, she visited countless schools and universities in thirty-two countries. At her last stop in India, homeland of the Buddha, she shaved her head and received full ordination in Hong Kong the next day. At the age of forty-seven, she became Hiuwan, a disciple of Bhikṣu Tanxu. Bhikṣuṇī Hiuwan then promptly established the

Wise Compassion Elementary School and the Spring of Wisdom Elementary School, both of which offered educational opportunities for the children of newly arrived Chinese refugees. Two years later, she founded the Lotus Night School and the Sea of Wisdom High School. She also founded the Hong Kong Association of Culture and Arts and taught Buddhist arts classes on the radio. It is significant that these schools incorporated many elements of pedagogy and educational administration from Christian schools.

Unfortunately, Hiuwan's devotion to education did not succeed in Hong Kong, mostly because of the 1956 riots, when violence perpetrated by pro-KMT civilians against pro-communist civilians seriously threatened the safety of immigrants from mainland China. When she accepted an invitation to teach Buddhist art and culture in Taiwan, she became the first Buddhist nun to become a professor there. At the same time, Bhikṣuṇī Miaoran, the abbess of Dharma Cloud Temple, asked for her help as an honorary mentor in establishing a Buddhist institute for women.[10] Although Dharma Cloud Buddhist Institute lasted only three years, Hiuwan, in response to the request of nuns at Eternal Light Nunnery, went on to found the Lotus Ashram, a Buddhist institute for women, near the Chinese Cultural University in Taipei.[11]

In accordance with her ideals, Hiuwan refused to become the abbess and to have her own disciples, or to build temples. This meant that she had to support the Lotus Ashram with very limited resources, mostly her teaching salary and her paintings. Beginning in 1974, Hiuwan exhibited her paintings annually in order to raise funds. She also attended many international conferences to spread her ideas about education. By the 1980s, she was probably the most prolific Buddhist scholar producing English conference papers. Her gender and religious identity make this record especially notable. For example, in 1991 she was the special guest speaker of the 2nd Sakyadhita International Conference on Buddhist Women in Bangkok.[12] After establishing Huafan University, from 1980 to 2002, Hiuwan held a series of twelve International Conferences on Buddhist Education.

The turning point in Hiuwan's career in Taiwan occurred in 1987, when she established Huafan Science and Technology College. She devoted herself to establishing a Buddhist university, because at the time the government only allowed Christian organizations to establish private universities. Even the Buddhist Association of the Republic of China had been unsuccessful. Despite this failure, Hiuwan began to raise funds in 1983, obtained a government permit in 1987, started construction in 1989, and opened the college in 1990. Huafan Science and Technology College was finally recognized as a university in 1997. Thus, the first Buddhist university in Chinese history was established by a poor Buddhist nun at the age of eighty-five.

The Legend of Bhikṣuṇī Hiuwan

Bhikṣuṇī Hiuwan once remarked that her life in Hong Kong and Taiwan had been a journey to "three mountains and two islands" that represented successive stages of her monastic life. Traditionally in Buddhist circles, the term "mountain" refers both to the location of certain religious organizations and also to their lineages. In the case of Hiuwan, the three mountains refer to Mount Dayu in Hong Kong, Mount Yangming in Taipei, and Mount Dalun in Shenkeng, Taiwan. Hiuwan received the Tiantai lineage at Mount Dayu in Hong Kong. It was only when she founded the Lotus Ashram at Mount Yangming in Taiwan, however, that the teachers and students realized she was a Tiantai lineage holder. Later, when Huiwan founded Huafan University at Mount Dalun, her initiative marked the beginning of secular Buddhist education in Taiwan. These three "mountains" therefore represent stages in Hiuwan's extraordinary religious career as a Buddhist nun and her distinctive devotion to education. The two islands of Hong Kong and Taiwan represent special places of refuge, evolution, and growth for Hiuwan.

Hiuwan's religious career unfolded as she made two world tours with the purpose of investigating education systems around the world. After returning from these tours, she established a number of educational institutes, one after the other, in Hong Kong and Taipei. Most importantly, Hiuwan established a complete education system from elementary school through junior high school, and then high school, college, university, and research institutes. It seems that in the beginning, circa 1945, the blueprint in Hiuwan's mind was of a Western-style education system. Historically, as a British colony, Hong Kong followed the British educational model of encouraging various social groups to establish private schools, a trend that was also encouraged by the surge in immigration from mainland China and consequent shortage of resources in the 1950s. Some might argue that it was this historical precedent that inspired Hiuwan's devotion to public education. However, official policy in Taiwan during the 1970s, which prohibited the establishment of private colleges and universities, did not prevent Hiuwan from looking for an ideal location to establish a private Buddhist university. For me, this raises a question: Why did she ultimately choose to join forces with the modern educational system rather than promote educational reform within the monastic community?

I believe that Hiuwan, because of her personal experience in Christian schools, had a very different concept of "modern Buddhist education" from that of her contemporary Buddhist fellows. Her educational background would have been considered privileged by most Chinese at the beginning of the twentieth century. During her lifetime, most eminent monks received their education in the traditional system of monastic discipline, which naturally influenced their interpretations of educational reform. The case studies of the four most famous monks in the first half of twentieth century exemplify this. Taixu (1889–1947) conducted an educational revolution within the monastic community.[13] Yinguang (1861–1940) strictly refined his own practice and that of his lay followers by focusing on chanting the Buddha's name.[14] Hongyi (1880–1942) revised the monastic regulations of the Dharmagupta Vinaya School.[15] Xuyun (1840–1959) revived the tradition of meditation at Chan monasteries.[16] These four eminent monks all promoted traditional Buddhist education but limited their modernizing activities to within the walls of Buddhist monasteries. These male leaders tried very hard to establish Buddhist institutes and "lotus societies" rather than conventional public schools.[17] Indeed, many monasteries had been confiscated by local gentry and governments for the purpose of building Western-style schools. As for lay education, Taixu only went so far as to suggest that monks write novels to attract the youth. In other words, although these monks recognized the necessity of modernizing Buddhist education in the monastic community, they did not move beyond the traditional monastic framework to establish a systematic presentation of Buddhism as part of a lay educational curriculum.

In many ways, Hiuwan's approach was different from that of her male counterparts. She had not been trained in the monastic system, but had received a traditional Confucian education at home and a modern Christian education at school. Moreover, she did not become a Buddhist nun until she was thirty-seven years old. Initially, the educational programs she established were primarily intended for youngsters at general public schools. From her perspective, I suggest, religion can and should play an important role in general education, a perspective that echoes both Confucian and Christian educational philosophies, based on her own experience. Finally, and significantly, Hiuwan had always supported herself as a teacher before she became ordained as a nun. It seems that she was determined to lead an independent, intellectual, and celibate life, an unusual career path for a woman of her day. To some extent, her rejection of monastic roles such as abbess, ordination master, and temple proprietor kept her from fully living a traditional monastic life. Indeed, she never gave up teaching and lived in faculty housing most of her life, even after she became a nun.

During the first half of the twentieth century, it was not difficult to find laywomen like Hiuwan who were active in Buddhist circles. These women had similar backgrounds, usually graduating from Western-style schools, becoming interested in Buddhism during middle age, and, most importantly, being recognized as elites on the basis of their intellectual achievements. These Buddhist women intellectuals were viewed as exceptional because of their superior educational backgrounds and their intellectual endeavors, which included writing and translating Buddhist works and educating Buddhist nuns. These women did not necessarily remain single, however. Though the monastic community was not overly concerned about their marital status, these elite women generally considered celibate Buddhist monastic life an ideal way for women to live.

It is not yet clear whether Chinese women in those days pursued careers as a result of the inspiration they received from Christian nuns or whether it was simply that job opportunities opened up for them because of the education they had received. However, Hiuwan lived independently as a scholar nun and artist, apart from any monastic community. Considering her role and endeavors in the field of education, Hiuwan's lifestyle seems similar to that of a Christian nun teacher. On the other hand, because of her privileged status in Chinese Buddhism, Hiuwan created a new lifestyle for Buddhist nuns in the Chinese tradition, that is, a class of scholarly nuns and educators who worked for society in general.

In a sense, Hiuwan embodied spiritual freedom through her independence from communal monastic structures. Her journey to the distant sacred homeland of Buddhism during wartime shows her independent spirit; the fact that she learned English and was able to travel around the world indicates her intellectual independence. To learn a foreign language and to travel the world unaccompanied were, at that time, rare and precious experiences for women. Even in the 1990s, Hiuwan's extensive travel experience marked her as a pioneer in Taiwan, including among Buddhist women and nuns. Hiuwan justified these extraordinary personal adventures as religious practice—a noble goal. Her travels played a significant a role in constructing the legend of Hiuwan, as did her outstanding educational endeavors.

The legend of Bhikṣuṇī Hiuwan attracted Taiwanese Buddhist nuns to support her educational programs. In the process, the students of the Lotus Ashram have created a close and efficient network. Even though she was the primary instructor at the Lotus Ashram, Hiuwan usually identified herself as a gardener rather than as a proprietor. She expanded the traditional content of Buddhist teachings considerably; in addition to meditation and monastic regulations, students were required to learn Chan painting, classical Chinese, editing, and news publication and were encouraged to audit advanced classes at the Chinese Culture University where she taught. On the one hand, Hiuwan offered higher education for her students at the Lotus Ashram; on the other hand, she treated them as regular students, not disciples. This approach helped to avoid conflicts between the students and the Buddhist temples that had sent them there to study. Senior members of these temples had no worries that their younger nuns would shift their loyalties from their home temples and original teachers to the Lotus Ashram and Hiuwan, and junior nuns appreciated the opportunity to study at a "college." After graduation, these students and the members of their home temples tended to become followers and supporter of Hiuwan.[18]

The Taiwanese nuns who studied and trained at the Lotus Ashram came from small nunneries around the island. After returning to their home temples, they gathered teams of volunteers who organized fund-raising activities to support Hiuwan's educational endeavors. These nuns were able to accumulate such substantial donations that their activities even affected similar projects organized by much larger Buddhist organizations, such as Foguangshan. Hiuwan's students advised her to give public talks as a means to connect personally with Buddhist followers and to hold auctions of her paintings in order to get higher prices. Most importantly, they urged her to conduct Dharma gatherings and ritual assemblies to raise funds. These nuns made preparations for Hiuwan to appear at their nunneries and took turns donating the income generated by certain ritual assemblies that they conducted at their nunneries to Hiuwan. In addition to fund-raising, the nuns at each nunnery also offered their labor and public relations networks.[19]

As the founder of the Huafan University, the first university established by Buddhists in Chinese history, Hiuwan has had extensive influence. She created a model for a Buddhist university that adapted Buddhism in the public schools as a means of spiritual cultivation. In Taiwan in the 1990s, the image of Hiuwan changed in the popular imagination from scholar nun to great educator as a result of her founding of Huafan University. This change indicates the profound effect her commitment to the modernization of both religious and institutional education within the context of Buddhism has had, especially for women.

In this chapter, I have examined Hiuwan's success as a female religious leader who established the first Buddhist university in Taiwan. Because she was able to reach out to the general public through her art and writings, Hiuwan's influence extended far beyond the monastic community. Her philosophy of a modern education that incorporates Buddhist thought and culture, influenced by her own educational experience, created a new ideal for nuns as professional scholars and educators, as well as a new standard for Buddhist education. Her achievements were supported by nuns who were attracted by her independence, insight, and creativity to offer their practical skills in fund raising to fulfill her dreams. In this complex process, Hiuwan and these nuns all received much more than a standard academic education. Their efforts and ideals influenced not only the world of Buddhist education, but also a new generation of public school education in Taiwan.

Notes

1. For a more detailed biography of Bhikṣuṇī Hiuwan, see Yu-chen Li, "*Yunshui buzhu: xiaoyun fashi de biqiuni dianfan*" (The Clouds and Rivers Never Ceased: The Paradigm of Bhikṣuṇī Xiaoyun), in Huafan University, ed., *The Anniversary Memorial of Venerable Xiaoyun and the Sixth International Symposium of Tiantai School* (Taipei: Huafan University, 2007), pp. 11–38.

2. This spelling of her name follows the Cantonese usage; it is Xiaoyun in Mandarin.

3. Xing Fuqua, *Taiwanese Buddhism and Buddhist Temples* (Taiwan de fojiao yu fosi) (Taipei: Shangwu, 1991).

4. The Chinese Culture University was established in 1962 as a college and started the first Buddhist institutes in Taiwan by appointing Bhikṣus Yinxun, Xinyun, and Shengyan as chairpersons of the Institute of Indian Cultural Studies and the Institute of Buddhist Cultural Studies from 1977 to 1984. Bhikṣuṇī Xiuwen was invited to teach in the Department of Chinese Culture and Arts and the Department of Philosophy in 1966; later, she was in charge of the Institute of Buddhist Cultural Studies. She retired in 1983.

5. Huafan University follows the educational principles of Bhikṣuṇī Hiuwan, http://eng.hfu.edu.tw/introduction.html, accessed February 9, 2013.

6. Xiuhui Chen, *Venerable Xiuwen's Commitment and Innovation to Education* (Xiaoyun fashi de jiaoyu qinghuai yu zhiye) (Taipei: Wanjunlou, 2006).

7. Gao devoted himself to political reform in his youth but could not stand the corruption of his colleagues. Instead, he concentrated his efforts on painting and improving his traditional Chinese ink-painting skills, with influences from Japanese culture. See Wang Dan, *The Biography of Master Jianfu Gao, the Founder of Lingnan Painting School* (Lingnan Huapai Dashi Go Jianfu) (Guangdong: Guangdong Press, 2009).

8. Grace S. Fong, "Alternative Modernities, or a Classical Woman of Modern China: The Challenging Trajectory of Lü Bicheng's (1883–1943) Life and Song Lyrics," *Beyond Tradition and Modernity: Gender, Genre, and Cosmopolitanism in Late Qing China*, edited by Grace S. Fong, Nanxiu Qian, and Harriet Thelma Zurndorfer (Leiden: Brill, 2004), pp. 12–59.

9. For more on the master–disciple relationship between Tanxu and Xiuwen, especially his decision to transmit his Dharma lineage to a nun, which was the first time in history, see Chen Xiuhui, "Huixiao xiangda: Tanxu fashi dui xiaoyun fashi de yingxiang" (Intensively, Inward Promoting Greater Freedom: Tanxu's Influence on Xiuwan), *Huafan Journal of Humanities* 3(June 2004): 195–226.

10. Chinese Buddhist Institute, ed., "*Fayunsi*" (Dharma Cloud Temple), *Taiwan foxu yuansuo jiaoyu nianjian chuangkanhao* (The First Issue of the Taiwanese Buddhist Institutes' Yearbook) (Taipei: Dongchu, 1998), pp. 171–73.

11. It was Bhikṣuṇī Xiuci who proposed the establishment of a Buddhist school at Eternal Light Nunnery. Like other students of Hiuwan at Chinese Cultural University, Xiuci stayed at nearby Eternal Light Nunnery. See Lotus Ashram, ed., *The History of Lotus Ashram* (Lianhuayuan ji) (Taipei: Yuan Chuan Press, 1985).

12. Karma Lekshe Tsomo, "*Prajña*: The Philosophy and Life of Venerable Shig Hiu Wan," *Festschrift for Venerable Hui Wan* (Taipei: Institute of Asian Humanities of Huafan University and Institute of Sino-Indian Buddhist Studies, 2005).

13. Don A. Pittman, *Toward a Modern Chinese Buddhism: Taixu's Reforms* (Honolulu: University of Hawai'i Press, 2001).

14. Charles B. Jones, "Transitions in the Practice and Defense of Chinese Pure Land Buddhism," *Buddhism in the Modern World: Adaptations of an Ancient Tradition*, ed. Steven Heine and Charles S. Prebish (Oxford: Oxford University Press, 2003), pp. 125–42.

15. Raoul Birnbaum, "Master Hongyi Looks Back: A Modern Man Becomes a Monk in Twentieth-Century China," ibid., pp. 75–124.

16. Richard Hunn, ed. (trans. Charles Luk), *Empty Cloud: The Autobiography of the Chinese Zen Master Hsu Yun* (Salisbury, UK: Element Books, 1988).

17. Yu-chen Li, "Lay Buddhist Female Piety in Shanghai during the 1930s," paper presented at the Fifth Animal International Conference of the Lay Buddhist Forum (Seoul: Lay Buddhist Forum, 2011), pp. 26–30.

18. One of the reasons that Hiuwan stayed at the professors' housing rather than at the nunnery may have been to take care of her mother.

19. For instance, the first chairperson of the Huafan Board of Trustees, Bhikṣuṇī Jingding, sent all of her disciples to study at the Lotus Ashram; the present chairperson, Bhikṣuṇī Dijiao, herself graduated from the Lotus Ashram.

10

Pongnyŏgwan

The Eminent *Bhikṣuṇī* of Cheju Island

Hyangsoon Yi

Bhikṣuṇī Pongnyŏgwan (1865–1938) has left an indelible mark on the socio-cultural history of Cheju Island in Korea. She transformed the religious topography of Cheju in the early twentieth century by reviving Buddhism, which had disappeared for nearly two centuries. Despite her vital contribution to today's Buddhist community on the island, the details of Pongnyŏgwan's extraordinary life were not fully known to mainlanders until recently. It was in 2006 that her fifth-generation Dharma heir Bhikṣuṇī Hyejŏn introduced her at a conference on the lives and practices of Korean Buddhist nuns, held by the National Bhikṣuṇī Assembly of Korea.

In this chapter, I first survey the state of Buddhism on Cheju Island in the premodern period. Against this historical backdrop, I trace the amazing life path of Pongnyŏgwan. While covering salient aspects of Pongnyŏgwan's biography, special attention is paid to her unusual pattern of practice and especially her well-known miracle work, which is still vividly remembered by islanders. In the last part of this chapter, I briefly address a problematic relationship between gender and supernatural ability as a sign of eminence in the context of Korean Buddhism.

Cheju in the Korean Buddhist World

Cheju is the largest island in Korea, located off the southwestern coast of the Korean peninsula. Because of its size and distance from the mainland, this island has enjoyed a considerable degree of political and cultural autonomy throughout its history. The importance of this island in the contemporary Korean administrative system is demonstrated by its status as a "special autonomous province."[1]

During the Three Kingdoms era (57 BCE–668 CE), Cheju Island was called T'amna. As a small island state, T'amna maintained independence from the political powers of the peninsula, claiming its own lineage of hereditary rulers. With regard to islanders' religious life, a native shamanistic belief system was dominant. The earliest documented record of the relationship between Cheju and Buddhism dates back to the Koryŏ Dynasty (918–1392).[2] Although Buddhism flourished, shamanistic practices also remained strong, as suggested by the old adage that "five hundred temples and five hundred shrines" existed on Cheju.[3] It was during the Koryŏ Dynasty that the name of the island was changed from T'amna to Cheju.

Buddhism was popular in Cheju throughout the history of the Koryŏ Dynasty and even until the early years of the Chosŏn Dynasty (1392–1910). The Koryŏ court sponsored Buddhist institutions, and temples on Cheju were no exceptions. For example, the state extended economic support to Pŏphwasa and Sujŏngsa Temples, which owned 280 and 130 slaves, respectively.[4] A hermitage called Chonjaam also received a financial subsidy from the court for rituals it conducted for the prosperity of the state.[5] As the Koryŏ Dynasty declined, many aristocrats who resisted newly rising Chosŏn moved to Cheju Island voluntarily or involuntarily as defectors or exiles. The Buddhist orientation of these Koryŏ noblemen contributed further to the high status that Buddhist institutions enjoyed in Cheju. The vigorous religious activities of the Buddhist community on the island can be glimpsed in the *sūtras* printed by means of woodblocks that were carved at Myoryŏnsa Temple in Cheju.[6]

With the founding of the Chosŏn Dynasty, Cheju, as with other regions of the country, became subject to an anti-Buddhist policy that the Confucian Chosŏn court officially adopted. Although Buddhism was still practiced on Cheju in the first few decades of the new dynasty, this continuity was largely due to the legacies of Koryŏ. In the political sphere, the position of an independent ruler of Cheju Island and his crown prince's right to succeed the throne were abolished in 1404 by King T'aejong (ruled 1400–1418). In the eighth year of his reign, King T'aejong also reduced the number of slaves belonging to the Pŏphwasa and Sujŏngsa Temples to thirty each.[7] The Buddhist monastic community in Cheju was persecuted with increasing severity. In official records, reports on the deplorable state of Buddhism in Cheju began to appear as early as in 1426. In his report to King Sejong on the living conditions of islanders, Kim Wimin states that monks openly took wives and enjoyed family life with children. The reports also point out that Buddhist monks were exempt from labor taxes and that their "comfortable" lifestyle lured lay Buddhists across the sea to Cheju.[8]

Among all the anti-Buddhist measures implemented in Cheju, the most decisive one came with King Sukchong's appointment of Yi Hyŏngsang (1653–1733) as magistrate of the island. When this staunch Neo-Confucian scholar-official landed on the shores of Cheju in 1702, he surveyed various aspects of islanders' lives. In his book *Namhwanbangmul* (Various Things Observed in Cheju), it is recorded that there were two Buddhist temples on the island, Mansusa and Haeryunsa, but these temples had no resident monks.[9] Yi launched a major campaign to enforce Confucian rituals in Cheju; and in this process, he destroyed Buddhist temples and shamanistic shrines. Yi's devastating project virtually eliminated Buddhism from the region. It appears that, starting from the eighteenth century, the island had no Buddhist temples or shamanistic shrines for nearly two hundred years.

From 1702, the Buddhist community in Cheju was under the tight grip of the government. The Chosŏn court's efforts to Confucianize the ideological orientation of people in Cheju resulted in the disappearance of tangible signs of Buddhist faith from the island's sociocultural landscape. No written record of a public Buddhist gathering is found after Yi's demolition of the temples. Yet in spite of the large-scale destruction of old religious structures and institutions, shamanism continued to be followed clandestinely by islanders, especially the female population.

In reality, what came about on Cheju after Yi's militant campaign was a mixed form of Buddhism and shamanism in religious practice. In a sense, it can be said that Buddhist faith was carried on in a chaotic state by absorbing various shamanistic elements.[10] The absence of temples and monastic practitioners who could teach and guide lay Buddhists furthered the fusion of the two religions. The strong influence of shamanism on Buddhism can be traced, for instance, in the transformation of Yŏndŭnghoe, a traditional state-sponsored Buddhist festival from the Koryŏ period, into Yŏngdŭng *kut*, a representative shamanistic ritual today.[11]

Pongnyŏgwan and Cheju Buddhism

It was only in the opening decade of the twentieth century that Buddhism was reinstituted in Cheju. It was Bhikṣuṇī Pongnyŏgwan who nearly single-handedly accomplished this historic achievement by founding new temples and renovating old ones. She was born on June 14, 1865, to an ordinary farming couple in Cheju and was named Yŏgwan. No information on her youth is available except that in the spring of 1882, Yŏgwan married Hyŏn

Kuknam, a man from the same village. They had four daughters and a son.[12]

It is said that Pongnyŏgwan's initial encounter with Buddhism took place in 1899. One day, an old Buddhist monk came to her house during his begging round. When he was leaving, he gave her a small statue of Avalokiteśvara, telling her to put it in a clean place and chant the name of the *bodhisattva* diligently. He added that the incantation of the *bodhisattva*'s mercy would prevent her son and daughters from premature deaths. Needless to say, Pongnyŏgwan began her chanting immediately.

Soon afterward, however, Pongnyŏgwan's new faith caused a serious conflict in her family life. Her husband could not understand the nature of her religious devotion. In the course of two centuries, Buddhist doctrine and practice had gradually become alien to ordinary people in Cheju. Buddhism and shamanism had been mixed and could not be clearly distinguished from one another. For a long time, shamanistic rituals were officially banned, and shamans (*mudang*) were disparaged from the point of view of Confucian social norms. Ironically, the majority of shamans in Korea and particularly in Cheju were female. In light of this, it is not surprising that Pongnyŏgwan's *dhāraṇī* practice bewildered and even angered her husband.[13] Profoundly suspicious of her "superstitious" acts, Pongnyŏgwan's family burnt the statue of Avalokiteśvara and forced her to leave the home. Although she soon found a small place for herself, she was eventually expelled from the village by a group of hostile youths who threatened to kill her if she continued chanting. This incident occurred in 1900, one year after she took refuge in Buddhism.

As a total outcast, Pongnyŏgwan continued her practice outdoors. It is said that she found shelter in a tiny grotto in Mount Halla and prayed in it for several years. This small mountain cell later came to be named as the Grotto of Haewŏl after her Dharma name. Presently, the grotto marks the entrance to Kwanŭmsa, the first and the most important temple she founded on Cheju after her *śrāmaṇerika* ordination.

Pongnyŏgwan joined monastic life in 1907 as a disciple of Bhikṣuṇī Yujang.[14] She left Cheju for Taehŭngsa Temple in Chŏlla Province and was ordained there by Master Chŏngbong. Her *śrāmaṇerika* ordination seems to have taken place sometime in December that year.[15]

This critical turning point in her life is full of unusual incidents. When she decided to renounce household life, she dreamed that a white-robed Avalokiteśvara told her to go to Taehŭngsa Temple and shave her head. Guided by this dream, Pongnyŏgwan left for Taehŭngsa. Oddly enough, Bhikṣu Hyeo, the spiritual director of Taehŭngsa, dreamed of a white-robed Avalokiteśvara on the same night that Pongnyŏgwan had her dream. The *bodhisattva* told Hyeo that a queen would visit his temple the following day. Therefore, monks at Taehŭngsa were waiting all day long for a noblewoman, but no such visitor appeared that day. In the meantime, Pongnyŏgwan's journey was delayed, and she arrived at the temple in the late afternoon. Hyeo could not imagine that Pongnyŏgwan was a queen, so when she asked him to shave her head, he declined her request, saying that she should follow formal procedure for receiving precepts.

Frustrated, Pongnyŏgwan received permission to visit hermitages scattered around the nearby mountains. At one of the hermitages, she encountered a young monk who was suffering gravely from leprosy. Pongnyŏgwan volunteered to relieve him from severe pain. With permission from Hyeo, she applied three-year-old soybean paste on the body of the patient and covered it with ashes. After a few days, the painful wounds miraculously healed. Deeply impressed by Pongnyŏgwan's healing power, the monks at Taehŭngsa Temple made the unusual decision to grant her wish and allow her to receive the *śrāmaṇerika* precepts.[16] Thus, in December 1907, she was finally ordained as a nun by the *bhikṣu* precept master Chŏngbong.

Although Pongnyŏgwan took the vows of a nun, her life did not become any easier. Upon returning to Cheju Island in 1908 with a Buddha statue from Taehŭngsa, she found a small temple and began propagating the Dharma. Hardly had she set up a ritual altar to celebrate the Buddha's birthday when she was confronted with an angry mob that ruined the statue and set her place on fire, claiming that a Buddha statue would confuse the world and dupe people.[17] Expelled from her village, Pongnyŏgwan again wandered Mount Halla and prayed near Nŭnghwabong Peak for seven days. After a week of prayer and fasting in the mountains, she accidentally fell into a deep valley. Luckily, her fall was broken by an outcropping on the cliff side. The story of this incident recounts that when she landed there, thousands of crows flocked to her. Catching her robe and lifting her with their beaks, they carried her to a safe place.

The story of Pongnyŏgwan's sojourn on Mount Halla contains another anecdote of a prophetic dream. As soon as she was rescued by the crows, Pongnyŏgwan dreamed of an old man. According to this vision, she would soon encounter a special person who came from afar with a robe for her. Indeed, when she woke up from the dream and came down to a place called Sanchŏndan, an old monk from Mount Kyeryong in Ch'ungchŏng Province showed up and stated:

> The Buddha appeared in my dream several months ago and said that there would be an enlightened monk in the south. So I searched many southern islands but could not find him. Now as I encounter you, I would like to offer you this robe. Please accept it and take good care of yourself. I hope you will make great achievements.[18]

After these words, the old man gave her a *kāṣāya* (outer robe) and suddenly disappeared.[19]

All the fantastic elements aside, the above episodes contain vital information on the process by which Pongnyŏgwan established herself as a legitimate member of the monastic order in the same hometown where she experienced great antagonism. Two elements in the story of her escape to Mount Halla—her intense prayer and reception of a *kāṣāya*—draw special attention because they cement her newly acquired monastic identity. The prayer motif proves Pongnyŏgwan's inner power, creating an aura surrounding her in the eyes of the world, whereas the *kāṣāya* confers religious authority upon her as the reviver of Buddhism on Cheju. The combination of her exceptional spirituality and the institutional symbol completes her transformation into a monastic practitioner and, furthermore, a religious reformer.

One question raised by the above anecdote is the identity of the mysterious person who gave the *kāṣāya* to Pongnyŏgwan. In his *T'amna kihaeng* (Travelogue on Cheju), the renowned writer Yi Ŭnsang describes him as "a strange monk called Un *taesa* (Master Un)."[20] This same figure is referred to as "Sŭng'un *taesa* (Master Sŭng'un)" in the *Hoemyŏng munjip* (Collected Writings by Hoemyŏng).[21] Analyzing these two texts and related materials, Han Geum-soon identifies the person as Kim Sŏgyun, one of the *bhikṣu*s who assisted Pongnyŏgwan in founding Kwanŭmsa Temple in 1908. Han interprets the character "*un*" as implying Kim's Dharma name, "Sang'un," arguing that his involvement in an underground anti-Japanese movement made it impossible to openly mention his full name.[22]

According to my research, the old man whom Pongnyŏgwan encountered at Sanch'ŏndan seems to be Bhikṣu Hyeo of Taehŭngsa Temple. Hyeo's other Dharma name, Ch'wiun, ends with the character *un*. This speculation is feasible given that Taehŭngsa is where Pongnyŏgwan was ordained with special permission from Hyeo.[23] Moreover, Sŏgyun was not a fully ordained *bhikṣu* in 1908.[24] As a *śrāmaṇera* in his early thirties, he was too young to be revered as "Master." In light of these factors, three possibilities can be considered: First, it was Ch'wiun who either brought the *kāṣāya* directly to Pongnyŏgwan or dispatched a monk to Cheju to deliver the outer garment to her. The second possibility is that the mysterious person was Sŏgyun. Last, it was neither Ch'wiun nor Sŏgyun but a third person whose Dharma name contains the character *un*. Although this issue will not be resolved until incontestable material evidence emerges, this incident apparently confirmed Pongnyŏgwan's monastic status in the eyes of islanders, enabling and empowering her to engage in public activities as a religious leader in the mainstream society of Cheju without blatant harassment from mobsters.

Revival and Resistance

Pongnyŏgwan pursued Buddhist practice against all odds. Her spirituality was not properly understood by the majority of people in Cheju, including her own family members. Nevertheless, she was determined to revive Buddhism on the island. Toward this goal, she made two kinds of efforts. One was to secure temples as centers for spreading the Buddhist teachings. Hence, she renovated old, abandoned temples such as Pŏptolsa (later called Pŏpjŏngsa) and Pŏphwasa. She also constructed new temples such as Kwanŭmsa, Pult'apsa, Wŏlsŏngsa, and Paengnyŏnsa. Furthermore, she established Taegaksa in the center of the city to expand Kwanŭmsa's urban mission. Among all these, the founding of Kwanŭmsa Temple is considered the official birth of modern Buddhism in Cheju.[25] To this day, Kwanŭmsa has been pivotal in all Buddhist activities in Cheju.

The second important propagation work that Pongnyŏgwan carried out was the organization of Dharma meetings involving eminent monks. She invited famous Dharma teachers, ordained and lay, from the mainland. For example, Sŏn master Hoemyŏng toured the island, delivering a series of Dharma talks in different places, including Taegaksa Temple. By involving well-known Buddhist teachers in her propagation projects, such as Masters Manam and Manha, Pongnyŏgwan earned respect from local people and thereby could effectively rebuild the Buddhist community in Cheju after a long vacuum. Bhikṣuṇīs Kyŏnghwa and Kyŏng'u, Pongnyŏgwan's daughters who followed in the footsteps of their mother and became nuns, assisted her closely in managing temple finances and rites.

Pongnyŏgwan was also involved in establishing new organizations for the growing Buddhist population, starting with the Buddhist Association of Cheju (BAC). A major step forward in the history of modern Buddhism in Cheju, BAC was formed in 1924 under a colonial ideological policy to control religious activities in Korea. By sponsoring a number of public Buddhist gatherings and campaigns, BAC was very useful in Pongnyŏgwan's dissemination of the Dharma until her death in 1938. But the organization's pro-Japanese orientation is often held responsible for her ambivalent political stance, causing a thorny problem in assessing her achievements.

Represented by Hyejŏn, Pongnyŏgwan's Dharma heirs proposed a strong possibility of Pongnyŏgwan's financial support of the independence movement during the colonial period. In November 1918, an armed protest against the Japanese occupation broke out in Cheju. Led by Buddhist monks, this large-scale fight for independence preceded the famous 1919 March First Movement, a nationwide peaceful rally against Japanese rule. Although only circumstantial evidence is available for Pongnyŏgwan's cooperation

with underground anticolonial fighters, the possibility cannot be ruled out
that she secretly provided funds for Bhikṣu Tonghwa, a key figure in the
resistance organizations of Cheju. It is said that he often accompanied her
"alms-begging" rounds whose purpose, according to Hyejŏn, was unques-
tionably to help resistance fighters.[26] Moreover, Pŏpjŏngsa, a temple that
Pongnyŏgwan rebuilt, functioned as a clandestine hub for all anti-Japanese
activities.

However, as a prominent religious figure, Pongnyŏgwan maintained a
friendly relationship with the local colonial power. Obviously, the Japanese
governor of Cheju Island treated her respectfully, making large donations
to Kwanŭmsa, which functioned as the BAC headquarters throughout the
1920s and 1930s. Along with the governor and other influential Japanese
residents in Cheju, Pongnyŏgwan served as an officer in BAC. On the basis
of her close ties with the local political authorities, Han Geum-soon argues
that Pongnyŏgwan's collaboration with the colonial government was a major
factor in bolstering Kwanŭmsa as the focal point of all the Buddhist institutions in Cheju, and more importantly, in successfully restoring Buddhist faith
on the island.[27]

Conformist or nonconformist to the colonial policy, Pongnyŏgwan's
seemingly contradictory attitudes toward the political milieu of the time
were not unique. Similar ambiguities are discerned in the biographies of
monastic leaders who were under constant surveillance by the colonial
police. A number of Buddhist temples funded the exiled Korean government in Shanghai, China. But hidden channels of communication between
the monastic community in Korea and the overseas exiled government were
known only to a very few in the order's administration. To protect members
of their community and its lay supporters, some abbots and abbesses created
a smoke screen by keeping up good relationships with the local colonial
representatives. Their "collaboration" with the Japanese has generated much
misunderstanding and controversy in the postcolonial era in terms of their
true intentions. A pointed example is Bhikṣu Kuha, the abbot of T'ongdosa,
who had been condemned for his alleged cooperation with the Japanese until
documents surfaced recently attesting his allegiance to the exiled government.[28] Pongnyŏgwan's relationship with the Japanese politicians and busi-
nessmen may be one such case. Such murkiness notwithstanding, it is clear
that she did not advocate colonialism or partake in Japan's war propaganda
in the 1930s, just as she did not openly affiliate with secret patriotic organizations. It seems that her aspiration to revitalize Buddhism in Cheju might
have overridden the necessity to directly engage in anti-Japanese activities.
This sensitive and complex issue remains to be investigated in depth for a
fuller portrait of Pongnyŏgwan.

Pongnyŏgwan's *Dhāraṇī* Practice

Another recurrent question in Pongnyŏgwan's life story is related to a misconception about her practice method and miracle work. As mentioned above, she mainly practiced the recitation of *dhāraṇī*s and *mantras*. While such recitation is recognized as a legitimate mode of practice in Korean Buddhism, it was not understood adequately by the people of Cheju Island who had long lost touch with Buddhism. It was easily mistaken for a form of shamanistic superstition, which, although strictly banned by the pro-Confucian government, remained popular among islanders in late Chosŏn.

The perception of Pongnyŏgwan's *dhāraṇī* practice as a superstitious ritual act clearly demonstrates the profound influence of shamanism on the island. Indeed, Cheju is one of the prime sites in which the ancient shamanistic legacy has been well preserved.[29] There are several geopolitical reasons for this, the most conspicuous of which is the high death rate of the male population at sea. Throughout most of the history of Cheju, women have outnumbered men. But dangers at sea are not sufficient to explain the gender imbalance in the island's demography. Because Cheju had been used as a popular place for political exiles, men were always vulnerable to periodic military cleansing by the central government.

Faced with various socioeconomic hardships in their day-to-day lives, many islanders, especially women, relied on shamanism, the only readily accessible source of spiritual comfort. Less institutionalized as a religious system compared with Buddhism, however, shamanism was looked down upon. Nonetheless, it was able to survive harsh persecution during the Chosŏn Dynasty largely because of the support of the female population.[30] In Cheju, therefore, religious acts associated with women were often suspected to be shamanistic. Considering these historical and sociocultural factors in the religious topography of Cheju, the negative attitudes toward Pongnyŏgwan's *dhāraṇī* practice were not exceptional at all.

The prevalence of the shamanistic belief system among women sheds light on the general tendency in Korean culture to relegate Buddhist nuns with miracle powers to the category of shamans. It can even be argued that a male monastic who demonstrates supernatural ability is promoted to the status of an eminent monk,[31] whereas a female monastic who works miracles is downgraded to the status of a shaman.[32] In this cultural milieu, it is not difficult to imagine that solitary female practitioners such as Pongnyŏgwan who displayed extraordinary spiritual abilities but had no supportive community of nuns around them would face more criticism than those living in a monastic community (*saṅgha*). Obviously, Pongnyŏgwan had a very special ability to find water on the volcanic island, heal the sick, intuit others' thoughts from a distance, and so on. It is said that although she never received formal education, she was able to read not only Korean but also Chinese characters. Various writings attest to the fact that her followers marveled at her remarkable accomplishments. But at the same time, many detractors cited her unusual spiritual power as proof that she was engaged in shamanistic practices. Miracles as a "means of religious expression and communication" have been far more closely associated with women than men. The conflicting views on Pongnyŏgwan's spiritual power epitomize "the stereotypical ideas about faith versus rationality and femininity versus masculinity."[33]

Nearly all the Buddhist institutions in Cheju today reflect Pongnyŏgwan's touch. She is the pioneer of modern Buddhism on this island. But a thorough and comprehensive assessment of her role in reviving Buddhism in Cheju has yet to be conducted. Of particular importance in this task is documenting her relationship with the Japanese colonial government. Because of the absence of reliable information on the final phase of her life, her position in the sociopolitical history of Cheju, including the independence movement, tends to be overlooked.[34]

In order to reconstruct Pongnyŏgwan's biography as the eminent nun of Cheju, it is imperative to collect historical materials, written and oral. Along with pursuing fieldwork, it will be necessary to clarify various theoretical issues about the relationship between shamanism and Buddhism and their relevance to gender politics in Korean society and more specifically in the insular culture of Cheju.

Notes

1. South Korea is divided into eight provinces, one special autonomous province, six metropolitan cities, and one special city.

2. Chejudoji p'yŏnch'anwiwŏnhoe, ed., *Chejudoji* (Gazetteer of Cheju Island), vol. 6 (Cheju: Chejudo, 2006), pp. 975–78.

3. Wŏnhye kŏsa, "Cheju Pulgyo ŭi yurae" (Origin of Cheju Buddhism), *Pulgyo* 32(February 2, 1927); and *Mailsinbo*, November 12, 1937, p. 3. These two articles are quoted from Cheju Pulgyosa yŏn'guhoe, ed., *Kŭndae Cheju Pulgyosa charyojip* (Collected Materials on the Modern History of Buddhism on Cheju) (Cheju: Cheju Pulgyosa yŏn'guhoe, 2002), p. 68 and p. 35, respectively.

4. *T'aejong sillok* (Veritable Records of King T'aejong), eighth year, lunar February 28.

5. Hong Yuson, *Soch'ong yugo* (Soch'ong's Posthumous Work) (Seoul: Soch'ong yugo kanhaengwiwŏnhoe, 1997), p. 60.

6. A photocopy of *Kŭmgwangmyŏnggyŏng* (*Suvarnaprabha Sūtra*) that was printed from the Myoryŏnsa woodblocks is kept at Songgwangsa. For details, see Yun Pongt'aek, "13segi Myoryŏnsap'an *Kŭmgwangmyŏnggyŏngmun'gu* ŭi sasil chomyŏng: Sunch'ŏn Songgwangsajang Koryŏp'an Chŏnsunp'an Puljŏn ŭl chungsim ŭro" (A his-

torical light cast on the *Suvarnaprabha Sūtra* printed from the thirteenth-century Myoryŏnsa woodblocks: focusing on the Buddhist *sūtras* at Songgwangsa Temple in Sunchŏn that were printed in the Tiānshùn era from the Koryŏ woodblocks), *Tamna munhwa* 29(2006): 193–227.

7. *T'aejong sillok* (Veritable Records of King T'aejong), eighth year, lunar February 28.

8. *Sejong sillok* (Veritable Records of King Sejong), ninth year, lunar June 10.

9. Yi Hyŏngsang, *Namhwanbangmul* (Various Things Observed in Cheju), trans. Yi Sanggyu and O Ch'angmyŏng (Seoul: P'urŭn yŏksa, 2009), p. 113.

10. For a survey of the increasing mixture of Buddhism and shamanism, see O Sŏng, "Kŭndae Cheju Pulgyo ŭi t'aedong kwa Kwanŭmsa ch'anggŏn" (The beginnings of Cheju Buddhism and the founding of Kwanŭmsa Temple), *Taegaksasang* 9(2006): 245–50.

11. This change took place between the sixteenth and seventeenth centuries. Han Geum-soon, "Chejudo Yŏngdŭnggut ŭi yurae: Yŏndŭnghoe esŏ yŏngdŭnggut ŭroŭi pyŏnchŏn" (The Origin of the Lotus Lantern Ritual of Cheju Island: From Lotus Lantern Festival to Lotus Lantern Shamanistic Ritual), *Chŏngt'ohak yŏn'gu* 11(2008): 463–502.

12. Chin Wŏnil, "An Pongnyŏgwan sŭnim" (Bhikṣuṇī An Pongnyŏgwan), *Chejudoji* 42(December 1969), quoted from Cheju Pulgyosa yŏn'guhoe, ed., *Kŭndae Cheju Pulgyosa charyojip*, p. 338. Most of the miracle stories related to Pongnyŏgwan that are cited in this chapter were taken from Chin's above article and "Chejudo Amisan Pongnyŏgwan ŭi kijŏk (Pongnyŏgwan's miracle in Mountain Ami), *Mailsinbo*, March 2, 1918, p. 3 and March 3, 1918, p. 3. These two sources are reprinted in *Kŭndae Cheju Pulgyosa charyojip*, pp. 14–15. It should also be noted that there is conflicting information on the dates of Pongnyŏgwan's birth, *śrāmaṇerika* ordination, return trip to Cheju after the ordination, and death. In this article, I adopt, as Han Geum-soon suggests, the dates presented by Yi Hoemyŏng, who worked closely with Pongnyŏgwan for a number of years. Yi Hoemyŏng, *Hoemyŏng munjip* (Collected Writings by Hoemyŏng) (Seoul: Yŏrae, 1991).

13. A *dhāraṇī* is a sacred Sanskrit phrase used in a ritual incantation. *Dhāraṇī* practice relies on the recitation of such phrases, which are generally not translated.

14. No information is available on Bhikṣuṇī Yujang, except that she was a disciple of Bhikṣuṇī Tuok. *Tuok mundohoe hoewŏn suchŏp* (Membership Booklet for the Tuok Dharma Family), p. 51.

15. December 28 is listed as her ordination date in two places: Paik Hwanyang's "Hallasan sullyegi, sok" (Records of a journey to Mountain Halla, a sequel), *Pulgyo* 71(May 1930); and Yi Ŭnsang, *T'amna kihaeng* (Travelogue on T'amna) (Seoul: Chosŏnilbosa, 1936). These two sources are quoted from *Kŭndae Cheju Pulgyosa charyojip*, p. 89 and p. 325, respectively. In the meantime, Pongnyŏgwan's monastic register at the Jogye Order of Korean Buddhism reports that she received the *śrāmaṇerika* precepts on December 8. Although an official document, the register contains errors. It is likely that the information in the register was hastily put together by Chin Wŏnil between 1969 and 1971 when he was organizing various records related to Kwanŭmsa. Given that Chin's memoir offers wrong information on key dates in Pongnyŏgwan's life, including her birth and death, the accuracy of his information on her ordination date is also doubtful.

16. The legend of her miraculous cure of the leper at Taehŭngsa is quoted from "Cheju Pulgyo chungsijo An Pongnyŏgwan sŭnim lin" (Short information on Bhikṣuṇī An Pongnyŏgwan, the reviver of Cheju Buddhism). This short biographical information on Pongnyŏgwan was collected and organized by Kim Yŏngt'ae, a reporter of the *Pulgyo sinmun* (Buddhist Newspaper). This material was printed by Podŏksa Temple, where Bhikṣuṇī Hyejŏn has served as abbess.

17. Hyejŏn, "Pongryŏgwan sŭnim kwa Cheju Pulgyo ŭi chunghŭng" (Bhikṣuṇī Pongryŏgwan and the revival of Buddhism in Cheju), in *Hanguk Piguni ŭi suhaeng kwa sam* (The Practices and Lives of Korean Bhikṣuṇīs) (Seoul: Yemunsŏwŏn, 2007), p. 353.

18. *Maeilsinbo*, March 2, 1918; and Yi Ŭnsang, *T'amna kihaeng*, quoted from *Kŭndae Cheju Pulgyosa charyojip*, p. 15 and p. 325, respectively.

19. The *kāṣāya* is an outer monastic robe with a prescribed pattern of patches that is worn over a sleeved monastic robe.

20. Yi Ŭnsang, *T'amna kihaeng*, quoted from *Kŭndae Cheju Pulgyosa charyojip*, p. 325.

21. Yi Hoemyŏng, "Cheju Hallasan Kwanŭmsa pŏptang chunggŏn sangryang-mun" (Essay written to celebrate the raising of the ridge beam in the Dharma hall of Kwanŭmsa Temple in Mountain Halla, Cheju), in *Hoemyŏng munjip*, pp. 88–91.

22. For a short description of Sŏgyun's anti-Japanese activities, see Han Geum-soon, "Kŭndae Cheju Pulgyosa yŏn'gu" (A study of the modern history of Buddhism in Cheju), PhD dissertation, Cheju National University, 2010, pp. 44–47. For the development of the anti-Japanese movement at Pŏpjŏng-sa and Sŏgyun's participation in it, see Han Geum-soon, "1918 nyŏn Cheju Pŏpjŏngsa hang'il undong e taehan saeroun insik" (A new perspective on the 1918 anti-Japanese movement at Pŏpjŏngsa Temple), *Chŏngt'ohakhoe* 10(2007): 429–67.

23. Official documents prepared by the colonial government show that Hyeo served as the abbot of Taehŭngsa in 1912, but it is likely that he was the abbot and/or spiritual director of Taehŭngsa in 1908 as well. Because 1908 precedes Japan's forceful annexation of Korea in 1910, his monastic administrative position was not included in the colonial documents. Hyeo served as the abbot of this temple until 1933, except for the years from 1918 to 1923. Taehan Pulgyo Jogyejong Ch'ongmuwŏn Ch'ongmubu, *Ilchesidae Pulgyo chŏngch'aek kwa hyŏnhwang* (Buddhist Policies and the State of Buddhism during the Japanese Colonial Period), vol. 1 (Seoul: Taehan Pulgyo Jogyejong, 2001), pp. 155, 157, 163, 167, 169, and 173.

24. Sŏgyun was fully ordained in 1916.

25. Han Geum-soon, "An Pongnyŏgwan kwa kŭndae Cheju Pulgyo ŭi chunghŭng," pp. 254–55.

26. Hyejŏn, "Pongnyŏgwan sŭnim kwa Cheju Pulgyo ŭi chunghŭng," pp. 360–62.

27. Han Geum-soon, "An Pongnyŏgwan kwa kŭndae Cheju Pulgyo ŭi chunghŭng," pp. 265–84.

28. For a controversy on this issue, see Pak Iksun, "Pulgyogye ch'inil insa myŏngdan muŏsi munjein'ga?" (What is the problem with the list of pro-Japanese persons in the Buddhist community?), *Hyŏndae Pulgyo*, September 4, 2005.

29. The enduring religious and cultural forces of shamanism on Cheju Island are best illustrated by the story of Princess Pari. Detailed discussions of this native shamanistic-Buddhist myth of Cheju are found in Michael Pettid, "Late Choson Society as Reflected in a Shamanistic Narrative: An Analysis of the Pari Kongju Muga," *Korean Studies* 24(2000): 113–41; Clark Sorensen, "The Myth of Princess Pari and the Self Image of Korean Women," *Anthropos* 83(1988): 403–19; and O Sejŏng, "Musoksinhwa e nat'anan Mu-Pul ŭi kyoryu wa pyŏnju" (Buddhist-shamanistic exchanges and variations in shamanistic myths), *Pulgyo p'yŏngron* 41(2009): 171–87.

30. For example, it was largely women who contributed to the survival of the Lotus Lantern Ritual in Cheju during Chosŏn. For a discussion of the continued practice of shamanism among women in Confucian Chosŏn society, see Yi Sunku, "Chosŏn chŏn'gi yŏsŏng ŭi sinangsaenghwal" (Women's religious activities in early Chosŏn), *Yŏksahakpo* 150(1996): 41–82.

31. Miracles attributed to Master Samyŏng epitomize this tendency. Samyŏng, the famous leader of the Chosŏn monk army during the Imjin War (1592–1598), worked various fantastic miracles in Japan, where he was negotiating with the Japanese to bring back Korean prisoners of war kept there.

32. For instance, in his article "Kŭndae Cheju Pulgyo ŭi t'aedong kwa Kwanŭmsa ch'anggŏn," O Sŏng calls her outright a "*munyŏ*" (female shaman) who "took refuge in Avalokiteśvara and prayed for one hundred days" before she was ordained in 1907 (pp. 245–46). He quotes Chin Wŏnil's essay "Kodae sach'al kwa Arari Kwanŭmsa" (Ancient Buddhist temples and Kwanŭmsa in Arari) as the basis of his reference of Pongnyŏgwan as a shaman. In Chin's original writing, however, she is described as a "faithful Buddhist from the age of thirty." See Chin Wŏnil, "Kodae sach'al kwa Arari Kwanŭmsa," *Chejudoji* 39(July 1969), quoted from Cheju Pulgyosa yŏn'guhoe, ed., *Kŭndae Cheju Pulgyosa charyojip*, p. 333.

33. Anne-Marie Korte, "Women and Miracle Stories: Introduction," in *Women and Miracle Stories: A Multidisciplinary Exploration*, ed. Anne-Marie Korte (Leiden: Brill, 2001), pp. 2–3.

34. During my fieldwork in Cheju in the summer of 2010, Bhikṣuṇī Ŭnyŏng, a disciple of Hyejŏn, told me a rumor that Pongnyŏgwan was probably murdered by means of poisonous mushrooms. The story about the circumstances of her death insinuates that Pongnyŏgwan was aware of her impending death by poison. Ŭnyŏng suspected that Pongnyŏgwan's friendly relationship with Japanese colonialists might have been "misunderstood" and indeed misled someone to assassinate her. Bizarre as it is, this rumor testifies to the degree of sensitivity and complexity of which a researcher needs to be aware in interpreting the sociopolitical implications of Pongnyŏgwan's religious activities.

11

A Resolute Vision of the Future

Hyechun Sunim's Founding of the National Bhikṣuṇī Association of Korea

Eun-su Cho

Hyechun (Hyech'un) Sunim is an example of a great meditator who became a powerful social mobilizer. Although Buddhist practice and enlightenment are commonly considered an individual achievement that occurs in the private domain, Buddhists just as often engage the larger, more complicated frameworks of culture and society. The life of Hyechun Sunim (1919–1998) illustrates how one woman was able to dramatically restructure herself, first as a fierce meditator and then as a leader who mobilized social support to achieve her vision—a vision that culminated in the creation of the National Bhikṣuṇī Association of Korea.

Hyechun Sunim never in her life relaxed the reins of her own Sŏn (Chinese: Chan; Japanese: Zen) practice. Not only was she was an exemplary practitioner in her own right, but in the eyes of the public she was a luminary with a grand vision for society. Tales of her twenty years of relentless effort to practice under the great masters of the time—effort that required of her an immense resolve, devotion, and endurance in order to overcome the extreme ordeals she met as she roamed the entire country—are still retold in Sŏn meditation halls today. Her adamant determination to practice the Dharma was extraordinary in itself, but she channeled the power of her practice further through the many connections she made and exchanges she had with the sages, both men and women, she met along the way. She was able to obtain the support of men such as Sŏngch'ŏl Sunim (1912–1993), a towering figure who dominated Korean Sŏn Buddhism for fifty years, while also faithfully inheriting the teachings and practice traditions of the revered figure Mansŏng Sunim (1897–1975), arguably the greatest Korean woman practitioner of the time.

Hyechun Sunim's life was a combination of personal dedication and self-confidence, plus she had a unique gift for negotiating politics and soliciting social cooperation—special qualities necessary for a religious leader in modern society. She incorporated wisdom and strength to forge a new concept of a Korean *bhikṣuṇī*, and she developed an innovative model of leadership in which she was able to cultivate a cadre of socially adept and highly motivated practitioners. As a nun, she departed from the traditional focus on meditation practice after her enlightenment in order to pioneer the social engagement of nuns, and in so doing, she offered them an inspiring example for the future. For, even though she denied that she was a visionary, the course of her life demonstrates a clear example of how the fruits of one individual's practice can have value that extends far beyond the realm of the personal and makes a broad and lasting impact on society at large. In traditional Korean society, the practice and accomplishments of Buddhist women were not the product of personal effort and dedication alone, but also reflected a confident vision of dedicating such efforts to others, assisted and reinforced by a network of family and community support that was even more important than their individual efforts. Not only did Hyechun Sunim aspire to the path of the *bodhisattva* with all her heart, but she also manifested it in practice. She even utilized the support of her natal family ties, using her father's talent as a lawyer for the cause of reforming Korean Buddhism.

The Life of Hyechun Sunim

Early twentieth-century Korea was not a favorable place for women to go out and forge their own purpose in life. Had Hyechun Sunim's experience not been unique in so many ways, her life might have been forgotten and buried in the mundane—immersed in a litany of unappreciated domestic work, as were the lives of so many women at the time. Hyechun Sunim's path differed even from those of other Korean *bhikṣuṇī*s, especially in regard to her close ties with an extensive network of male monastics. The circumstances that led Hyechun Sunim to enter the *saṅgha* were quite different from those of other *bhikṣuṇī*s in premodern Korea, many of whom were sent to temples early in life because of discrimination against girls, economic hardship, or the loss of their parents. In contrast, Hyechun Sunim was motivated to leave the secular world when she gained insight into the transience of life. At that time, most other great *bhikṣuṇī*s had entered the *saṅgha* at a very early age, without any experience of marriage, whereas Hyechun Sunim entered at the relatively late age of thirty-one after losing her husband in the chaos of war and becoming a widow.

No doubt, a measure of shared sympathy for the fate of human beings caught in the indiscriminate and inescapable forces of war influenced Hyechun Sunim's decision to abandon the dust of the world, a choice that eventually enabled her to become a great master even though she once had been married. After becoming a widow, Hyechun Sunim took the unusual step of embarking on the path to enlightenment. Had there been no experience of war or personal loss in her life, she might never have become a *bhikṣuṇī* or gone on to form the National Bhikṣuṇī Association of Korea. Hyechun Sunim's story raises interesting questions about human relationships and interactions within the larger context of history and society and how they intersect with dedication and effort in individual lives.

Born and Raised in Privilege

Hyechun Sunim's early life was very privileged. In the early twentieth century, most Koreans were suffering in conditions of hardship because of the economic and political pillaging taking place during the Japanese occupation and colonialization. But Hyechun was fortunate to live a comfortable life in a wealthy household because her father was the judge of a local court. She was born Yu Song-juk in Pukchŏng in Hamgyŏng-do Province (the northeast of what is now North Korea) in 1919, the third daughter of three sons and four daughters. As a child, she was cheerful, outgoing, and adept at fostering harmony with others. In an interview, she stated that her father particularly adored her and that his outside stresses would disappear whenever he saw her, although he sometimes said that it would have been nice if she had been a boy."[1] A bright student, she rarely forgot things, even those that she learned only once. She often helped her father by writing replies for him when he was serving on a governmental advisory council. Her mother was a typical housewife, gentle and domestic. She later recalled, "Because I came to South Korea from North Korea [when I married] at the age of twenty-two, that was the last time I saw my mother [because of the outbreak of the Korean War]. Looking back now, I was terrible to my mother. When she told me to sew or crochet, I would reply that I wouldn't become a housewife like her. I think nowadays that doing wrong to my parents was the lowest thing I have done as a human being."[2]

Hyechun Sunim graduated from Hamhŭng Women's High School in 1937 with an impressive record of scholarly aptitude. Although there were sixty-three students in her graduating class, only three of them were Korean. The other sixty were Japanese, because at the time Korea was a Japanese colony. Yet even the Japanese students remarked that they felt cheerful when they saw her. Attending a women's high school meant that she received the highest quality of education a woman could possibly obtain in the country-side.[3] She was a model student, later recalling that, because there were only three Koreans in the class, "We figured that we had nothing going for us except learning and so we all worked hard and excelled in our studies."[4] She was very active in school and played guard on a basketball team. Almost nothing was beyond her capabilities, especially because she was determined not to be bested by the Japanese. She loved music, played the piano, and often traveled to Seoul to listen to operas such as *Carmen* and *La Traviata* performed by Japanese troupes.

Becoming a Widow and Renouncing Family Ties

In 1940, at the age of twenty-two, prior to her renunciation, Hyechun Sunim had been married to a prodigy who was the youngest person to pass the Higher Civil Service Examination at the time. Just after the marriage, her husband was appointed to the position of magistrate in Yŏnggwang County in Hamgyŏng Nam-do Province (now North Korea). Her husband respected her and gave her a considerable amount of individual freedom. They were ideal for one another; their married life could not have been better. As a housewife, with a cook to prepare meals for her, she enjoyed an easy life. After marriage, she spent most of her time absorbed in books. She particularly liked reading philosophy and was deeply interested in the writings of Goethe. During ten years of marriage, she gave birth to one son and three daughters. Although she was an affectionate wife and mother, with a happy married life, she was able to shed all ties to the mundane world with one thought.

In 1950, the Korean War broke out and her entire life changed. Her husband was kidnapped by the North Koreans, but little else is known about what she went through during the war years from 1950 to 1953. In fact, traditionally, details about a person's life before having entered a monastery are regarded as private.

Hyechun Sunim's long association with Buddhism began in 1950 while she was a refugee in Pusan, the temporary capital of South Korea where most North Koreans resided during the war. A neighbor took her, a lamenting widow, to Pulgap-sa Monastery, where she heard Chaun Sunim teach on the *Sūtra of Brahma's Net* (Chinese: *Fanwang jing*). As she listened to the words of the teaching, she felt as if the Buddha himself were speaking them. Filled with joy, she experienced a spiritual awakening that kindled her monastic aspirations.

Amid the confusion and devastation of the war, her father searched for her for three months. He was not very fond of Buddhism, and when he eventually found her, he opposed her decision to live a monastic life. But she remained at the temple, and as surely as ripe fruit falls from the tree, as she put it, she renounced all the ties that bound her to the mundane world and decided to become a nun. At that time, she had four children. Her parents arranged for her children to be raised by her brothers-in-law. The separation was not easy for her; she once had a tearful reunion with her eldest son, who visited her to announce that he had started middle school.

Her father-in-law, a man who had at one point been a provincial governor, one of the highest government positions, was more sympathetic. He sent her a letter saying that he understood her decision to sever all her ties and attachments and become a nun. Once, when her father and her father-in-law met over drinks, they commiserated with each other about having lost two children: one who had been kidnapped and the other who had become a nun.

Although her decision to leave her children in others' care and pursue a life at the monastery can be criticized as abandoning her maternal responsibilities to seek her own religious goals, her decision mirrors the Buddha's own renunciation of privilege and family ties. Rather than being seen as selfish, renunciation in the Buddhist ideal places enlightenment, and the benefit of humanity, above the benefit of one's own family.

Confrontation: A Fateful Meeting with Sŏngch'ŏl Sunim

After having awakened to her monastic aspirations while listening to Chaun Sunim's teaching, Hyechun Sunim set out to receive Dharma training from Sŏngch'ŏl Sunim, the most famous Sŏn master at the time. She made her way to the nearby Ch'ŏnje Cave near Anjŏng-sa Temple in Tongyeong, Kyŏngsangnam-do Province, where Sŏngch'ŏl Sunim was engaged in meditation. In the following passages, Hyechun Sunim describes her encounter with Sŏngch'ŏl Sunim:

> It was a late night during winter, just after the Korean War broke out. Only the moon was a Dharma friend to the practitioner sitting cross-legged under a big pine tree, with the appearance of a laywoman. She looked just like a snowman under the moonlight against the dark mountain. A novice monk, holding a blanket at his side, called out to her: "Sunim, Sunim," but there was no

reply. Instead, a very soft voice repeated, "Amitābha Buddha, Avalokiteśvara Bodhisattva. . . ."

The novice monk approached with great concern. Her eyes shone like stars, reflecting the moonlight. "Bosalnim, please cover yourself with this," he said. "What is it?" she asked. "A blanket," he replied. "Please take it with you," she responded. "But Sunim, you might die of cold," he implored. "Novice monk, I am engaged in practice here. I will live here if I can. I will die here if I die."

One week passed. She survived on the rice balls offered by the village people. When the rice balls froze, she made them edible by thawing them in the river. Nobody could begin to match her resolve for enlightenment.

Eventually, the great master Sŏngch'ŏl sent a message through a novice monk: "I will teach her the Dharma if she successfully finishes 100,000 bows to the Buddha image at Songju-sa temple." This was a test to see whether the woman had a strong mind of enlightenment. It was scarcely imagined that anyone would be able to do it. However, she finished 100,000 bows in a week and returned after accomplishing the task.

When she arrived at the cave, however, Master Sŏngch'ŏl did not accept her as a student and told her to leave before dark. Yet she could not leave, and asked again for him to teach her. Again, he refused. The night became darker and darker, colder and colder, but she did not move. Finally, the master replied to her with a big bowl of water. He poured the water right on Hyechun, in the midst of a rigorous winter.[5]

Hyechun Sunim later recalled Sŏngch'ŏl Sunim's words—that she must pay the price of receiving training—as he pushed her to bow ten thousand times, then thirty thousand times. She pledged to atone for all her sins, wondering whether the Buddha would forgive her for leaving her parents and children behind to become a nun. She resolved to be a good nun to make amends for these misdeeds. She said that when Sŏngch'ŏl Sunim caught sight of her, he threw stones at her; he hit her with sticks to discipline her and never had any kind words for her. Although harsh treatment was a trademark of Sŏngch'ŏl Sunim, as a practitioner of the Imje Sŏn tradition,[6] his treatment of her was harsher than usual. This was probably a test of her resolve, especially in light of her previous life of ease and luxury in a wealthy family and the fact that she had been married and had children already.

Sŏngch'ŏl Sunim sent her for further training to Sŏngju-sa, a *bhikṣuṇī* temple in nearby Changwŏn.[7] At the temple, Inhong Sunim, a renowned Sŏn practitioner, was presiding over a meditation retreat with a group of some of the most dedicated nuns of the time. Sŏngch'ŏl Sunim had instructed Inhong

Sunim in advance to accept Hyechun Sunim as a practitioner but not to let her enter the meditation hall. Still a thirty-two-year-old widowed laywoman, she had to study her *hwadu* (Japanese: *koan*) sitting on a straw mat under the eaves of the meditation hall, without permission to shave her hair or even to enter the room. Sustaining herself with only a handful of barley rice and salted kimchi (pickled vegetables) every day, she conducted all her meditation and devotions on the damp straw mat outdoors. Only after two months of this practice was she finally allowed to cut her hair and enter the hall.

Hyechun Sunim reminisced, "At the time there were seventy *bhikṣunīs* meditating under the aegis of Inhong Sunim. Each one was fiercely devoted to her practice, to the point where each considered sleep her worst enemy. When snow began to fall, everyone stepped outside to contemplate her *hwadu*. I had a hard time then, because of drowsiness. My thighs were bruised from pinching them to stay awake. Because my mind was focused on comforts, I was sloppy in studying my *hwadu*. Everyone worked very hard, focusing on nothing but her own practice." The dedicated efforts of nuns like these, who overcame the privations of the times through fierce practice and the steadfast search for truth, are no doubt the reason why the Korean *bhikṣunī saṅgha* has become one of the greatest in the world.

Formally Entering the *Saṅgha*

At last, Hyechun Sunim formally entered the *saṅgha* in 1951 as a postulant at Yaksu-am Bhikṣunī Hermitage in Haein-sa Monastery, with the *bhikṣunī* Changho Sunim as her tonsure master. She was thirty-three years old at the time. The next year, in 1952, she received the ten *śrāmaṇerika* precepts, with the *bhikṣu* In'gok Sunim as her precept master. Only then was she known as Hyechun Sunim. That year she spent her first retreat season at Yunp'il-am Hermitage in Taesŭng-sa Temple, located in Mun'gyŏng, Kyŏngsangbukdo Province.

The conditions for living and practice for nuns at that time were extremely poor. Ancient hermitages assigned to nuns, such as Yunp'il-am Hermitage, were generally the long-neglected appendages of larger monasteries. This meant that nuns often had to rebuild and refurbish these structures from the ground up. Traveling by foot, they gathered wood for repairing the buildings and collected rice and other necessities. Sometimes their trips to other parts of the country to collect donations took many months. They also had to walk many miles to find a master and to listen to Dharma talks and teachings. Stories of these brave women circulated in meditation halls and temples, encouraging many serious practitioners to become dedicated to the religious path.[8]

The Korean War was a time of particular hardship. Sometimes monks and nuns would secretly go off to the mountains and weep from hunger.

Most Buddhist temples were burned down during the fighting. The monasteries that were assigned to nuns were often in particularly bad condition. These pioneer nuns had to scrape materials together to build and repair the compounds on their own. Hyechun Sunim recalled that Myojŏn Sunim, the caretaker of Yunp'il-am Hermitage at the time, used to go around asking for alms, cooking and feeding the nuns engaged in meditation retreat with the proceeds: "That was an enormous act of generosity and altruistic *bodhisattva*-like care that is almost inconceivable today. Serving as a caretaker, she went out to request alms every day, then made food for sixty to seventy practicing nuns. The extent of her benevolence and kind-heartedness is something that ordinary people cannot even imagine. She was like a shadow, protecting these nuns. That is much more meritorious than practicing for oneself."[9] These words are a testimony to the hardships *bhikṣuṇī*s endured in order to painstakingly carve out a space for their practice in a harsh environment.

Studying under Mansŏng Sunim at Taesŏng-am in Busan

Hyechun Sunim meditated for ten years under Mansŏng Sunim, the greatest *bhikṣuṇī* Sŏn master in the modern period. Hyechun Sunim related this story about her training with Mansŏng Sunim:

> In 1950, I entered the temple. In 1951, I became a postulant and, in 1952, became ordained [as a *śrāmaṇerika*]. I felt that existence was false and vain, and had no interest in worldly life. I wanted only to discover the truth and to become a liberated being. When I was a laywoman, I had already received a *hwadu* and was practicing meditation. Upon ordination, I meditated for ten years in Taesŏng-am Hermitage under the direction of Mansŏng Sunim.[10]

When Mansŏng Sunim was practicing at Kyŏnsŏng Hermitage, laypeople frequently came to request various ceremonies. Each day, the nuns beat a wooden bell calling everyone to work together. One day, Mansŏng Sunim wanted to practice meditation so badly that she quietly took her cushion to go sit in the mountains. The two nuns in charge of work duties ran after her, shouting: "Sunim, Sunim, the bell calling us to work has been struck. You must go work!" Mansŏng Sunim was frustrated, because there was always something in the way of her meditating as much as she wanted. So she shouted back: "You two, there are places where people who prevent someone from meditating go. You will end up in hell!" Then she disappeared into the forest. As a result of her experience, when she later created a Sŏn training hall at Daesŏng-am Hermitage, she showed great concern for the meditators under her care. They could sit in meditation as much as they wanted. The wooden bell was not struck and she did much of the work by herself, every day, all day long. Inspired by Mansŏng Sunim, Hyechun Sunim also focused all her energy on intensive meditation practice: "Once I did a week of non-sleep practice all by myself. Mansŏng Sunim came by and told me, 'Hyechun, in this lifetime you will awaken to your nature; continue to put as much effort into your practice as you are doing now.'"

Meditators such as Mansŏng Sunim and Hyechun Sunim pursued their practice with fervor, despite their monastic duties. Undaunted by the many obstacles they faced, each persevered in her practice and each emerged from that practice as a consummate inspiration for the Korean *bhikṣuṇī* practice tradition at large.

Deepening Her Practice

In 1961, Hyechun Sunim received full *bhikṣuṇī* ordination at Tongdo-sa Temple, with Chaun Sunim as her precept master. Ten years had passed since she had received the *śrāmaṇerika* precepts. Soon after receiving full ordination, she took up residence at the Sŏn retreat center at Sŏknam-sa Hermitage, where she served as an *ipsŭng* (one who teaches and guides other practitioners), a position she held for ten years.

Next, she entered a special three-year retreat and made a commitment to meditate intensively, without interruption or venturing outside, practicing alongside other great nuns such as Inhong, Changil, and Sŏngu. To finish a three-year retreat such as this is considered a great achievement for any practitioner. Although she never mentioned it herself, she is said to have attained enlightenment while practicing at Tong-am Hermitage at Kakhwa-sa Temple, located in the middle of the Taebaek Mountains.[11] Her *hwadu* (*koan*) was "What is it?" Until her death, she completed a total of thirty-six summer meditation retreats. During her lifetime, wandering like a cloud during the spring and autumn seasons, she visited many Sŏn centers across the country, including Sŏknam-sa Temple, Naewŏn-sa Temple, and Pudo-am Hermitage at Tonghwa-sa Temple.

Returning to the World, Awakening the Power of Bhikṣuṇīs

An intriguing question is how such a fearless meditator became a community organizer. She was certainly respected by others for her character, education, and practice history, but these qualities alone do not explain her rise to leadership. One motivating factor may have been the social discrimination that *bhikṣuṇī*s faced. In 1985, a movie called *Aje Aje Para Aje*[12] appeared that centered on a very negative representation of nuns. Hyechun Sunim joined other nuns to protest against this misrepresentation and to demonstrate by seeking an injunction against the film. This solidarity movement united the *bhikṣuṇīs* and affirmed the power of their collective voices. This demonstration brought prominence to activist nuns and contributed to the formation of the National Bhikṣuṇī Association. In an interview with Martine Batchelor, Hyechun Sunim explained her involvement in a humorous way:

> I continued to practice in various meditation halls over the years. One day, we heard that a film was being made by a Korean filmmaker about a nun. The scenario and script were terrible; the nun in the film breaks the precepts many times. When we heard about this, we decided that the film would not be good for Buddhism; furthermore, it was not good art, nor beneficial for the *sangha* or for Korean Buddhists. . . . For the first time, Korean nuns organized themselves to prevent the movie from being made.
>
> During the previous ten years, there had been an organization called Udambara, mainly comprised of senior nuns, which met from time to time. They had not had much to discuss or do, so they had stopped meeting, but the infrastructure was there. When the film issue came up, they began to gather again. All the nuns came together and we formed the National Bhikṣuṇī Association. Being unlucky, I was elected as the head of the association. The number of nuns registered with us was three thousand. The number of nuns in the order was about five thousand.

Encouraged by their newfound solidarity and sense of purpose, the National Bhikṣuṇī Association was established with Hyechun Sunim as president. She served two five-year terms as president, from 1985 to 1995. The roots of the association and the mobilization of *bhikṣuṇīs* in modern Korea go back to earlier decades, however, with Hyechun Sunim at its center. Her active social engagement was spurred by a profound sense of justice, and her abundance of political energy placed her at the vanguard of social engagement. She was well known for her activism during the Buddhist "purification movement" (1954–1964), which sought to purge married monks from the *sangha*, and she served as one of the ten *bhikṣuṇī* representatives of the movement.[13]

Indeed, the Korean *bhikṣuṇī* community was at the forefront of the purification movement. The presence of married monks in the *sangha* was viewed as a legacy left by the Japanese religious culture that permitted monks to marry, in contrast to the Korean Buddhist tradition of monastic celibacy. The nuns saw this movement as providing the strategic momentum necessary to gain their rightful place in the *sangha* as a whole. After the Japanese colonial period, only a handful of celibate *bhikṣus* remained in Korea. Most of the elite, well-educated monks had either converted to Japanese Buddhism or joined the order of married monks. At the peak of the movement, married monks were purged through street demonstrations and lawsuits, and *bhikṣuṇī*s outnumbered *bhikṣu*s.

Though Hyechun Sunim had only been ordained for a short time, she threw herself into the purification movement with great enthusiasm. By that time, her father had become a powerful lawyer in Seoul. However, when his daughter sought his help, he initially rejected her request. He thought, "Having renounced the secular world, was she now not throwing herself back into it?" Her earnest pleas eventually won him over, and he began arguing cases for the purification movement in the courts. By that time, the courts had ruled that the Jogye Order (practically the sole order of Buddhism in Korea at the time) was a celibate order. Through the efforts of her father, Hyechun Sunim became a key figure in the purification movement that eventually led to victory for the celibate monks.

In the 1950s, while married monks were being removed from monasteries in Korea at the height of the movement, and the effort to redistribute property and to redefine Korean Buddhism was beginning, there was a sentiment that at least one of the twenty-five monastic headquarters (*chongnim*, lit., grove of monasteries) should be given to the *bhikṣuṇī*s to recognize their central contributions to the purification movement. However, when the *bhikṣu*s finally attained power, they denied the *bhikṣuṇī*s a rightful place of their own. These monastic headquarters are critically important, because each of the twenty-five headquarters selects one representative to the national body. This group of twenty-five representatives makes important decisions for the Korean *saṅgha* as a whole, one of which is to elect the head of the Jogye Order of Korean Buddhism, akin to the College of Cardinals electing the Pope in Catholicism. To this day, because of *bhikṣu* resistance to change, all twenty-five headquarters remain *bhikṣu* institutions, effectively disenfranchising *bhikṣuṇī*s from the highest level of decision making in the Jogye Order.

Tonghwa-sa Temple was discussed as the prospective site for such a *bhikṣuṇī* monastic headquarters in 1954. In preparation, a group of nuns who participated in the movement took charge of Tonghwa-sa for one year, after it was recovered from a married monk. Immediately, opposition arose from the *bhikṣu*s. It is said that a particular senior monk protested, arguing that Tonghwa-sa Temple could not be entrusted to nuns because it was inconceivable that a woman could become the matriarch of a monastic headquarters. In the end, the backlash was too strong, and plans for a *bhikṣuṇī* headquarters never came to fruition.

In 1967, more than ten years after their hopes had been dashed, the *bhikṣuṇī*s' aspirations to organize resurfaced. On April 16, many nuns gathered at a Dharma lecture to celebrate the ninety-seventh birthday of Man'gong

Sunim, a renowned *bhikṣu* Sŏn master.[14] These nuns resolved to establish a monastic headquarters for *bhikṣuṇī*s near Sudŏk-sa Temple. The temple would be a place where they could engage in deep practice exclusively, without any other obligations, following the example set by Man'gong Sunim himself. At the time, Sudŏk-sa Temple was as close to a head temple of the Korean *bhikṣuṇī* order as one could find; it had special significance as the location of the first Sŏn meditation facility for nuns in modern Korea. Again, however, the nuns' plans ran into opposition from the monks. The nuns' organizational abilities were still far too weak.

On February 24, 1968, motivated by the rebuffs they had experienced, the nuns responded by founding the Udambara Association, the first *bhikṣuṇī* organization in Korea. This was the forerunner of the Korean National Bhikṣuṇī Association. While this was happening, the issue of finding and purchasing land to build a hall for the Udambara Association met with significant difficulties. After the mid-1970s, core members who had actively worked on the project began to drop out, and the Udambara Association went into hiatus. A decade later, in September 1985, a group of influential senior *bhikṣuṇī*s attended a special seminar on *bhikṣuṇī* precepts at Sŏknam-sa Temple and expressed the need to revive the *bhikṣuṇī* association. Right away, they organized a general meeting at the Samsŏn Buddhist Center in Seoul. They invited Hyechun Sunim to be its president, and they named it the National Bhikṣuṇī Association of the Jogye Order of Korean Buddhism.

It is important to note that the formation of the National Bhikṣuṇī Association and the construction of its assembly hall received little assistance from the *bhikṣu saṅgha* administration. It was the *bhikṣuṇī*s themselves who accomplished the great task of providing an environment for the generations of nuns to come. Even though Korean nuns were ignored in the central political body of the *saṅgha*, they accomplished their goals through their own self-sufficient efforts. Ironically, being alienated from the central administration worked in their favor, because it sheltered them from the battles that in the past had often divided factions of the *bhikṣu saṅgha*.

The establishment of the National Bhikṣuṇī Association in 1985 was the culmination of more than thirty years of sporadic attempts made by nuns to mobilize and unite their efforts. Their tumultuous history is a testament to the difficulties that nuns have faced while attempting to carve out a place for themselves to apply their solidarity and activism. Despite their most sincere aspirations, these nuns continued to lack the support, resources, and infrastructure to achieve their goal until 1985. Hyechun Sunim was behind their success. She had never given up her determination to mobilize the *bhikṣuṇī*s. Buddhist newspapers at the time reported that the eyes of the Buddhist world were focused on Sŏknam-sa Temple at Kaji-san Mountain near Ulsan on September 5, 1985. For the first time in the sixteen hundred years since Buddhism was transmitted to Korea, a united *bhikṣuṇī* association had been established.

In laying the institutional foundations for the National Bhikṣuṇī Association, Hyechun Sunim ensured that the intellectual, spiritual, and human resources she accrued would continually be passed down for the benefit of future generations. Keeping an eye on the future, she tirelessly worked, with great generosity and loving kindness toward those around her, to gather Korean *bhikṣuṇī*s together. Although this was at a time when *bhikṣuṇī*s lacked solidarity, she managed to pool their strengths and inspire them to social action. She was an exemplary leader who, by taking the crucial step of establishing institutional frameworks, went on to consolidate these human and material resources into something that united and served the greater community and society in general. She deftly made use of the networks she forged through her personal connections and social resources, leveraging considerable political influence in the formation of a national *bhikṣuṇī* association.

In a newspaper interview at the time, Hyechun Sunim expressed her feelings in anticipation of the founding of the association. She said that, considering all the different issues that had arisen both inside and outside the *saṅgha*, the *bhikṣuṇī*s needed to unite in solidarity and revive the spirit of the original *bhikṣuṇī*s and, in so doing, become the last stronghold in defense of the Buddhadharma. Her recognition of history in founding the National Bhikṣuṇī Association and her fervent sense of duty are clearly evident in her words.

Using Skillful Means: One Must Know about the World

Following these events, Hyechun Sunim became more interested in the outside world. For example, she took the Mokdong Youth Center under her care from the city of Seoul in 1988. She said, "The Mokdong Youth Center is the first time Buddhist monastics had been entrusted with running a social welfare facility. I was invited to direct the programs. I had to go to work every day! Because I tend to be the kind of person who works really hard, there were many difficulties, but the Buddha helped me. Assisting youth and spreading Buddhism are all important things."[15]

Although a *bhikṣuṇī* association had been formed, there was still no space for its members to congregate. Eventually, Hyechun Sunim was able to secure land to begin the construction of the National Bhikṣuṇī Association Hall. The construction project was treacherous and fraught with challenges and setbacks, such as corruption and ordinances that disallowed development. Nevertheless, she was able to overcome all of these obstacles. In 1992, she acquired land to build an assembly hall and began construction in 1998, although she passed away before the completion ceremony was held in 2003.

This 1991 interview with a Buddhist magazine indicates how much effort and anxiety went into building the assembly hall. The interviewer said:

> As soon as I met [Hyechun Sunim], she pointed her finger straight at a huge map of Seoul, big enough to fill one wall of her office. She highlighted the portions marked in red and told me that those were the areas planned for the construction of the *bhikṣuṇī* assembly hall. She said, "Because I spent all my time going around meditating with nothing but my knapsack, I don't know anything or have any special abilities. Even though I'm trying as hard as I can in taking on this enormous task, actual progress is slow and I only have thoughts of regret. But as long as we resolutely pursue our vision and work hard, I believe that the assembly hall will be built. It is the hope of the National Bhikṣuṇī Association to create this hall, so we can oversee the character of *bhikṣuṇī*s, gather together, and educate postulants who wish to join the *saṅ gha*. If there is anyone wracked with suffering who comes to the Association, we hope to be able to ease all their suffering by giving them Dharma lectures. It has already been six years since we first dreamt our resolute vision of constructing an assembly hall. Though I was supposed to let go of the chair after one term, I ended up serving another term, partly due to my own wishes and partly due to others' requests. This coming May marks the end of my second term and I'm sitting here alone, suffering from pangs of anxiety, because I need to finalize the purchase of this land by that time."[16]

Eventually, Hyechun Sunim began to take on an international role, receiving practitioners from around the world and supporting them. She practiced skillful means and had a heart big enough to embrace all those who sought guidance, knowledge, and inspiration. She strongly supported the full ordination of women, which is lacking in many Buddhist traditions. Her most well-known international disciple is Karma Lekshe Tsomo, who received *bhikṣuṇī* ordination from her in 1982 at Pŏmŏ-sa Temple in Pusan. Il Ta Sunim, an acclaimed *bhikṣu* scholar, calligrapher, and *vinaya* master, revived the tradition of dual ordination for *bhikṣuṇī*s, conducted by ten *bhikṣu*s and ten *bhikṣuṇī*s, in response to a letter that Tsomo had written to him while he was staying in Irvine, California. Unaware that Il Ta Sunim had reinstated the dual ordination procedure for *bhikṣuṇī*s, Tsomo arrived in Korea seeking *bhikṣuṇī* ordination and, by a fortuitous set of circumstances, arrived at

Pŏmŏ-sa Temple just in time for the dual ordination. Hyechun Sunim had been appointed to take the lead among the *bhikṣuṇī* precept masters. During breaks in the ordination schedule, she instructed Tsomo in the *hwadu* method of Sŏn meditation in the fluent Japanese she had learned during her school days decades earlier. After the ordination, Hyechun Sunim invited her to Pohyŏn-am Hermitage, where they continued their Dharma exchanges. Tsomo remembers her dynamism and clear insight: "She was like a mountain. She was the living memory of a thousand people."

Inspired largely by Hyechun Sunim's example, Tsomo became a founder and president (from 1987 to 2008) of the world's leading Buddhist women's organization, Sakyadhita International Association of Buddhist Women. If it was possible to bring *bhikṣuṇīs* together from around Korea, then why not bring them together from around the world? In 1991, Hyechun Sunim attended the 2nd Sakyadhita International Conference on Buddhist Women in Bangkok, where she spoke about the importance of Buddhist women working as a cohesive group. Expressing sentiments that were far ahead of her time, she stressed the importance of an international Buddhist women's alliance to consolidate women's strengths and encourage solidarity, while at the same time deepening their practice. Not only did she deliver a talk at an international conference, which was a rarity at the time for a senior monastic, but she also actively received guests from all over the world—serving as an ambassador for international Buddhist exchanges. In 1993, despite her advanced age and a raging infection on her foot, she intrepidly traveled to the 3rd Sakyadhita Conference in Colombo, Sri Lanka, where she again welcomed visitors from around the world, completely oblivious to her own physical discomfort. Even as medical personnel were summoned to treat her infected foot, Hyechun Sunim's sheer determination to overcome all obstacles and engage fully with Buddhists from around the world conveyed an important teaching to everyone she met.

Wrapping Up Her Life

Hyechun Sunim did not accept disciples until she was fifty years old, because she thought that guiding students might interfere with her practice. When she was the *ipsŭng* of Sŏknam-sa Temple, a nun named Soyŏng asked to be her student, so she left the temple—a way of telling the nun to seek a better teacher. Soyŏng waited three years before she was able to become her student, demonstrating the same kind of tenacity that Hyechun Sunim had modeled in seeking instruction from Sŏngchŏl Sunim. Hyechun Sunim eventually began to take students in 1972 after she founded Pohyŏn-am Hermitage (located near Haein-sa Temple on Mount Gaya Mountain), a feat that took twelve years and was not fully completed until 1984.

The words that Hyechun Sunim's disciples use to characterize her include "active in the midst of stillness." Paradoxically, she possessed both qualities simultaneously. She was lively and meticulous at the same time, commanding and calm, putting beginners both on alert and at ease. Her natural simplicity and humility were balanced by her profound practice of compassion.

Hyechun Sunim was known as a rigorous and strict master who did not play games, but she could also be delightful and playful. At special moments, one might find her playing the piano and singing, talents she learned as the daughter of a wealthy family. Her personal qualities would have been great assets for a cultured housewife, but she moved beyond the domestic sphere to national and international domains, sharing her razor-sharp insight with numerous students and colleagues. Unpretentious simplicity was perhaps her most impressive quality. She never lied and was at times even brutally honest.

Hyechun Sunim could not imagine skipping prayers. Early one morning on November 6, 1998, at Pohyŏn-am Hermitage, she joined in the prayers at daybreak as usual and then finished a bowl of gruel. She recited the following poem:

> Did I come like this and leave like this?
> Coming and going is all the same.
> The fresh wind goes on for miles.

Then she asked, "Isn't the weather nice?" and mindfully passed away. Her worldly age was eighty, and her Dharma age (counted by years of ordination) was forty-seven.

Hyechun Sunim'a life might be summed up in a few words. Most importantly, she was a consummate meditator who devoted herself to Sŏn practice with all her strength and determined willpower. She was strong, noble, and dignified, with a generous heart. The fact that she had been married did not pose an obstacle in her monastic career. In fact, she was able to use her education and the social capital she had accrued in the secular sphere to help her direct fellow nuns toward a greater goal. Samhaeng Sunim, the current abbess of Pohyŏn-am Hermitage, described her as an openhearted person who would do exactly what she said. The force of her determination was unimaginable.[17]

Even as an enlightened practitioner with thirty-six years in Sŏn meditation halls, Hyechun Sunim did not leave behind any writings about her own practice. True to form, she steadfastly avoided pretension. When Martine Batchelor asked her about Sŏn, she responded:

> For us, to be alive is to practice. The question is our life. If we
> hold the question continuously, this is proof that we are alive.
> "What is it?" is everything. Because I cultivate the question, I can

be in Seoul [at the National Bhikṣuṇī Association, remote from the meditation halls that were her spiritual center]. If I did not practice like this, I could not be there. I became a nun because I was not fond of worldly life. If I were not to practice, how could I live in Seoul?

This thought epitomizes her life: Each busy moment is complete with insight and compassion. For modern-day practitioners, this thought can also serve as a guidepost. Most of us often wonder how intensive practice is possible in the frantic mundane world. Perhaps Hyechun Sunim's life holds some answers.

Notes

1. Buddhist Broadcasting Service (BBS) interview, November 2, 1996. This is part of a series of interviews conducted with Hyechun Sunim from November 1–10, 1996, two years before her death.
2. BBS Interview, November 5, 1996.
3. The first women's college (Ewha Women's University) was founded by American missionaries only in 1925. For more on higher education for women at this time, see Jihang Park, "Trailblazers in a Traditional World: Korea's First Women College Graduates, 1910–45," *Social Science History* 14:4(1990): 533–58.
4. BBS Interview, November 2, 1996.
5. Oksun An, trans., "100,000 Bows in One Week," *Sakyadhita Newsletter* 11:2(2000), http://www.sakyadhita.org/home/newsletters/11-2.htm.
6. Chinese: Linji, Japanese: Rinzai.
7. In Korea, *bhikṣuṇī*s can only practice at facilities for *bhikṣuṇī*s and not at facilities for *bhikṣu*s.
8. For a further account on the state of *bhikṣuṇī* society in modern Korea, please see Pori Park, *Trial and Error in Modernist Reforms: Korean Buddhism under Colonial Rule* (Institute of East Asian Studies at University of California, Berkeley, 2009); and Chapter 2, "Female Buddhist Practice in Korea: A Historical Account," in Eun-su Cho, *Korean Buddhist Nuns and Laywomen: Hidden Histories, Enduring Vitality* (Albany: State University of New York Press, 2011).
9. BBS Interview on November 9, 1996.
10. This passage is from an interview with Hyechun Sunim conducted by Martine Batchelor, who lived in Korea as a Buddhist nun from 1975 to 1985 and now teaches Buddhism in Europe. I wish to express my gratitude to her for sharing this unpublished manuscript.
11. Interview with Samhaeng Sunim, abbot of Pohyŏn-am Hermitage, July 11, 2011.
12. This is a transcription of the beginning of the Sanskrit mantra, *gate gate pāragate*, that concludes the famed *Heart of Wisdom Sūtra*.
13. The term "purification movement" was coined by Rhee Syngman, the first president of South Korea, a Princeton Ph.D. graduate who returned to Korea after liberation in 1945, after many years of foreign exile. His explicit agenda was the removal

of all Japanese cultural taints from Korea. Although he was a devout Christian, it is said that he was furious about the practice of married monks in Korean Buddhism. His exhortation to "purify" the established system of married monks provided the legal and political grounds for removing these monks during the struggle that would follow over the next ten years.

14. In many ways Man'gong Sunim (1871–1946), a renowned Sŏn master monk of the time, was the founding father of the *bhikṣuṇī* practice tradition that resumed in modern times. With Man'gong Sunim's leadership and support, a center for *bhikṣuṇī* Sŏn meditation (*sŏnwon*) was established at Kyŏngsŏng-am Hermitage at Sudŏk-sa Temple that accepted *bhikṣuṇī* meditators for the retreat season in January 1916. This is the first recorded instance of such a meditation facility for nuns in modern Korea. Many of the nuns whom he accepted as his disciples and encouraged to practice later became leading *bhikṣuṇī*s. See Cho, *Korean Buddhist Nuns and Laywomen*, p. 45.

15. BBS interview, November 11, 1996.

16. Yi Chŏlsu, "The Efforts to Establish a National Bhikṣuṇī Association Hall," *Haein: Monthly Magazine on Buddhism*, February 1991, p. 108.

17. Interview with Samhaeng Sunim, abbess of Pohyŏn-am Hermitage, July 11, 2011.

12

From Mountains to Metropolis

Sŏn Master Daehaeng's Teachings on Contemporary Buddhist Practice

Hyeseon Sunim (Kyunhee Lee)

Located on the outskirts of metropolitan Seoul, Hanmaum (One-mind) Sŏn Center is one of the most flourishing urban temples in Korea today.[1] Despite its short history, this temple, along with Nŭng'in Sŏn Center and An'guk Sŏn Center, is considered to be a successful example of Buddhist propagation among city dwellers.[2] The founder and spiritual director of this popular meditation center was the *bhikṣuṇī* master Daehaeng (1927–2012),[3] a charismatic Sŏn nun who spent nearly a decade engaged in ascetic practices deep in the mountains. Daehaeng's extraordinary practice history provides important background information for understanding her innovative ideas on contemporary Buddhism.

The modernization of Korean society over the last hundred years or so necessitated a new way of spreading the Dharma. Various aspects of traditional Buddhist institutions, rituals, and customs have been modified to meet the changing needs of Koreans caught in the rapid urbanization and westernization of their lifestyles. Daehaeng's exemplary endeavors to modernize Buddhist practice amid this shifting sociocultural milieu deserve particular attention.

Daehaeng spent more than ten years in the mountains as an itinerant Sŏn practitioner. This is remarkable given the rugged terrain of the region through which she wandered. In Korean Buddhism, this mode of spiritual training is almost always associated with monks. Consequently, the expression "*sansŭng*" (mountain monastic) tends to conjure up the image of a monk, not a nun. While "*sanjung kido*" (praying in the mountains)[4] and "*unsuhaenggak*" (wandering like clouds and water)[5] are commonly undertaken by nuns as well as monks, long-term itinerant meditation is adopted almost exclusively by monks because of the various physical challenges involved.

Traditionally, itinerant practice has fostered the rich monastic lore of a spiritual breakthrough that monastics experience on their path to awakening. The winter mountains, in particular, are regarded as the most challenging and yet ultimately ideal location for Sŏn meditation. This view derives from the six years of ascetic practice undertaken by the Buddha. Actually, the place where the Buddha stayed for six years was a small hill in the forest. In Korea, however, many biographies of the Buddha present the site of his intense meditation as a snow-covered mountain in the Himalayas. Hence, this phase of his life is typically referred to as the period of "*sŏlsan kohaeng*" (ascetic practice in the snow mountains)."[6] Because the Buddha became enlightened at the end of this period, the cold mountains are regarded not only as spiritually auspicious places but also as penultimate points of meditation.

Daehaeng's decade-long retreat in the wilderness marks the rare instance of a nun's ascetic practice in modern Korean Buddhist history. Her penchant for the outdoors developed early in her childhood. She recollects that she spent much of her time outside her family home, which suffered heavy political and economic blows from the Japanese colonial forces because of her father's service in the Korean army.[7] After the family house was confiscated by the Japanese military government, Daehaeng, although quite young, became both physically and psychologically homeless. These disruptive circumstances and the experience of subsistence living drove the precocious young girl to ask herself fundamental existential questions, such as why she existed and why people suffered so much from hunger and disease.[8]

In 1950, as a result of deeply questioning the meaning of life, Daehaeng renounced household life. Soon after, she received the *śrāmaṇerika* precepts (vows of a novice nun), then retreated to the mountains. Wandering through Kangwŏn and Kyŏnggi Provinces and the area around Seoul, Daehaeng continued her itinerant, open air meditation practice for four years. She ran into many sorts of life-threatening situations on her journey, which spanned the time of the Korean War and its aftermath. A strong anti-communist sentiment swept South Korea during this period. North Korean guerillas and spies used the remote mountain ranges to infiltrate South Korea; consequently, people were suspicious of strangers who lived in the forests and mountains. Daehaeng was sometimes bullied and beaten by strangers and even arrested and tortured by the police, who suspected her of being a North Korean spy.[9] Daehaeng's four years of wandering were followed by another six years of solitary retreat on Mount Ch'iak in Wonju of Kangwon Province. At this time, she stayed in a small hut near Sangwŏn Temple.[10]

Several salient features characterized Daehaeng's life in the wilderness. Above all, she faced gender-specific challenges as an itinerant female practitioner. As a way of protecting herself from the potentially dangerous men she might run across, she covered her face with mud. As a result, her facial skin cracked and bled in the cold weather, giving her a terrible appearance. With her repulsive face, indifference to clothing, and total immersion in her own inner world, it is not surprising that she was treated as a mad vagrant. Once a question arose in her mind, Daehaeng stopped on the spot and stayed there day and night until she found an answer.[11] When she felt hungry, she ate whatever leaves and grasses lay near her.[12] Although she was unconcerned about her bodily appearance, needs, and functions, Daehaeng never considered the form of practice she was undertaking to be asceticism; she simply had no interest in things related to her physical form.

Monastic institutions could not function properly during the war and postwar years. Further, the monastic establishment during this period placed excessive emphasis on formal sitting meditation and narrow adherence to a rigid set of rules for daily life.[13] Daehaeng felt compelled to be outdoors, as she yearned to investigate questions directly, not by means of scriptural study or ritual performance. She had already awakened to her true nature and could see that a rote adherence to rule and structure wouldn't help her. The natural environment provided her with a wide range of occasions on which she could investigate the subtle workings of the mind. Of particular interest in this process was her communication with flora and fauna. Her interaction with animals and plants helped her gain insight into the interconnectedness of all forms of sentient beings. The *Fundamentals of One Mind* contains numerous nonverbal dialogues she had with wild animals, including a tiger and a snake, and with trees and flowers.[14]

Daehaeng developed her compassion for the sick through her study of nature and through her travels. During her travels after the Korean War, she encountered many people suffering from various maladies. This led her to contemplate the cycle of birth, sickness, aging, and death and the causes of suffering, especially the effects of the mind on bodily suffering.[15] Because of her profound compassion and ability to heal others, developed during long years of mountain practice,[16] she was highly respected as a "*bodhisattva* of medicine."

Daehaeng's long mountain practice finally came to an end in 1972, when she felt that "the time was right to settle down."[17] In 1972, she founded

Hanmaum Sŏn Center in Anyang, a satellite city of the nation's capital. Her selection of an urban locale as the main site for her Dharma teaching was significant. Although her own practice followed Korea's long tradition of mountain Buddhism, she realized after awakening that one does not have to seek a special place for meditation. When asked why she had spent so much time in the mountains, she laughed and replied that it was because she was poor and had no place to go. In essence, those were just her circumstances, so that was where she practiced.[18] She did not insist that her disciples practice the kind of asceticism she herself undertook in the wilderness.[19] On the contrary, she stressed that one can, and in a sense should, practice where one's day-to-day life unfolds. "The Buddhadharma is the law of reality and the law of daily life," she said. Therefore, "as long as you think that enlightenment is something apart from your daily life, you will never realize enlightenment."[20]

To city dwellers, Daehaeng taught that the "here and now" is the right time and place for practice. Just as the wilderness naturally became a place of walking meditation for her as a homeless wanderer, so does the modern cityscape naturally become a practice site for contemporary urban adherents. She encouraged her listeners to accept the problems faced in frantic modern life as the raw material for mental cultivation. It is not wise to avoid, reject, or be depressed by such hardships. Instead, difficulties are to be embraced as opportunities to learn and grow, knowing that they are inherently empty. Hardships serve as objects of our contemplative investigation and should be treated as teachers in spiritual training.

Daehaeng's emphasis on Sŏn as an everyday activity explains her open attitude toward social change. This is clearly reflected in her innovative ideas about mainstream Korean practice traditions. For example, the tradition of sitting meditation as practiced in quiet natural surroundings emerged from and established itself in accordance with the historical conditions of premodern Korean society. But extensive sitting meditation has become somewhat outdated in contemporary cultural environments. While we should honor the spiritual legacy of such a tradition, we should simultaneously try to adapt it to new circumstances.

In order to propagate the Dharma effectively in ultra-modern Korean society, Daehaeng emphasized three concepts: simplicity, accessibility, and clarity of focus. She brought these concepts into practice programs, temple structures, and ritual forms. One example of simplicity and accessibility is an innovation she implemented in ritual forms and practice methodology: the use of vernacular Korean in ritual language. By translating old-fashioned Chinese terms into modern Korean expressions, she helped many lay Buddhists understand the Dharma more easily. In Korea, traditional Buddhist chanting is based on the transcription of classical Chinese. However, this transcription method represents sound, not meaning. Consequently, lay Buddhists tend to recite a *sūtra* without grasping its precise meaning. This deplorable situation led Daehaeng to adopt vernacular Korean as the formal ritual medium. Her decision was not only brave but also democratic, given that its primary beneficiaries have been undereducated women who constitute the majority of the laity.[21]

The simple interior of Hanmaum Sŏn Center's main hall is another distinctive feature of simplicity, accessibility, and clarity of focus. In a typical Korean temple, the main Dharma hall is dedicated to Sakyamuni, whose image is traditionally accompanied by two attendant *bodhisattvas*, Mañjuśrī and Samantabhadra. Along with these three figures on the central platform, paintings of protective deities appear in the background and on the two side walls of the main hall. In one corner of the hall, one can find small votive candles or lanterns as well. By contrast, Hanmaum Sŏn Center enshrines a Sakyamuni statue only. The exclusive focus on the historical Buddha is intended to help practitioners concentrate on Hanmaum—One-mind—from which various phenomena arise. Images and statues can divert the attention of uninformed people away from a direct investigation of their own Buddha-nature toward devotional practice for self-interest. The simple iconic design at Hanmaum Sŏn Center works to avoid these kinds of distractions and misunderstandings. Its bright and spacious halls provide urban workers with peace and tranquility amid cluttered cityscapes and noise.

The principles of simplicity and a clear focus on One-mind also apply to the arrangement of a ritual altar. In contrast to the great variety of foods and offerings used in traditional Korean Buddhist and Confucian ceremonies, the items offered on the altar at Hanmaum Sŏn Center include only incense, pure water, flowers, candles, fruit, and rice cakes. Daehaeng considered it unwise to spend hours preparing elaborate, old-style ritual food. Koreans' diets have changed considerably under the influence of Western culture. In light of today's changing food culture, Daehaeng maintained that insofar as ritual offerings embody one's sincerity and respect, a few simple offerings will suffice.

One popular custom for Korean Buddhists is releasing live fish or turtles into rivers or lakes. This custom purports to reinforce the importance of compassion for all forms of sentient life. To a degree, such a purpose is lost on urban residents, whose daily routine is alienated from nature. They liberate animals with noble intentions, but without proper knowledge of the local ecosystem or the animals' place within it. Such life-releasing rituals often end up killing the very animals one would save. Daehaeng advised that, however busy practitioners may be, it is important not to perform a ritual act simply for the sake of ritual. In lieu of fish and turtles, she recommended a true object of release: attending to the sick and poor among one's neighbors. This is a way of drawing attention to those who have been socially and economically marginalized in the nation's relentless modernization process.

In a similar vein, Hanmanum Sŏn Center does not offer fixed-term prayer sessions. In many temples, nuns and monks pray for a hundred or a thousand days at the request of a lay donor. Daehaeng deemphasized these types of sessions, commenting that Buddhists must earn merit by praying themselves, not by delegating their practice to monastics.[22] She encouraged ongoing prayer in day-to-day life.

Last, in the most avant-garde of her reforms, Daehaeng recognized the impact of modernity on Buddhism, particularly the role science and technology play in contemporary culture. She also acknowledged that science ultimately confirms the infinite power of the mind, as was taught by the Buddha. Unlike many traditionalists, who are wary of the impact of science on spirituality, Daehaeng encouraged the use of cutting-edge communication technology and adopted the use of digital media as an effective way of teaching Buddhism to urban dwellers and young people. Likewise, she promoted the study of science, as shown in her establishment of Hanmaum Science Institute, an integral branch of the temple organization.[23]

Daehaeng's pioneering project offers one example of how a Buddhist institution can reform itself to cope with issues of spirituality in the vortex of modernization. Her firsthand experience of mountain asceticism provided her with religious authority, which in turn helped her implement new practice methods for contemporary Buddhists whose way of life differs drastically from that of earlier generations of Koreans. Daehaeng's farsightedness is especially demonstrated by the vitality of the youth organizations at Hanmaum Sŏn Center. The growing numbers of children, young adults, and college students who participate in ongoing practice programs at Hanmaum Sŏn Center are a most welcome sign for the Korean Buddhist community at large.[24] Daehaeng's endeavors may be applicable only to the Korean situation, but her sensitivity and openness to social change in general can provide valuable lessons for those who engage in similar efforts to innovate in their own local practice traditions.

Notes

1. Sŏn is the Korean word for Chan or Zen. The Jogye Order of Korean Buddhism has officially adopted the Romanized form Seon in accordance with the revised system used by the Korean Ministry of Culture. Throughout this chapter, however, I use the form Sŏn consistently to avoid confusion. Therefore, Hanmaum Seon Center is transcribed as Hanmaum Sŏn Center. It should also be noted that

Hanmaum is transcribed as Hanmaŭm except as the institutional name specifically related to Daehaeng Sunim.

2. Hanmaum Sŏn Center, Nŭng'in Sŏn Center, and An'guk Sŏn Center all belong to the Jogye Order of Korean Buddhism and were founded in 1972, 1985, and 1989, respectively

3. The spiritual directors of Nŭng'in Sŏn Center and An'guk Sŏn Center are the *bhikṣu* masters Chigwang and Subul, respectively.

4. A *sanjung kido* is an intensive prayer session. When Korean nuns, like monks, devote themselves to praying for a fixed period of time, they prefer a remote mountain hermitage to a large urban temple. The duration of such a session can range from a few months to several years. Because tranquility is crucial in this practice, monks and nuns favor small, secluded places off the beaten track.

5. When summer and winter retreats end, a number of monks and nuns travel to visit eminent Sŏn masters in faraway places. In olden times, such spiritual teachers used to be located up in mountains. Although industrialization and urbanization have changed the monastic topography of the country, many renowned teachers still tend to stay away from large temples that attract crowds of tourists.

6. For instance, the fifth chapter of *Tohae p'alsangrok* (Pictorial Interpretation of the Eight Phases of the Buddha's Life) is titled "Sŏlsansudosang" (The picture of the snow mountain practice)." O Kosan, Yi Chong'ik, and Sim Chaeyŏl, eds., *Tohae p'alsangrok* (Seoul: Poryŏn'gak, 1979), pp. 178–99.

7. For the precarious conditions of Daehaeng's family and especially for her troubled relationship with her father, see Daehaeng Sunim, *No River to Cross: Trusting the Enlightenment That's Always Right Here* (Somerville, MA: Wisdom Publications, 2007), pp. xiii–xv.

8. Ibid., p. xv.

9. Daehaeng Sunim, *Hanmaŭm Yojŏn* (Fundamentals of One Mind) (Anyang: Hanmaum Sŏn Center, 1996), p. 91.

10. Although identical in name, this temple differs from Sangnwŏn Temple in Mountain Odae.

11. Daehaeng Sunim, *Hanmaŭm Yojŏn*, pp. 70–71.

12. Daehaeng Sunim, *No River to Cross*, p. xix

13. Daehaeng Sunim, *Hanmaŭm Yojŏn*, p. 50.

14. For example, one day she started coughing up blood. Thinking that she would die soon, she lay down on the ground, at which point a snake brought her an herbal leaf. Mustering her last bit of energy, she pounded the leaf on a rock and swallowed it. As her coughing stopped, she realized that during her journeys, she had once rescued that very same snake. According to her, the snake communicated to her in tears that it wanted to hug her to warm her up, but it was unable to because of its snake body. Daehaeng's episodes about her "mountain friends" include one involving a tiger that left dry tree branches and straw in front of her shabby hut in the ice-cold winter. Sunim, *Hanmaŭm Yojŏn*, pp. 68, 83.

15. Ibid., pp. 97–98.

16. For Daehaeng's reputation as a healer, see Chong Go Sunim, "Educating Unborn Children: A Sŏn Master Daehaeng's Teachings on T'aegyo," in *Religions of*

Korea in Practice, ed. Robert Buswell (Princeton: Princeton University Press, 2007), pp. 225–57.

17. Daehaeng Sunim, *The Inner Path of Freedom* (Anyang: Hanmaum Sŏn Center, 1999), p. 19.

18. Daehaeng Sunim, *No River to Cross*, p. xxii.

19. Sunim, *No River to Cross*, p. xxii.

20. Ibid., p. 70.

21. For the sociohistorical implications of Daehaeng Sunim's use of the vernacular Korean, see Hyangsoon Yi, "Pomunjong and Hanmaŭm Sŏnwŏn: New Monastic Paths in Contemporary Korea," in *Out of the Shadows: Socially Engaged Buddhist Women*, ed. Karma Lekshe Tsomo (Delhi: Sri Satguru Publications, 2006), pp. 232–33.

22. For a similar reason, Daehaeng objected to issuing amulets by Buddhist temples.

23. For more information on Daehaeng's perspective on science and technology, see Park Chong-rae, et al., "Daehaeng Sunim's Views on Science," in *Korean Nuns within the Context of East Asian Buddhist Traditions* (Conference Proceedings) (Anyang: Hanmaum Sŏn Center, 2004), pp. 327–43.

24. Propagation of the Dharma among children has emerged as an urgent task in the Buddhist community in Korea. According to a survey carried out in 2007 by the Bureau of Missionary Activities of the Jogye Order, only 180 of 1,886 temples hold Dharma meetings for children on a regular basis. In view of such a "shocking" or "dismal" report, the programs for children run by Hanmaum Sŏn Center have drawn much attention from the Buddhist media. For more detail, see *Ibulgyo* (Buddhist Newspaper) 2319, April 18, 2007, http://www.ibulgyo.com/news/read.asp?news_seq=80066, accessed December 20, 2010.

BUDDHIST WOMEN IN
THE TIBETAN CULTURAL REGION

13

The Importance of Jetsun Mingyur Paldron in the Development of Sikkimese Buddhism

Kalzang Dorjee Bhutia

Jetsun Mingyur Paldron (*Rje btsun Mi 'gyur dpal sgron*, 1699–1769) is famed as a member of the Jetsunma institution of female practitioners in the Mindroling (*Smin gro gling*) tradition of Tibetan Buddhism. The women of the Jetsunma institution are renowned as female practitioners of the highest order in Tibetan Buddhism. Historically, they have been the daughters of the Mindroling hierarchs, the important throne holders (*khri rab*) who descended from the founder of the Mindroling tradition, Terdag Lingpa (*Gter bdag gling pa*, 1646–1714). Jetsun Mingyur Paldron herself was the daughter of Terdag Lingpa, and today she is considered to have been one of his major lineage holders. Many references to her life link her inexorably with her father, particularly her efforts to continue his lineage after his death in 1714. She is famous for the work she did with her brother to rebuild Mindroling Monastery after it was destroyed in 1718 by the Dzungar Mongol forces. By transmitting many of her father's most important teachings, she thus ensured the continuity of the lineage even after her uncle, the other Mindroling hierarch and *vinaya* holder (*khen rab*) Lochen Dharmashri (1654–1718), and her brother, the next in the lineage Pema Gyurme Gyatso (*Pad ma 'gyur med rgya mtsho*) (1686–1718), were both executed by the Mongols. Jetsun Mingyur Paldron ensured that the Mindroling tradition continued to flourish, and she reconsolidated the institution's position as the premier center of the Nyingma (*Rnying ma*) tradition in Central Tibet.

Aside from her relationship with her famous father and her rebuilding of Mindroling Monastery, Jetsun Mingyur Paldron was a remarkable religious practitioner and teacher in her own right. A biography of Jetsun Mingyur Paldron, written by her student Khyungpo Repa Gyurme Osel (*Khyung po ras pa 'gyur med od gsal*, 1715–1782) thirteen years after her death, is a fascinating text that documents the broad extent of her Buddhist activities.[1]

In this chapter, I focus on a part of Jetsun Mingyur Paldron's life that is less well known. It took place when she and her family escaped the Mongol troops in 1718 and fled to the small Vajrayāna kingdom of Sikkim in the eastern Himalayas. Previously, Lhatsun Tulku Dzogchen Lama Jigme Pao (*Lha btsun sprul sku rdzog chen bla ma 'Jigs med dpa' bo*, 1682–1733?) had repeatedly tried to invite Jetsun Mingyur Paldron to give teachings in Sikkim. Thus, she and her family sought refuge there during their exile. Her time in Sikkim was a historic occasion for both the Mindroling tradition and for Sikkimese Buddhism. While there, she transmitted many important teachings and consolidated the position of the Mindoling tradition in Sikkim. Some say that she remained there for two months, while other sources state she was there for two years.

Jetsun Mingyur Paldron's autobiography outlines this period, and Sikkimese records add even more information regarding her stay in Sikkim. Two of these Sikkimese records are the autobiography of Jigme Pao[2] and the text *The History of Sikkim*, written between the 1890s and early 1900s by the ninth king of Sikkim, Thuthop Namgyal (*Mthu stobs rnam rgyal*, 1860–1914) and his Tibetan wife, Yeshe Dolma (*Ye shes sgrol ma*, exact dates unknown).[3] Both accounts include further information about Jetsun Mingyur Paldron's life during this period of time. For example, the ill-fated marriage between the fourth king of Sikkim, Gyurme Namgyal (*Gyur med rnam rgyal*, 1706–?), and Jetsun Mingyur Paldron's sister Mingyur Dolma (*Mi 'gyur sgrol ma*, dates unknown) is detailed and reveals interesting perspectives on the relationship between the Mindroling lineage and the Sikkimese state. This written material provides further evidence of the important relationship of Jetsun Mingyur Paldron and the Buddhist hierarchs of Sikkim, as well as new insights into the development of satellite institutions of Tibetan Buddhist lineages.

Jetsun Mingyur Paldron's Early Life

In order to deepen our understanding of Jetsun Mingyur Paldron and how she became such an extraordinary teacher, we must first know something of her early life and education. She was the fourth of seven children born to the treasure revealer and teacher Terdag Lingpa and his consort Yum Phuntsog Palzom (*Yum Phun tshogs dpal 'dzom*). She was born in Drachi Valley in central Tibet on the twenty-fifth day of the tenth month of 1699 amid many miraculous signs, which in the Tibetan tradition are indicators of the birth of an extraordinary being. On the day of Jetsun Mingyur Paldron's birth, Terdag Lingpa pronounced that she would bring great benefit to sentient beings. And from a young age, she did exhibit many unusual characteristics, such as great intelligence, innate knowledge of Buddhism, and boundless compassion. She spent most of her young life receiving empowerments and teachings from both her father as well as other teachers, and she practiced in retreat. Jetsun Mingyur Paldron was enthroned as a full lineage holder in the Mindroling tradition, and her father repeatedly told her and other members of the family that she would be a powerful and great teacher. Her father, Terdag Lingpa, passed away when she was sixteen years old. When she was seventeen, her uncle Lochen Dharmasri, later executed by the Mongols, ordained her as a nun and prophesized that she would be a significant lineage holder in the future.

Jetsun Mingyur Paldron's Activities in Sikkim

Lochen Dharmasri's prediction exhibited great foresight, for on the horizon dangers were looming that would ultimately lead to the deaths of several important Mindroling hierarchs. The arrival of the Dzungar Mongols in Tibet in 1718 heralded their ambitious desire to consolidate authority over Tibetan territory. They destroyed many monasteries and threatened the safety of the people. It was during this time that Lochen Dharmasri and Mingyur Paldron's brother, Pema Gyurme Gyatso, the main lineage holders of the Mindroling tradition, were imprisoned in Lhasa. Jetsun Mingyur Paldron had been in retreat following her father's death, but news about the captivity of both her uncle and her brother made her concerned about Mindroling's future, and she left her retreat. The community members who had managed to escape being captured by the Mongols urged Mingyur Paldron to avoid capture by fleeing into exile.

According to both the biography of Jigme Pao as well as *The History of Sikkim*, Mingyur Paldron foresaw the best course of action contained in an instruction given by her father before his death. *The History of Sikkim* records:

> The reason why they [Mingyur Paldron and family] fled to Sik-kim was that Terdag Lingpa had repeatedly mentioned before he died that people should pay attention to the offering cake (*gtor ma*) called Durtro Lhamo (*Dur khro lha mo*) in the main hall of Mindroling. He said that the rice cake should be examined for signs regularly. Later on, the cake began to fall over repeatedly

and cracks appeared in its surface. When it was examined, a
piece of paper was discovered on which a message was written
in the Great Treasure Discover [Terdag Lingpa's] own hand. It
said: "Mingyur Paldron, take your mother and brother and flee
to Sikkim!" According to that warning, the Treasure Discover's
consort (*gter yum*), son, and daughter all fled to Sikkim as the
war approached Mindroling.[4]

Although there remains some discrepancy about whether Mingyur Paldron's
mother and brother originally fled with her to Sikkim, she herself donned
the disguise of a layperson and left on foot, accompanied by a small group
of companions who walked with her across the mountains and escaped the
fighting. As they fled, the monastery was razed to the ground and the local
area devastated.

Mingyur Paldron's mother and sister were captured by the Mongols and
inadvertently revealed to them that Mingyur Paldron had escaped and was
still alive, whereupon the Mongol army pursued her all the way to Sikkim.
Her escape had been a treacherous one, and she had become quite ill from
exhaustion as they fled. However, when she finally did arrive in Sikkim, she
was received with a royal welcome. The king sponsored her to give public
empowerments and teachings, and many people gathered to meet her. She
taught Terdag Lingpa's treasure texts along with her own Ati cycle of teachings, as well as many other important Mindroling lineage teachings. She also
exchanged teachings with Jigme Pao; along with other teachings, she received
from him the *Rigzin Sroggrub* (*Rig 'dzin srog grub*), which had been discovered
by his first incarnation, Lhatsun Namkhai Jigme (*Lha btsun nam mkha' 'jigs
med*, 1597–1654).[5]

Mingyur Paldron visited many of the sacred sites of Sikkim. It is said
that she gave a public teaching just below the premiere royal monastery of
Sikkim, Pemayangtse (*Pad ma dbyang brtse*). Local oral history also reveals
that she had been invited up to the monastery but had declined on the
grounds that it was inappropriate for a nun to visit an institution for male
Vinaya holders (*dge slong*). This tale is intriguing because it suggests that the
Pemayangtse monastics, who for the past century at least have been nonceli-
bate, may have indeed been celibate at an earlier time.

Another story from Mingyur Paldron's biography tells about the escape
of her mother and sister from the Mongols and their rush to join her with the
Mongols in hot pursuit. Mingyur Paldron apparently performed a wrathful
ritual that caused many obstacles to arise for the pursuing Mongols, foil-
ing their arrival altogether. As time passed, the Mongolian army in Lhasa,
impaired by internal feuding, finally began to fall apart. Mingyur Paldron
eventually received notice that she and the others could return to Mindroling.

The Marriage between the Sikkimese Royal Family and the Mindroling Lineage

Before the return of Mingyur Paldron and the others to Mindroling, another crucial event occurred that was intended to consolidate links between Mindroling and Sikkim. *The History of Sikkim* records the following:

> Mingyur Paldron's sister, who was named Mingyur Dolma, along with Jigme Pao, Khenchen Rolpa'i Dorje, and the lamas and laypeople all requested permission from Terdag Lingpa's wife for the king to take Mingyur Dolma as his consort. After permission was granted, the king married Mingyur Dolma on the eleventh day of the first month in the Iron Bull year of the 12th year cycle (*rab byung*) [1721]. After the marriage, Mingyur Paldron returned to Tibet. . . . Two monks from Pemayangtse Monastery traveled to Mindroling to accompany Jetsunma and after accompanying the family the king and Jigme Pao returned from halfway.[6]

While the marriage was intended to consolidate the relationship between the different branches of the Mindroling lineage, it was not to last. The marriage was not a happy one, and within only a few years it was dissolved. At the time, this event was seen as just part of Sikkim's "bad luck" at a time of great upheaval and conflict with Nepal and Bhutan, Sikkim's neighboring states in the Himalayas; however, it is also attributed to the sister's "ugliness" (*mtshar po med*). The king and queen were increasingly unable to get along with each other, and their behavior toward one another gradually cooled. Sikkim's political situation had become progressively unstable because of Gorkha activity, and this gave Mingyur Dolma an excuse to return to Mindroling.[7]

Conclusion

Despite the unsuccessful marriage between Mingyur Dolma and the king, the relationship between Mindroling and Sikkim remained a strong one. After Jetsun Mingyur Paldron returned to Mindroling to begin her rebuilding efforts, her reputation as a teacher continued to grow. She transmitted many important empowerments to the *saṅgha* and local laypeople, went on pilgrimages, and eventually became acclaimed throughout Tibet to such an extent that she was requested to perform important ceremonies for the central Tibetan government. She established an archive of documents and published many rare lineage texts, thereby ensuring their survival. Jetsun Mingyur Paldron was also committed to the women in her lineage and established several institutions where nuns and *yoginī*s could commit themselves to practice.

In 1769, Mingyur Paldron passed away at the age of seventy. Her important contributions to Sikkimese Buddhism are still remembered. During the period of her exile in Sikkim, she transmitted many important teachings that remain vital parts of the Nyingmapa tradition there. Her influence and tireless activities in Sikkim, as well as in Central Tibet, have ensured that Jetsun Mingyur Paldron will continue to be remembered throughout even the most remote areas of the Himalayas as an extremely important and beloved female teacher.

Notes

1. Khyung po ras pa 'gyur med 'od gsal, *Rje btsun mi 'gyur dpal gyi sgron ma'i rnam thar dad pa'i gdung sel* (Thimphu: National Library of Bhutan, 1984). This document has been partially translated by the Mindrolling History Project and is available online at the Mindrolling International Web site. "The History of the Mindrolling Family, Parts 5, 6, 7," http://mindrollinginternational.org/mindrollinghistoryproject, accessed March 16, 2010. The summaries of Mingyur Paldron's life in this essay are based on the Tibetan text, with reference to the English translation.

2. 'Jigs med dpa' bo, *Rdzogs chen rig 'dzin 'Jigs med dpa' bo'i bka' 'bum mthong grol chen mo* (The autobiography of Lha bstun Sprul sku 'Jigs med Dpa' bo of Sikkim) (Gangtok: Dzongsar Khyentse Labrang, Palace Monastery, 1983).

3. HRH Mthu stobs Rnam rgyal the Chos rgyal of Sikkim and HRH the Maharani Rgyal mo Ye shes sgrol ma, *'Bra ljongs rgyal rabs* (Gangtok: The Tsuklhakhang Trust [Henceforth BJGR], 1908 [2003]).

4. BJGR: 85–86.

5. BJGR: 86.

6. BJGR: 86.

7. BJGR: 89–90.

14

The Legacy of a Female Sikkimese Buddhist Teacher

The Lineage of Pelling Ani Wangdzin and Gendered Religious Experience in Modern Sikkim

Amy Holmes-Tagchungdarpa

What makes a Buddhist woman eminent? Is it because she has an important, demarcated space in Buddhist institutional history? Or is it because of her extraordinary commitment to social, political, or spiritual issues, which draws attention to her from well beyond her community? While these types of women are certainly deserving of the title "eminent," many other women in the broader history of Buddhist cultures have also demonstrated commitment, compassion, and community awareness. Though their stories may not be recorded or the focus of significant institutional attention, and though they may not be officially recognized within a Buddhist hierarchy as ordained or affiliated with powerful male teachers, these women need to be recognized and considered in order to generate a truly representative archive of eminent Buddhist women.

This chapter focuses on one such woman, who, although not part of any official record or institution, transmitted a lineage within the eastern Himalayas. Pelling Ani Wangdzin (*Pad gling A ni dbang 'dzin*, 187?–192?) originally brought to the Eastern Himalayan state of Sikkim in the early twentieth century a Sikkimese Buddhist lineage that is still active today.

Pelling Ani Wangdzin's oral biography remains an extraordinary story of the determination and resilience she exhibited during her short life as she traveled the length of the Himalayas alone, from Sikkim in the east to the Kathmandu Valley of Nepal in the west and then on to the meditation communities of eastern Tibet. After receiving a premier tantric education of her era from some of the leading Buddhist teachers in the Himalayas, she returned to Sikkim and established a community of students that she led until her death. For her time period and milieu, Pelling Ani Wangdzin was unusual—she forfeited the life of a conventional Sikkimese Lhopo aristocrat to follow the path of a Tibetan Buddhist *yoginī* and became a renowned teacher within her community.

The lineage that is the focus of this chapter is remarkable not only because of the life story of its original teacher, but also because it continues to be practiced in contemporary times and propagated predominantly by Sikkimese women. Pelling Ani Wangdzin's legacy remains an example of the potential that female practitioners in wider Tibetan Buddhist cultures have to become leaders and also demonstrates how the lineage that she brought back to Sikkim from her travels has been passed on in unexpected and original ways. The Avalokiteśvara practices that she transmitted to students are now the specialty of groups of older women known as "Mani Amlas" (*Ma ni A ma lags*, or mothers who perform the practice of Avalokiteśvara's *mantra: om mani pad me hum*). The activities of these groups of women depict interesting potentials for older women to practice Buddhism in an intensive, collective environment in modern Sikkim. Their activities also suggest how women in minority communities in South Asia, such as Lhopo and Lepcha, who make up the demographically significant portions of Mani Amla communities, have continued to sustain their traditions in the face of new mainstream cultural institutions in a postcolonial era. These communities are made up women who are deserving of the title of eminent Buddhist women but who are often overlooked. Therefore, an overview of their community and its development affords us an opportunity to recognize a subaltern group of practitioners—women from outside large institutions—who make significant contributions to Buddhist transmission.

The Life of Pelling Ani Wangdzin

In order to convey the uniqueness of this lineage, something more must be said of its founder, Pelling Ani Wangdzin.[1] Ani Wangdzin was born sometime in the 1870s[2] in the Pelling (*Pad gling*) area of West Sikkim in the village of Singyang (orthography uncertain). Singyang had been the traditional home of her family, the Tagchungdarpa (*Stag chung dar pa*) clan, for several generations. Though predominantly made up of households engaged in agriculture, Singyang's Tagchungdarpa clan members also were often members of Pemayangtse (*Pad ma dbyang brtse*) Monastery, located just up the hill from the village. This monastery dated back to the seventeenth century and was closely affiliated with a set of families known as the Lhopo (*Lho po*) Thongtho ruzhi besengay (*Thong tho rus bzhi 'bed seng ge*).[3] The several Lhopo (or Bhutia, as they are known today) families in this group traced their family lines back to the thirteenth century and were among those whom the kings of Sikkim married.[4] Pelling Ani Wangdzin was therefore born into a well-connected and religiously oriented family: her father was a generous patron of Buddhism, and her two older brothers were ritual specialists at Pemayangtse, counted among the important religious advisors to the king.

Little information remains about the circumstances of Pelling Ani Wangdzin's childhood. However, oral traditions state that from her teen years, Ani Wangdzin wore the robes of a *bhikṣuṇī*. Later, she resisted attempts to secure her a marital alliance with another wealthy or religious family. Her style of dress and unmarried status led to rumors that she had in fact taken the vows of a *bhikṣuṇī*; however, this cannot be confirmed. Further adding to the mystery of Ani Wangdzin's official status is that the existence of a historical *bhikṣuṇī* lineage in West Sikkim (or in Sikkim generally) is contested. It is therefore unclear where she may have taken her vows and where she might have studied.[5]

Ultimately, however, the legitimacy that is often afforded by official ordination status in contemporary times for female practitioners was not important for Pelling Ani Wangzin. Instead, her legitimacy was self-created. One obvious place where she may have received at least preliminary religious education was at home. When Ani Wangdzin later decided to pursue her religious education outside Sikkim, her family was enthusiastic about supporting her plans. In her teens, Ani Wangdzin left Sikkim on her own to travel to Bodhgaya (*Rgya dkar rdo rje ldan*). After visiting the historical sites of the Buddha, she traveled north again to visit the *stūpa*s of Kathmandu Valley in Nepal. From there, she traveled on to Tibet. She eventually reached Kham (*Khams*), where she studied with the renowned meditation teacher Tokden Shakya Shri (*Rtogs ldan Śākya shrī*, 1853–1919). While many sources are available regarding the historical composition of Tokden Shakya Shri's community, few of these sources mention the women who were present.[6]

The oral stories of women such as Pelling Ani Wangdzin, however, confirm that women were active participants in this community, where meditation instructions along with teachings about physical and inner yogas were emphasized for lay as well as ordained people. Either after or during her time in Kham, she also visited Tsari, the sacred mountain on the southeastern border of Tibet. This detail is particularly important, because in Sikkimese oral memory, no one is sure how long her travels lasted, and there are no records of her in Shakya Shri's biography, *The Garland of Flowers*, or other writings. One memory that remains clear, however, is that she took part in the Tsari Rongkhor Chenmo (*Rong skor chen mo*, literally "the great circumambulation of the valleys"), a physically grueling and spiritually challenging pilgrimage that went the entire way around Tsari, traveling a circuit that went through jungles and over mountain tracks.[7] Because of the scale of this event, it was staged only once every twelve years, during the Year of the Monkey in the Tibetan calendrical cycle.[8] Considering that Ani Wangdzin only lived until her forties or fifties, only three of these events took place in her lifetime: in 1884, 1896, and 1908.[9] Assuming that she did the Tsari Rongkhor Chenmo in 1908, while she was in her late teens or early twenties, it seems likely that she studied with Shakya Shri at about that same time.

Ani Wangdzin's presence in Kham and her participation in the Rongkhor Chenmo does not provide any explicit information about what she might have learned during her time in Tibet. She must have been quite an advanced practitioner, however, as when she returned to West Sikkim, she was encouraged by the local community to establish her own teaching center. She based herself in a cabin in Upper Pelling on the ridge near to Sangha Choeling retreat center.[10] At her center, Ani Wangdzin was known for her teaching of the *nyungne* (*smyung gnas*) fasting practice of Avalokiteśvara. She also taught meditation and more advanced inner yogic practices (*rtsa rlung*), which suggests that she was considered to have a high aptitude in these practices. She passed away of unknown causes at a young age, during the mid-1920s.

Continuity in the Lineage of Pelling Ani Wangdzin

The example of Pelling Ani Wangdzin offers us an intriguing glimpse into the opportunities for women to act as teachers in traditional Buddhist societies. Within her short life, Ani Wangzin achieved a remarkable amount. Her story also demonstrates how women participated in transnational Buddhist education and pilgrimage cycles that linked India, Nepal, Sikkim, Bhutan, Tibet, Mongolia, and China in the nineteenth and early twentieth centuries. These aspects of her life remain as interesting legacies within the present-day religious communities of Sikkim. However, her teachings also continue to be practiced, and thereby her legacy is embodied as well as imagined through physical participation and spiritual actualization.

Since the death of Ani Wangdzin in the 1920s, there have been dramatic changes in the Buddhist Himalayas, one of the most significant being the incorporation of Tibet into the People's Republic of China during the 1950s, which in turn led to an enormous exodus of refugees along with the Tibetan religious leader, the Dalai Lama, into India. Sikkim, a sympathetic Vajrayāna Buddhist country, acted as a site of refuge for many Tibetans, and for their lamas in particular. Sikkim had historically been considered to be a Hidden Land (*sbas yul*), one of the sites set aside by Guru Rinpoche as a place that would remain closed to the mundane world, only to be revealed to those of appropriate spiritual insight during a time of need.[11] It was therefore seen as a natural site of refuge for many Tibetans. Many lamas have since moved on to other places in India and the West, but a number have remained in Sikkim, where many of them have become renowned teachers of Avalokiteśvara practices within the local communities. This new influx of teachings represents new lineages of Avalokiteśvara fasting traditions that have since become predominant, leading to the disappearance of, or at times absorption of, the older traditions. These changes are indicative of even broader changes afoot in Sikkimese society. In 1975, Sikkim was officially absorbed into the Indian Union. Despite the enormous shifts rendered by the Indian takeover, religious lineages and other cultural institutions in Sikkim have been continued, albeit in methods appropriate to the rapidly changing contexts of twentieth- and twenty-first-century South Asia. The patterns of continuity between earlier eras of Sikkimese society and the present day are illuminated in considerations of the changing perception of gender in Sikkim.

Sikkim was traditionally a state founded on an intimately intertwined religious and political system that emulated Tibetan models of governance. Monasteries therefore were not only religious forces but also the seats of considerable political and economic power. The lamas within these monasteries held high social status as advisors to the kings and also served as ritual specialists to laypeople in the state.[12] However, they were always predominantly male in their focus. This is not to say that women had no social or political authority in traditional Sikkim. On the contrary, written and oral accounts prior to the incorporation of Sikkim into India in 1975 confirm that women enjoyed a considerable amount of power within Lhopo communities—they had equal rights with men to the family inheritance, and upon marriage were bestowed with their own estates and wealth rather than having a dowry transferred to their husband's families. Women were also given opportunities for secular education and in the aristocratic families were often literate.

Despite this relative equality, women are notably absent from the religious institutions that held political and spiritual power in Sikkim prior to 1975. There are no records of nunneries earlier than the 1950s, when Tibetan refugees began to arrive from the north, and also no tradition of female monasticism, which explains the ambivalence regarding whether Pelling Ani Wangdzin really was ordained and where she was ordained. Female monastics remain rare in Sikkim today. In the 2009 election, only thirty-seven nuns were enrolled to vote within the unique Sikkimese *sangha* constituency, in contrast with 3,021 monks.[3] These thirty-seven women are all either associated with exiled Tibetan nunneries or, although ordained, do not affiliate with a nunnery and still reside with their families. The many reasons for the scarcity of nuns in Sikkim are very complex and outside the limits of this chapter, but I do want to focus on one potential reason. It may well be that nuns are few in Sikkim because of the wide availability of other opportunities for women in the religious sphere.

The most prominent of these is the opportunity to join an institution known as a Mani Lhakhang (*Ma ni lha khang*). The Department of Ecclesiastical Affairs in the State Government of Sikkim estimates there are between 150 to 190 of these institutions throughout the state (compared to fewer than 100 monasteries). Mani Lhakhang are small, village-level structures that are used by groups of women to carry out fasting practices associated with Avalokiteśvara, the *bodhisattva* of compassion in the Tibetan Buddhist pantheon. The women who take part in these rituals are laywomen, often older than forty, who have teenaged or adult children and thus are deemed to have the sufficient time available to participate in the retreats associated with the practices. These retreats are intensive; they can last for up to sixteen days and involve intense physical and mental practices along with fasting on alternate days. In order to participate, women must go through training with a lama or a more senior member of the community who can train them in the appropriate prayers to recite and rituals to perform.

These communities remain as a prominent example of the legacy of Pelling Ani Wangdzin, because many of them continue to practice the lineage that she transmitted (and thus include her in their lineage supplications). It is a coincidence, but a remarkable one, that almost all of those who continue to carry out her lineage are women, and it suggests interesting patterns of gendered religious experience in modern Sikkim.

These emerging patterns that have been introduced to Sikkim since its incorporation into India in 1975 are harmonious with Pelling Ani Wangdzin's legacy because they also disrupt old gender norms about male authority in monastic matters. Prior to 1975, Sikkim was heavily influenced by British colonialism; even after Indian independence in 1947, Sikkim continued to have Indian government overseers. Against this backdrop, 1975 brought an unprecedented bombardment of new information and cultural norms to

Sikkim. Media, education systems, and the physical arrival of many Indians in Sikkim made many new norms pervasive in Sikkimese society, and within them mainstream attitudes about gender also began to influence societal expectations.

The idea of organized groups of older women leaving their families for sections of time to take part in retreats that they organize themselves challenges fundamental assumptions regarding Indian ideals of appropriate behavior for senior women. It also happens that the alternative communities for women created by these Mani Lhakhang organizations are usually extremely well organized, and their fundraisers often rival those of their male monastic counterparts in organization and efficiency, even though they are provided with far less state funding than monasteries. The ambivalent authority that these women hold is clear from their absence in the public sphere in Sikkim. The few portraits of them that have appeared in mainstream Indian-owned newspapers and media depict them as elderly, illiterate women who take part in religious practice as a form of social bonding, as opposed to the socially important, efficacious rites that are carried out by their male counterparts, the lamas, in monastic institutions. These attitudes now also influence broader societal discourse regarding the groups—these women are not often sought after for their ritual or religious knowledge, and there are no prominent female Buddhist teachers like Pelling Ani Wangdzin.

Conclusion: The Ambivalent Legacy of Pelling Ani Wangdzin

This leaves a wide chasm between mainstream concepts of the role of women in society and the more realistically conceived role of Sikkmese women in religious practice communities, in which some male lamas eagerly support them and offer them respect. The situation suggests a fundamental ambivalence regarding the nature of female power in different parts of the Indian nation state, because these older women disrupt conventional portrayals of ideal older women and find meaning and community beyond the domestic sphere. The contemporary legacy of Pelling Ani Wangdzin in Sikkim is an intriguing study of how traditional forms of religious practice and belonging in tribal India subvert other mainstream hegemonic imaginings of identity and community. Her current lineage holders represent how Sikkim has experienced modern South Asian history, challenging the conventional portrayal of Sikkim as being purely part of the Tibetan cultural realm and therefore alien to South Asia. Mani Amla constituents represent the potential for Sikkimese women to resist the mainstream Indian stereotype of women—a view that discourages or limits religious attainment for them. Mani Amla communities accomplish this by maintaining strong organizations that uphold and enact the religious ideals of their lineage predecessor, Pelling Ani Wangdzin, from a century ago. The greatest significance of Pelling Ani Wangdzin's story and the continuation today of her lineage lies with the ability of such narratives and community-based practices to allow for the recognition of truly eminent Buddhist women—women who, despite not having had official hierarchical positions or texts written about their lives, continue to inspire and encourage women today to challenge conventional views and recognize that they can pursue religious practices and live the teachings of the Buddha equally with men.

Notes

1. "Ani" is a term used for female ordained religious practitioners that is now commonly regarded as pejorative. While I support the removal of the term from discourse regarding ordained women in Tibetan societies, I persist in using it here for several reasons. First, Wangdzin was generally known as Pelling Ani Wangdzin in her community in Sikkim, and changing the title used for her may render her unidentifiable for readers interested in further research on her life. Second, "Ani" is also a term used to refer to a maternal aunt in Lhokyed (*Lho skad*), the Tibeto-Burman dialect used in Sikkim. Because many of the people who told me about Wangdzin are in fact related to her by blood or marriage, their use of this title may in fact refer to her family designation. The likelihood of this is supported by the ambiguity surrounding her ordination status, which I discuss further below. It is noteworthy that information regarding ordination lineages for women in Sikkim is extremely sparse, and therefore it has not been absolutely established that Wangdzin was ordained, though she did wear robes and never married.

2. This assumption is based on the fact that she died in the mid-1920s in her forties or fifties.

3. Orthography uncertain.

4. For more on these families, often referred to as clans or tribes, see Mthu stobs rnam rgyal and Ye shes grol ma, '*Bras ljongs rgyal rabs* (Gangtok: Tsuklakhang Trust, 2003 [1908]).

5. Some accounts suggest that Sangha Choeling retreat center near Pelling may have historically had a nuns' community present. There were certainly female practitioners present there. Mentions of these women can be found in Mthu stobs rnam rgyal and Ye shes sgrol ma, '*Bras ljongs rgyal rabs*.

6. These sources are surveyed in my book, *The Social Life of Tibetan Biography: Textuality, Community and Authority in the Lineage of Tokden Shakya Shri* (Lanham, MD: Lexington Books, 2014).

7. Toni Huber, *The Cult of the Pure Crystal Mountain* (Oxford: Oxford University Press, 1999). Chapter 8 from p. 128 onward describes this event in detail.

8. Ibid., p. 128.

9. These are based on dates from Huber. Ibid.

10. Sadly, this center is currently being built over in the tourist boom that is leading Pelling to become a leading tourist destination in the Eastern Indian Himalayas.

11. For more information on this phenomenon, see Franz-Karl Ehrhard, "The Role of 'Treasure Discoverers' and Their Search for Himalayan Sacred Lands,"in *Sacred Spaces and Powerful Places in Tibetan Culture*, ed. Toni Huber (Dharamsala: Library of Tibetan Works and Archives, 1999), pp. 227–39; and Franz-Karl Ehrhard, "Political and Ritual Aspects of the Search for Himalayan Sacred Lands," in ibid., pp. 240–57.

12. These institutions are also examined in Kalzang Bhutia, "Sikkimese Lay Practitioners: Mani Amlas, Gomchen, and Alternative Paths for Laypeople in the Religious Landscape of Guru Rinpoche's Hidden Land," in *Proceedings from the Chong-ji Buddhist Order Forum on Lay Buddhists in Society* (Seoul: Chong-ji Buddhist Order Education Centre, 2007), pp. 120–41.

13. IANS, "Special EVMS for Sikkim's Buddhist Monks, Nuns," *Thaindian News*, April 29, 2009, http://www.thaindian.com/newsportal/politics/special-evms-for-sikkims-buddhist-monks-nuns.100185797.html, accessed January 24, 2010.

15

Kunzang Drolkar

A *Delog* in Eastern Tibet

Alyson Prude

Although they usually spoke in Chinese, Cathy, my roommate and fellow student at Qinghai Nationalities University in Xining, China, was practicing her Tibetan with Kunzang as they were having lunch together in a noodle restaurant near Kunzang's home in Eastern Tibet.[1] Given Cathy's elementary Tibetan language skills, the conversation topics between the two were quickly exhausted, so Cathy mentioned my interest in *delog*s (*'das log*). Previously, I had shared with Cathy that in my experience many Tibetans are unfamiliar with the word *delog*. When Cathy mentioned it to Kunzang, however, Kunzang sat up and proclaimed, "I'm a *delog*!" Cathy thought she had misunderstood. To clarify that they were both referring to the same thing, Kunzang enacted a spontaneous pantomime of dying: she stuck out her tongue, rolled her eyes back into her head, and collapsed backward into her chair. It was clear that Kunzang understood the term.

At the time, I was enrolled as a research student at Qinghai Nationalities while I conducted my dissertation fieldwork on Tibetan *delog*s.[2] When I heard that Cathy's friend Kunzang claimed to be a *delog*, I quickly made preparations to leave Xining for Kunzang's nomadic region of Eastern Tibet. When I arrived in Kunzang's village, I enlisted the assistance of a dynamic local woman named Sonam to act as my translator, and over the course of two days, we interviewed Kunzang and recorded her life story. The following episodes are drawn from her oral autobiographical account.

169

Before turning to Kunzang's narrative, some explanatory comments about *delog*s may be helpful. A *delog* is a Tibetan revenant, someone who has seemingly died and returned to life. In this sense, a *delog* is similar to someone who has undergone a near-death experience. An important distinction, however, lies in the role *delog*s play in their communities. While the body is lying cold and motionless, the *delog*'s consciousness (*rnam shes*) travels to the *bardo* (*bar do*), the intermediate state between this life and the next. In the *bardo*, the *delog* witnesses the sufferings of the recently deceased and is charged with messages to convey back to the living. When the *delog* awakens, he or she reports on the fates of those he or she encountered in the intermediate state and relays personal messages from those who have recently died.

Both women and men can become *delog*s, the necessary criteria being a death experience and a willingness to talk about it. Tibetan accounts of *delog*s can be traced to the twelfth century, and according to Bryan Cuevas in *Travels in the Netherworld*, *delog* biographies available today are equally representative of both male and female *delog*s.[3] In my field research in contemporary Tibet and Tibetan Buddhist areas of the Himalayas, however, I have found that female *delog*s outnumber male *delog*s roughly four to one.[4] This difference between numbers of male and female *delog*s in written accounts versus contemporary society can be accounted for by the fact that unlike many of the male *delog*s, and male religious practitioners in general, female *delog*s' life stories are not often recorded in writing. Instead, stories of extraordinary women are recounted orally and spread via word of mouth. This was also true of Kunzang. Kunzang had shared her story with trusted friends, and people had come to her for information about the dead. Until now, however, her narrative had not been committed to writing.

People evaluate a *delog* based on the *delog*'s overall character and his or her track record for reliability. Are the details he or she provides about the deceased's place of birth, life events, and surviving family members accurate? Can any of the information, such as the location of a lost earring, be proved? Do the messages the *delog* delivers make sense to those who knew the deceased? I have found that it is never the case that all members of a community agree about the authenticity of a particular *delog*. Unless a *delog* is recognized and publicly supported by a high-ranking lama, his or her status remains ambivalent. Unlike other *delog*s I sought out after I heard their stories repeated by Tibetans, some of whom were living sometimes thousands of miles away, Kunzang's reputation did not precede her. When I saw her about town after our interviews, she was walking alone, not surrounded by the throngs of faithful who reportedly line the streets when another local *delog* passes through. Perhaps this is because Kunzang has never been publicly promoted by a high-ranking lama or formally recognized as a *khandroma* (*mkha' 'gro ma*).[5] It is possible that the social stigma she encountered as a young woman discouraged her from pursuing a more public image, or maybe she did attempt to make a name for herself but was unsuccessful. During the course of my research, I have observed that delineations between visionary figures and people marginalized for being mentally unstable are not always obvious or consistent.

As Kunzang's case demonstrates, the biographies and identities of extraordinary individuals are not necessarily common knowledge even within their own communities. Writing about Tibetan women who fought against Chinese troops during the Communist takeover, Carole McGranahan notes that the narrators' friends and relatives are often unaware of these women's remarkable tales. She states, "Those listening were not familiar with the stories being told except perhaps in the most general of outlines. Even among intimate acquaintances, these stories are not necessarily told, they do not have the well-polished sheen of family stories passed down through the generations or traded over the years between friends. Most Tibetans do not know these histories."[6] My roommate, Cathy, had known Kunzang for several years but was surprised to learn that she was a *delog* and to hear the amazing account of her life. Likewise, my translator, Sonam, who took pride in her region's Buddhist culture, had not heard of Kunzang and had been unaware that there was a *delog* living in her own small town. Kunzang resides in a nondescript, one-room dwelling hidden from the street by a modern, multistory apartment building and chooses to keep a low profile. Her name does not appear in the credits of a locally produced DVD that depicts the dying process, a film for which she served as a consultant.

Kunzang's story offers a glimpse into the lived realities of the life of a Buddhist woman in rural Eastern Tibet. She describes dislocation from her natal home, social ostracism, single motherhood, economic hardship, and loneliness, difficulties well known to many Tibetan nomad women. Yet Kunzang does not allow life's obstacles to hinder her religious efforts, and her words express her continued determination to surmount the hurdles that her sex and Tibetan ethnicity pose. As much as her struggles are struggles shared by any number of Asian women who live outside major urban centers like Beijing, Osaka, or even Xining, Kunzang is not an ordinary woman. As a *delog*, her life is one in which journeys beyond the visible, human world to the *bardo* or intermediate state and journeys to other realms are possible.

Delog practice is largely unorthodox, and *delog*s undergo no training, ceremonial or otherwise, before engaging in their postmortem journeys and message-bringing from the deceased. They operate outside the formal Buddhist system, and there is no established place for *delog*s in the hierarchy of nuns, monks, reincarnate lamas, abbots, and the like. As a result, *delog*s retain greater opportunities for personal expression and creativity than their monastic counterparts. This is particularly true for female *delog*s. Kunzang lives as an independent, self-supporting single woman who travels when and where she pleases and who regularly invites monks and lamas into her home to perform rituals at her request. Yet it is important to keep in mind that Kunzang is not an average *delog*, if there is such a thing. Several miraculous events, such as her son's immaculate conception while she was meditating in a cave and the appearance of a food-bearing hand when she was starving, distinguish her life story from those of other *delog*s whom I interviewed.

Kunzang did not offer much commentary on the meaning of her experiences. In later discussions with Sonam and Cathy, I found that Sonam accepted Kunzang's reports literally. For her, the marvelous occurrences make evident the power of the Buddhas and Kunzang's elevated spiritual state. The miracles thus lend authority to Kunzang's narrative; they do not call into question her credibility. For Cathy, the events Kunzang described are extraordinary and surprising but not implausible when contextualized within a religious framework. I was by far the most skeptical member of Kunzang's audience. In what follows, I leave it to each reader to interpret the narrative for him- or herself.

When Sonam and I met her in the one-room home she shares with her youngest son, Kunzang was fifty-five years old. She began by describing her father and the prophecy the local lama gave when she was born:

> My father was a lama with special vision.[7] He was like me, a little crazy sometimes. Sometimes a monk, sometimes a *tantrika*, sometimes an undertaker . . .[8] When I was a baby, he took me to Khenpo and asked him to name me. "Poor thing with blonde hair," Khenpo said. "Name her Kunzang Drolkar. She will suffer greatly. She will suffer greatly, but she will benefit Tibetans.

This is the only information Kunzang gave about her father, other than mentioning his absence. In contrast, she described her mother with warmth and intimacy:

> It's said that my mother fell from the sky. She was called the daughter of a local god (*gzhi bdag*) because she was conceived when her parents slept together on the god's road. People say she was very beautiful and her clothes never got wet when it rained. Because she had a patch of pig fur on her back, she was known as an incarnation of Dorjé Phagmo (Rdo rje phag mo, Sanskrit: Vajra Vārāhī). When I was small, she would ask me to scratch her back, and sometimes I would grab onto the patch of fur.

The child of a crazy visionary father and divine mother, Kunzang's blood lineage is endowed with spiritual potency. Faith in and devotion to the Dharma and merit built up over the course of previous lives are necessary requisites for manifesting as a *delog*. The fact that both of Kunzang's parents were recognized as special religious figures can be read as an indication of the positive karma Kunzang accumulated in the past. Her meritorious karma and exceptional parentage, however, did not protect her from facing hardship, even as a child. The suffering that Khenpo predicted was a recurring theme throughout her life:

> When I was still too small to recognize him, my father was put in prison [by Chinese authorities]. My mother was alone. This was during the Liberation (*bcings dkrol*, i.e., the Communist takeover of Tibet). During the Liberation, everyone was put in prison. Because [my mother] had a little bit of education, she was made a leader for the local townspeople. Later, she was criticized for being a lama's wife and imprisoned for five years. There was no one to look after me. When she was released, we were taken to Changri to herd yak. There were people who didn't like those who had held official jobs, so we were sent to Changri.

Kunzang experienced extreme anguish when she was forced to leave home and to move to Changri, a place known, even by Tibetan standards, for being cold and inhospitable. Kunzang suffered spells of insanity over the course of the following years and attributed this illness to her entrance into territory protected by unfamiliar land deities (*yul lha*):

> We moved to Changri, into the territory of other regional deities (*yul lha*) and land gods. I went crazy. I was fifteen, and I became crazy, crazy. I would wander around here and there. Sometimes I'd go to cemeteries, and people would say, "Kunzang's gone to the cemetery to eat flesh." Once I played a joke and brought some yak meat to them asking if they wanted to eat flesh. "Oh, the crazy one is here!" they cried as they ran away. To sentient beings like you, I'm just a crazy woman.

Despite her odd behavior, a local lama recognized Kunzang's spiritual potential. Kunzang did not explain what the lama saw in her. Instead, she emphasized the harshness of her initiation onto a path of religious training:

> Chamde Lama recognized me as special, but there was nothing he could do to keep me from acting crazy. He put me in a cave

and said, "Now eat flesh and meditate." When I asked him how to meditate, he replied, "Just meditate," and sealed the mouth of the cave with mud. I didn't know how to read or write, so I just recited prayers.

We are left to speculate about what the lama saw in Kunzang and the success of her prayers while she was in the cave, because before long, her practices were interrupted by unexpected motherhood:

> While I was staying there in the cave, a drop of water fell and landed on my left side. The skin in that spot turned red. It was just like the union of a husband and wife, and before even a month had passed, I felt a baby moving in my belly. I was scared and ran to my mother.
>
> "Oh, you've got something in your belly! You're pregnant!" my mother said. I was terribly ashamed. I told my mother the story, but she didn't believe me. "It's no different from you falling from the sky," I insisted, but she still didn't believe me. After a month, my son was born. Usually it takes nine months, but my pregnancy lasted only one month and fifteen days. I was around twenty-six or twenty-eight years old at the time.

Kunzang did not comment further on the miraculous nature of her first child's birth.[9] For her, it was more important to describe the doubt and skepticism she faced when she revealed the unusual manner of his conception. Later, when her son had gone to India, rumors that Kunzang had sold him there led her to threaten suicide if he would not return to Tibet. Consideration of these incidents as well as the ridicule Kunzang encountered as a young woman fond of wandering and unafraid of cemeteries highlights the power that gossip and social humiliation can have on Tibetan women's lives.

Like Kunzang's mother after her father was imprisoned, Kunzang raised her son without the support of a spouse. She remembered the first years of her son's life as a time of great difficulty and sorrow as she embarked on the begging, peripatetic lifestyle of a religious nomad. During these years of physical and emotional distress, Kunzang experienced her first *delog* episode:

> I had this son, and I carried him with me as I washed people's clothes and helped them fetch water. I collected discarded shoes to wear. In the past, there had been monasteries in the places I visited, but they were all destroyed, completely demolished. I cried and put stones where they used to be. Then I died (*dbugs chad song*). I had been sent out herding, and while I was out herding,

I passed out. Lhundrup was the leader of that area. He put me
on a piece of plastic and pulled me to his doorstep.

In correspondence with the details of many literary accounts, Kunzang's
death experience occurred during a period of intense sadness and depression.[10] Like other *delog*s I have met, Kunzang's first *delog* experience was both
unexpected and involuntary. In addition, it was but the first of a continuing
series of "deaths" and "returns to life." Kunzang described "going *delog*" (*'das
log song*) as difficult and painful yet unavoidable. For many contemporary
*delog*s, after their initial death experience, subsequent travels to the other
realms can be anticipated based on the phases of the moon. Kunzang's journeys, however, are irregular and occur with less frequency:

> This fall, I also must go *delog*. It's really tough (*dka' mo*). Every
> year, I have to go once. There's no way around it. I get intense
> pains, and I get angry at my children. I lose my temper with
> everything and everyone, and I talk nonsense.

Since her first, unanticipated *delog* experience, the female deity Drolma (Sgrol
ma, Sanskrit: Tārā) now visits Kunzang to inform her when it is time for her
to go *delog* again, thus giving Kunzang a day or two to prepare herself for
her next otherworldly journey:

> When the time draws near, Drolma appears and tells me, "It's time
> for you to go." Sometimes things like rainbows also manifest. A
> while back, I was passing through Dingchen with a friend when
> the clouds started moving towards me, right in front of me. My
> heart was going *tuk, tuk, tuk, tuk*, and I thought that I would
> die. "Oh, now it's time to die. I should finish what I need to
> do," I told myself. That evening, there were rainbows above my
> house. I went out and found a Chinese guy who helped me take
> a picture. When I came back home, I was so, so sick. I was really
> sick this past time.

Feelings of weakness and dizziness in the moments leading up to their
"deaths" and confusion and sickness when they return to report their experiences are ubiquitous in *delog*s' tales. Visits from a Buddha or *bodhisattva*
indicating that it will soon be time to repeat the *delog* experience, however,
are not common. More frequently, *delog*s depart on the eves of the new and/
or full moon. The regularity of the lunar schedule renders the appearance
of deities and omens unnecessary and makes it easier for a *delog*'s clients to
anticipate the *delog*'s next visit to the *bardo*.

Because *delog*s undertake their journeys repeatedly and return with
status reports on the deceased, they can function as couriers or, in Kunzang's
words, "postal workers." It is the individualized messages *delog*s deliver when
they return from the intermediate state that constitute *delog*s' significance to
their communities. People who have recently lost a loved one may consult a
delog about their late relative's fortune: "Have the funeral rituals been effective? Are further offerings needed to ensure the deceased a fortunate rebirth?"
and so on. *Delog*s also deliver messages at the request of the deceased. Most
of these messages consist of descriptions of unpleasant states and pleas for
ritual assistance. As Kunzang reported:

> A man sent me a message a while back. He said, "My home is in
> Domar. I have a daughter and a son there and lots of money. Look,
> I am boiling in this cauldron. Please, do some Dharma for me!"

"Doing Dharma" for the deceased is a means of creating merit so that
the dead will be released from their suffering and achieve a fortunate rebirth.
Common merit-making rituals include chanting mantras, lighting butter lamps,
sponsoring the recitation of scriptures, hanging prayer flags, commissioning the
carving of *mani* stones, purchasing and releasing animals intended for slaughter, and making donations to a monastery. *Delog*s often specify both the type
and quantity of ritual assistance needed by the individuals they meet in the
intermediate state. More serious sins require more extensive expiation, but it is
said that *delog*s are sensitive to people's means and never prescribe donations
or sponsorship that the message's recipients would be unable to provide.

Kunzang became most animated when she described the postmortem
torments inflicted on women who had abortions, a common practice in contemporary China:

> Women who have had abortions must experience birth pains
> three times over [while in the intermediate state]. The workers
> [there, minions of the Lord of Death] pour molten metal into their
> mouths. It boils inside their bodies and is difficult to expel. When
> they finally push it out, it explodes out of them. Sometimes it's
> so difficult to expel the molten metal that it blisters and destroys
> the women's flesh, making them into skeletons. They scream, "*Ah
> tsa!*" in pain, and their unbearable screams pervade all of space.

Kunzang's next example of karmic retribution centered on prostitutes
whose lower bodies, in the *bardo* state, are "rotten with worms." "In this
unfortunate time, everyone is becoming [sinful] like this. People fall into hell,
where they're boiled and roasted and don't recognize their own nature," she

continued. Robert Barnett, writing in 2005, states that "in Tibet the urgency of the national question has so far overridden other issues," notably those concerning gender and sexuality.[11] He predicts that problems regarding birth control, women's employment, and prostitution will "become more relevant to women" as globalization and Chinese economic policies increasingly affect Tibet.[12] Kunzang's attention to abortion and prostitution may signal that issues related to women and women's bodies are significant to Tibetan women, even if they have yet to gain prominence in public forums.

Not all reports of the dead are of humans. Kunzang described delivering complaints from animals as well:

> Several years ago, I gave messages to those who had been selling horses and dogs. The horses told me that they had carried those people in summer and in winter and had won prizes for the family. "In the end, you sold me to Han Chinese who poured water in my nose to wash out my body. Chant *mani* for me," [one horse requested]. I also told those people not to sell dogs. "If you sell dogs, it will be like such-and-such," I explained. The dogs had also sent spoken messages (literally, "sent messages through their teeth," *so gi sgo nas bskur*): "In winter and in the heat of summer, I guarded the door. You didn't feed me well, and finally you sold me for 10,000 RMB." They sent these messages. The owners do Dharma for the animals when I tell them this.

*Delog*s expose themselves to criticism and rebuke as they fulfill their responsibility to deliver unwelcome bad news. Tasked by the Lord of Death, Shinjé Chögyal (Gshin rje chos rgyal), to deliver messages in spite of the consequences to his or her own life and limb, the *delog* fulfills the obligation, often at great risk to him- or herself. Kunzang never elaborated on the punishments she has undergone, but other *delog*s whom I have interviewed reported being threatened or beaten by angry recipients of the unwelcome messages that they delivered. In extreme cases, a *delog* may be tortured or even killed by those who are offended by her testimonies. Kunzang continued:

> There have been many messages, but I mustn't reveal the people's names. A long time ago, Khandro Delog used to say such things. A policeman asked her about his father who had died. "When he was alive, your father stole a butterlamp from an altar. Now he's suffering in hell with a rope tied tight around his waist. If you do some Dharma, he'll be released," she told him. The policeman got angry and cursed her. "Damn you, woman! My father only died last night. You're insulting me," he said. He tied and dragged

her behind his horse. This also happened to Pema Khandro.[13] She told someone that his dead son was in hell. The man heated an iron in the fire and used it to burn her forehead.

As Kunzang's memories of the fates of other *delog*s makes clear, being a *delog* is not easy. Apart from the danger of arousing her community's ire, the repressive policies of the current Chinese government pose a challenge for *delog*s as they attempt to carry out their religious duty in the People's Republic of China. Because they operate independently of the organized Buddhist monastic system, *delog*s are difficult for the state to monitor and control. Furthermore, *delog*s are notorious for criticizing people in positions of power, both religious and political. As a result, Chinese officials are especially quick to penalize anyone said to possess a *delog*'s unusual capacities. *Delog*s in Tibet are therefore reluctant to reveal themselves to people they do not know and trust.[14]

Kunzang is intimately familiar with the problems her contemporary, Khandro Delog, has had with Chinese officials, including prison and lifetime house arrest, and was initially hesitant to tell her story. When I first talked with her, she said, "I don't dare to say this. Do you think it's okay to talk? I usually don't speak about these things." As McGranahan points out, fear of negative political repercussions can lead to narrative withholding and thus the absence of important events from historical records. Concern that attention from a foreigner might expose Kunzang to state scrutiny initially made me reluctant to solicit and record her autobiography. But for Sonam, my assistant, the fear of losing a facet of Tibet's cultural heritage was a graver risk. Sonam wasted no time launching into an impassioned and persuasive argument about the benefits, indeed the necessity, of Kunzang's telling us her story:

> The status of our [Tibetan] nationality (*mi rigs*) is especially low, but we have a special and unique culture, and we should let others know about it. If you keep this to yourself, others won't know that we are a great nationality. They won't know the deep (*rting*) parts of our culture. . . . Even though I'm Tibetan, I don't know anything about [*delog*s]. . . . If you don't talk about these things, [the tradition] will disappear. . . . We must repeat these things, one person to the next. If you tell us these things, it will be beneficial for [the foreigners], it will be beneficial for me, it will be beneficial for you, and it will be beneficial for our nationality.

Sonam's plea brings to mind McGranahan's probing questions: "If the event is that which can be narrated . . . then what happens to events that cannot be narrated? Is historical recognition predicated on narratability . . . ? As multiple scholars have argued, events are real not because they happened, but because they are told in culturally meaningful ways. . . ."[15] Sonam's urging also highlights a fear among Tibetans that their histories must be told, not in order to be made "real," but so as not to be forgotten.

Kunzang's subsequent agreement to have her words recorded points to the importance of Tibetan culture and religion to both her and Sonam. Their willingness to take a risk in order to benefit the Tibetan people and preserve Tibetan culture supports McGranahan's observation that "with the notion of beneficial action in mind and with the hope, if not belief, that telling will benefit the Tibetan cause," Tibetans will indeed speak out.[16] In fact, Kunzang later encouraged me to visit another local *delog* with whom she is acquainted, giving me this advice: "Tell him that you're doing this for Tibet. Otherwise, he may not talk to you; he'll say, 'I don't know. I don't know anything.'"

In her daily life, Kunzang disguises her *delog* reports as divinations (*mo*). This is her own strategy for evading government censorship and punishment:

> People always come and ask me for a divination. They have a lot of faith in me. Even along the road, people ask me to do divinations. They say, "Do a divination, please!" but they really want to ask me these things. I can't say these things directly, but I pretend to do a divination. By telling people to do certain rituals, in fact, I'm relaying messages.

As Kunzang related the events of her life to Sonam and me, she was often interrupted by female friends and neighbors, some stopping by to chat and to request a divination. The political situation in contemporary Tibet makes engaging in *delog* practices a risky endeavor, but throughout Kunzang's life, she has repeatedly faced and overcome daunting obstacles. As a nomad living in a remote area of Eastern Tibet, she does not have the financial resources to sponsor great acts of religious merit. As an illiterate woman, she is not in a position to be able to embark on a teaching career. Nevertheless, Kunzang has found avenues suitable for someone of her sex and background, for fulfilling her religious obligations and personal goals. Despite her insistence that she is not special and does not know how to meditate or understand the Dharma, at several points during the interview Kunzang revealed a positive self-image, unfailing determination, and sense of empowerment and agency:

> I want to spread the Dharma. I printed and hung prayer flags all over Changri. The Dharma had never flourished there like that before. I've traveled all over India. I like India; I was happy

there, [but] I came back. When I returned to Tibet, I came to this place where there was a large *mai* house, some stones, and a few kids making prayer flags. Other than that, there was nothing here. I had a mold for making *tsa-tsa*, you know, those little statues. I worked, regardless of the weather—whether it was cold or hot, and even when I was hungry and tired. After I completed three million *tsa-tsa*, Akhu Chöyang's temple was built. I've gone everywhere and really suffered. There's no place that I haven't been. Even though I get carsick, I still travel.

Kunzang has journeyed to India on more than one occasion, visiting important pilgrimage sites and educating herself about the customs and languages of other countries. Likewise, she has learned a few words of Hindi and is proud to demonstrate her knowledge of some English-language greetings.

Tibetans are not free to travel outside China without a permit, and India, home to the 14th Dalai Lama and the Tibetan Government in Exile, is a particularly taboo destination. Like many Tibetan pilgrims, Kunzang did not have government permission to go to India. She was apprehended during her reentry into China and spent time in Chinese jails as a result. Even imprisonment, however, did not prevent her from carrying out her duties as a *delog*:

Because I escaped to India, they put me in prison. Again, it was time for me to die. In my cell was a small window, and at midnight, Drolma came through it. Her body was green, and she brought three pieces of fruit and a stalk of wild rhubarb. She gave me the fruits and told me to eat them. After that, I didn't feel hungry. I didn't feel sad. Before she came, I had been distraught. "Why am I in prison? I didn't do anything wrong. I may never see my mother again," I worried. But afterwards, I no longer felt sad. Then she was gone and I went *delog*.

In Kunzang's words, her story is one of adversity and suffering.[17] But I interpret Kunzang's narrative as a tale of hope and miracles. In presenting her life, she makes frequent reference to extraordinary happenings, prophecies, and marvels; and the element of divine protection is a recurrent theme in Kunzang's narrative. No matter the degree of hardship she has faced, she has been routinely saved by the intervention of a deity or helpful spirit. Sometime after the birth of her first child, Kunzang was wandering alone in a remote area of Eastern Tibet when an unidentified being came to her aid:

Once I went to some rocky valleys in western Kham and got so hungry I thought I would die. I crawled onto a patch of grass thinking that if I died in that spot, someone might see my bones and chant *mai* for me. All of a sudden, there was a "*Skob!*" sound, and a blue hand appeared. It was like the hand was holding meat and butter tea, and it fed me. When I finished eating, it disappeared. Because it'd been so long since I'd eaten, I fell asleep. After that, I didn't feel hungry for a long time. Sometimes it would rain, and I'd feel like someone was pouring water into my mouth. Then, again, I wouldn't feel hungry.

In her conclusion to the collected volume *Women and Miracle Stories*, Anne-Marie Korte points out that women's miracles are "often more physical in nature, involving a change either in her body or brought about by her body, and serve less often to establish religious authority" than men's, and the unbelievable occurrences that Kunzang experiences conform to this trend.[18] First, there was the unusual conception and remarkably rapid development and birth of her first child. Then there are the occasions when Kunzang has been fed by the goddess Drolma as well as by a mysterious blue hand. Furthermore, when Kunzang goes *delog*, she experiences significant bodily changes. While she is touring the intermediate state, her body lies lifeless, becoming, as she put it, "an empty container, like a bowl, a box, or a plastic bag." When she revives, she is sometimes sick for days. As has also been noted about the extraordinary religious activities in which women typically engage, the miracles Kunzang reports are not performed *by* her but, rather, happen *to* her. She is less an active agent than a vehicle through which sacred powers reveal their presence.

Like most of the female *delog*s I met in the course of my research, Kunzang is highly articulate and impresses me as being extremely intelligent. Despite her lack of formal education, Kunzang is well versed in Buddhist cosmology. Her descriptions of the intermediate state and other realms of existence fit well with standard Tibetan doctrine, suggesting that she has found alternative ways to access Buddhist teachings. When I asked her to describe what happens when we die, she gave a detailed account based on her personal *delog* experiences:

When I go *delog*, I pass through a fog and arrive in a city of demons (*srin po*). Everyone there has the head of a tiger or snow leopard. When I leave that city, I arrive in front of the Lord of Death. The workers tie iron chains around our necks and drag us through the *bardo* to the Lord of Death. It doesn't matter to them if you're a *delog*. They tie their rope around your neck and drag you. Cries of "Die! Die! Kill! Kill!" pervade all of space.

When you get there, you speak the Dharma and beg, and they let you go. The chains of iron become ceremonial silk scarves (*kha btags*) due to the blessings of the Dharma. All the workers

turn into deities. Those who are really lucky are liberated and go
to the Great Compassionate One, Arya Avalokiteśvara's Pure Land,
passing through the lights of white rainbows. Attaining rebirth in
the Pure Land of Arya Avalokiteśvara is no easier than passing
through the eye of a needle. Those who are reborn in the Pure
Land of Amitābha emerge from an eight-petaled lotus.

Kunzang described with great animation the journey through the *bardo*, and
then she opened a cabinet near her bed and handed me a locally produced
DVD. The recording was an animated simulation of the dying process, and
Kunzang seemed proud to say that the monk who created it had consulted
her about the accuracy of its depictions.

   Judgment by the Lord of Death and his animal-headed minions is ubiquitous in Tibetan literature describing the afterlife. Not only do texts such
as the *Bardo Thödrol*, or *Tibetan Book of the Dead*, describe the damnation
of those who engaged in evil and the liberation of those who followed the
Dharma, but popular Buddhist art and sermons also explain the postmortem
consequences of virtue and sin. Details about the intermediate state differ
from text to text and from teacher to teacher as well as from *delog* to *delog*.
One woman I interviewed in the Nepal Himalayas emphasized the compul-
sory interrogation that everyone, *delog*s included, faces. Each individual must
recount his or her virtuous and sinful deeds before being shown the "mirror
of karma" (*las kyi me long*) and reminded of any omissions. Those who are
unable to speak are beaten and thrown into thickets of iron thorns. Comparatively, Kunzang's account of what happens at death is mild and optimistic.

   At the end of our interview, I queried Kunzang about the near-death
experience as it is described in Western sources. "If a foreigner does something like *delog* but returns without any messages, is he a *delog*?" I asked.

   That's not a *delog*. People like that don't have awakened perception
   (*rig sad*). It's like a TV that isn't getting enough electricity so the
   picture is fuzzy. That kind of person didn't have enough electricity. Perhaps he was too hungry [i.e., attached to this world]. He
   wasn't able to awaken his perception because he wasn't able to
   practice the Dharma in his previous life.

In this way, Kunzang ended her narrative with reference to the value and
uniqueness of Tibetan religion. She emphasizes the necessity of Buddhist
practice for spiritual development and states, unconditionally, that Westerners
who have near-death experiences are not *delog*s.

   Although they are rarely famous, *delog*s like Kunzang play important
roles in their communities. The messages they relay comfort the bereaved

as well as keep local leaders, both religious and secular, in check. *Delogs'* reports of the death process and intermediate state confirm Buddhist teachings and are used by lamas to illustrate and add weight to their discourses. The amazing events of Kunzang's life, her ability to act as a *delog*, and the model of female courage and fortitude she provides for local women make her an eminent figure within the Tibetan cultural sphere. It is likely that there are many more exceptional religious persons like Kunzang in contemporary Tibet pursuing their remarkable lives quietly and privately, out of the public eye. Because we deal largely with texts and elite members of society, scholars encounter but a few of these people. Unless a highly literate member of the religious establishment chooses to commit Kunzang's biography to writing and circulate it within the local and exile communities, she will continue her life in relative obscurity, unknown to but a few trusted friends.

Notes

1. Kunzang is a pseudonym. All personal names and names of locations have been changed.

2. The research for this paper was supported by a graduate research fellowship from the University of California Pacific Rim Research Program.

3. Bryan Cuevas, *Travels in the Netherworld: Buddhist Popular Narratives of Death and the Afterlife in Tibet* (Oxford and New York: Oxford University Press, 2008), pp. 13–14.

4. More precise figures and an analysis of the reasons for the gender difference can be found in my dissertation, *Death, Gender, and Extraordinary Knowing: The Delog ('das log) Tradition in Nepal and Eastern Tibet* (University of California, Santa Barbara, 2011).

5. The literal meaning of the term *khandroma* (Sanskrit: *ḍākinī*) is "she who travels in space." *Khandromas* are believed to be incarnations of wisdom energy (*shes rab* or *ye shes*) and play an important role in Tantric Buddhism, where they convey guidance and inspiration to practitioners. *Khandromas* can also manifest as human women.

6. Carole McGranahan, "Narrative Dispossession: Tibet and the Gendered Logics of Historical Possibility," *Comparative Studies in Society and History* 52:4(2010): 776.

7. "Special vision" (*mig mthong ba*) can refer to an ability to perceive beings that others cannot, to see through solid matter, to see into the future, or to recognize others' spiritual qualities.

8. I am translating the Tibetan term *chöpa* (*gcod pa*) as *tantrika*. *Chö* (*gcod*), however, literally means "cutting." It is a particular tantric practice aimed at severing one's ego-attachment. *Chö* meditations involve visualizing the dismemberment and distribution of one's body as a feast for various spirits and lesser deities. For this reason, and because the rituals are often performed in charnel grounds, Kunzang's

father's work as an undertaker (literally, "corpse chopper") would have reinforced his *chö* practice and, perhaps, vice versa.

9. Kunzang conceived the rest of her four children normally. Her ex-husband is the father of her second and third children, and she identified the father of the youngest as a farmer she met when she was traveling. She carried these three children for nine months each.

10. On this aspect of the *delog* experience, see Cuevas, *Travels in the Netherworld*, pp. 76–77.

11. Robert Barnett, "Women and Politics in Contemporary Tibet," in *Women in Tibet*, ed. Janet Gyatso and Hanna Havnevik (New York: Columbia University Press, 2005), p. 288.

12. Ibid., p. 289.

13. Pema Khandro was an Eastern Tibetan *delog* who died in the 1950s.

14. An additional reason for this hesitancy is the Buddhist belief that skeptics who ridicule the Dharma will accrue negative karma.

15. Carole McGranahan, "Truth, Fear, and Lies: Exile Politics and Arrested Histories of the Tibetan Resistance," *Cultural Anthropology* 20:4(2005): 580.

16. Ibid., p. 590.

17. Given the South Asian context in which Kunzang imagines her life, this is not uncommon. Indic religious traditions have long maintained a positive relationship between women's suffering and spiritual power.

18. Anne-Marie Korte, "A Different Grace: Epilogue," in *Women and Miracle Stories: A Multidisciplinary Exploration* (Leiden: Brill, 2004), p. 332.

16

Courage as Eminence

Tibetan Nuns at Yarchen Monastery in Kham

Padma'tsho

The lives of Buddhist women are marked by a certain quality of courage, developed over lifetimes of religious practice in ever-changing circumstances. In our current age of development, Tibetan nuns have the opportunity and responsibility to explore their Buddha nature and to realize their value in today's society. Women are key to the redressing of longstanding gender discriminations that have historically permeated cultural attitudes, even in Vajrayāna Buddhism, and women play a special role in the recasting of women's image in popular culture.[1]

The doctrines of Vajrayāna Buddhism hold women in high esteem. As early as 2,500 years ago, the Buddha taught that women could reach enlightenment. The Vajrayāna precepts, moreover, accord women a lofty status; it is written that one must not vilify or disrespect women. Vajrayāna Buddhism promotes wisdom and compassion and teaches that "wisdom is the mother of all Buddhas."

Women have thus come to symbolize wisdom in Vajrayāna Buddhism, and therefore the merits of women in these teachings are both acknowledged and celebrated. The story of Tārā in Tibetan Buddhism is a useful example. Tārā, a female *bodhisattva* who embodied wisdom and compassion, descended into the world and took rebirth as a princess. Whenever she made offerings to the Buddha, she generated the altruistic attitude of *bodhicitta*.[2]

All the *bhikṣus* around her urged the princess, "If you pray that your deeds accord with the teachings, then indeed then on that account you will change your form to that of a man, as is befitting."[3] After several exchanges with these monks, the princess announced her conclusion: "In this life there is no such distinction as male or female, neither of 'self-identity' or a 'person' nor any perception (of such), and therefore attachment to ideas of 'male' or 'female' is quite worthless. Weakminded worldlings are always deluded by this." And so she vowed, "There are many who wish to gain enlightenment in a man's form and there are but few who wish to work for the welfare of sentient beings in a female form. Therefore may I, in a female body, work for the welfare of beings until *samsāra* has been emptied." She then became enlightened by skillfully utilizing the five kinds of sensual pleasures and contemplation. Therefore, the princess is respectfully called the "Mother who Saves and Transports." Tārā is both mythic confirmation that women have the prerequisites for awakening as well as affirmation of the quality and value of women's achievements in Buddhist practice. At the same time, her story can be used as a powerful denunciation of gender discrimination in society.

In contrast to the scriptural esteem for women found in Vajrayāna Buddhism, the realities of contemporary Tibetan culture and the day-to-day functioning of the monastic world betray a far more derogatory perspective toward the roles and capacities of women. Although the hard work that women do is acknowledged and respected within the domestic sphere, this esteem often seems to end outside the kitchen door. At home, husbands listen to women's opinions and value their suggestions when it comes to caring for children and the elderly, where compassion and loving kindness are most evident, but at public events or social gatherings, Tibetan men typically demand compliance and subservience. The customary roles for women and men during these events are quite distinct in their responsibilities: the women make the tea and cook the meals while the men engage in loud and empty talk. Whenever unrelated people are present, Tibetan men seem to presume that women are ignorant. A pattern of silencing extends to all interactions and activities in the community, even to festivals and folk gatherings, such as summer village gatherings in agricultural areas and horse-racing festivals in pastoral areas. On these festive occasions, the men are front and center. They sit inside the central yurt, talking boistrously, while the women make tea and cook meals outside on open-air stoves and serve the men inside. While humble service may well be one of the virtues of Tibetan women, their own intelligence and confidence are undermined and stifled by this unfair division of labor.

Through the lens of Tibetan culture, I note three important characteristics that play a role in my assessment of women's status. First, women are held in high esteem in the doctrines of Vajrayāna Buddhism, as we have seen in our short analysis of the figure of Tārā. The second quality is that women's diligence and good-heartedness are respected. Nevertheless—and this is the third characteristic—women traditionally have had very little opportunity to be heard in the public sphere, and their opinions are generally undervalued. The contradictions that exist between private and public also exist between the spiritual and social. In Buddhist teachings, women embody the ideals of selfless service and humility, and they also have the clear potential to become fully enlightened. However, in traditional Tibetan cultural and social norms, there are great restraints and limitations imposed on women. The difference between the esteem granted to women in Vajrayāna Buddhist scripture and the manner in which women are discounted within monastic institutions represents another large contradiction. To illustrate, I analyze the material I gleaned from firsthand experiences and interviews that describe the everyday lives, Buddhist education, and Dharma practice of the nuns at Yarchen Monastery.[4]

The Nuns of Yarchen Monastery

Yarchen Monastery (also called Yaqing Wujin Meditation Center) is located 13,779 feet (4,200 meters) above sea level in Changtai District, Palgyu County in Gandze Prefecture. At present, there are more than 7,000 monastic residents at Yarchen, including 5,070 nuns and 1,500 monks. The monastery is administered in traditional style; all aspects of the lives of the monastics are managed through a system of hierarchically ordered posts. The great assembly hall for nuns (reg stsal dhi ma ta la'i pho brang) was completed in 2006. The hall has two stories and can hold up to 6,000 nuns. The monastery is said to be the manifestation of the Palace of Infinite Light of Padmasambhava, which indicates that it is an exceptional and auspicious site for practicing the Dharma.

I was curious to learn where these thousands of nuns came from and what motivated them to come to the monastery. Based on interviews, I learned that most of the nuns had come to Yarchen because conditions for advanced Buddhist learning were inadequate in their home temples, where they had no access to lamas, who are the transmitters of the Buddhadharma. They had heard that Achuk Rinpoche and many khenpos[5] were teaching at Yaqing. Through accounts given by their fellow villagers and relatives, they developed faith in Achuk Rinpoche and Asong Tülku and consequently came to the monastery to take refuge in them.

The study program at Yarchen Monastery focuses strongly on the Great Perfection (Dzogchen), which was taught by Lama Achuk Rinpoche from the time of the monastery's founding in 1985 until his passing in 2011.[6] Since 2001, Asong Tülku has been in charge of expounding this teaching and confirming a student's comprehension of the Great Perfection. In 2007, there were five long-term residential *khenpos* teaching in the program. In addition, there were twenty-six visiting *khenpos* who came from all over Tibet to teach. At the same time, there were more than forty *khenpos* in retreat and additional *tülkus* and *khenpos* from various areas combining retreat practice with teaching, leading rituals, and reading scriptures.[7]

Gathering Together from Far and Wide

In 2007, there were also five *khenmos* (female *khenpos*) in residence in the nuns' area of the monastery. They were primarily responsible for assisting Achuk Rinpoche and Asong Tülku with their Dharma talks. Before 2008, nuns went to the *khenpos'* teaching quarters to listen to the elucidation of the *sūtras*, which were held every day, except during ceremonies. Each of the twenty-six *khenpos* taught a different *sūtra*, or commentary, and the nuns selected the one they wished to study. In 2009, seven blocks of teaching quarters were built next to the Sūtra Hall in the nuns' area. Today, there are seven *khenpos* teaching in those new quarters every afternoon. With the new construction, nuns no longer have to go to the *khenpos* teaching quarters on the other side of the river to study.

In Yarchen Monastery, there are three chief *khenmos* who assist with Asong Tülku's Dharma talks by giving preliminary instructions and answering the nuns' questions. These *khenmos* guide the nuns' preliminary practices step by step. All of the nuns at Yarchen Monastery can freely choose which *khenmos* they wish to study with. Because there are no classrooms for the *khenmos'* assistant teaching, they perform this function in their own quarters or in the yard outside their room. One of the chief *khenmos* is Solang Drolma. She has been studying and practicing at Yarchen Monastery for almost thirty years and was personally appointed as a *khenmo* by Achuk Rinpoche. Every day from early morning to late afternoon, whenever there is no teaching by a *khenpo*, there is a long line of nuns in her yard waiting to ask questions.

In 2009, there were a total of thirty *khenmos* of different levels, including *delogmas* (*das log ma*), nuns who specialize in death rituals. All of these *khenmos* are capable of giving preliminary instructions, but they have not yet received permission to give other Dharma teachings or explain the *sūtras* on their own. In Larung Gar, another monastery in Kham, there are also *khenmos* who are primarily responsible for assisting the lama. Since 2005, *khenmos* have helped to explain the lama's instructions to the nuns, in both

Tibetan and Chinese, after he has given the teachings. I am currently doing research on the nuns' education system in Kham.

As we can see, a nun's knowledge and expertise is shared only within her own "domestic" sphere, which is strictly circumscribed. At present, the ability of nuns to operate in a more public sphere, and even to pass on higher teachings among themselves, is fairly limited. This teaching arrangement keeps the nuns looking outside their own community for the light of wisdom and learning. Psychologically, perhaps this encourages the nuns to continually look to the monks and lamas, rather than themselves, for instruction and guidance.

Nuns in the Life of the Monastery

Thousands of monks and nuns are gathered at Yarchen Monastery. A river divides the campus: the living quarters for the nuns are situated to the east of the river on the wetlands of Changtai County, surrounded and crisscrossed by many small streams. The living quarters for the monks are located on a hill to the west of the river, close to a major road. The monks' quarters are physically elevated and soundly constructed, whereas the nuns' quarters are situated below and are poorly put together. These obvious geographical and substantial disparities reflect the relative status of monks and nuns.

Further, unlike the monks, activities for the nuns are not limited to study and religious practice. In addition to providing for their own meals and personal needs of daily life, the nuns are also responsible for providing the basic physical labor needed around the monastery. These nuns who are already living in harsh conditions are also responsible for the construction work, including unloading the cargo trucks. Outside observers may find the living conditions of the nuns hard to endure, but the nuns themselves do not consider the circumstances of their lives unusual. They face all these hardships with a smile and even express feeling happy to take on the extra responsibilities. All the same, one wonders how much energy this labor diverts them from Dharma study and the pursuit of liberation. However, with heroism and great virtue, they continue to work even in these difficult circumstances.

Diligence in Mud Huts

Residences for the nuns are on the wetlands by the river, in huts, not houses. With no forest or stone nearby, almost all of the living quarters are made from pebbles and grass found by the river. The roofs are built from sticks and covered with plastic sheeting, and the sides of the huts are wrapped with shabby cloth or plastic, which barely shields them from the wind, sun, and biting cold. There is rarely any flooring inside these mud huts. Some of the nuns place thin foam mats on the ground on which to sleep.

Inside each of these small huts there are niches that serve as shrines, with Buddha images and material for rituals, such as water bowls, butter lamps, and scriptures. These shrines also house other daily necessities, which are usually shared between a couple of nuns who assist each other in their work and study. When there are blizzards and snow during winter, temperatures can drop to –4 degrees Fahrenheit (–20 degrees Celsius). At best, the mud huts are able to shield the nuns from wind and snow, but they cannot protect them from the low temperatures. In these humble huts, the nuns of Yarchen Monastery complete their preliminary practices and then practice the "direct crossing" of the Excellence of Wisdom. Nuns who are in retreat sit for four sessions of three hours each, every day. At the sound of a conch shell, they begin at 4:00 AM, and then again at 8:30 AM, 2:30 PM, and 7:30 PM, for a total of twelve hours a day. Day and night, regardless of the weather, they continue to sit in their quest to realize the light of wisdom within their own luminous minds. Each time the nuns describe the joy they experience practicing the Dharma at Yarchen Monastery, I see Tārā's enlightened qualities radiating from their faces.

If the nuns have questions about their thoughts or experiences during these sittings or wish to confirm their meditative state, they may ask the khenpos or khenmos in person. They may also request additional instructions from Asong Tülku or Achuk Rinpoche. Generally, they consult the specific khenpo or khenmo in whom they have taken refuge, and, as long as they are making diligent progress in their meditation, they may also receive secret oral transmissions. The khenmos at Yarchen are capable of assisting in the preliminary and basic practices,[8] based on the insights they have gained from their years of practice and experience, yet when it comes to confirming the level of practice that a disciple has attained or whether or not a disciple is ready to receive higher instructions, everything has to go through the khenpos and tülkus.

For those who are not yet qualified to practice the Excellence of Wisdom, the monastery arranges a retreat for completing the preliminary practices. In these retreats, the khenpos or khenmos provide instructions almost every morning. Some practitioners are advised to perform the preliminary practices more than once in order to accumulate further merit, eliminate mental obstacles, and enhance their insight and practice. This prepares them to pass the next year's examination and begin the higher level of chö (gcod, lit., "cutting through") and "direct crossing" contemplation.

Living expenses for the nuns are funded primarily by donations given to the monastery. The nuns receive modest donations of thirty to one hundred *renminbi* for chanting *sūtras* and performing rituals. All donations are administered by the monastery management committee, which distributes them equally to the nuns and monks. On occasion, the donations may be as much as three hundred *renminbi* (about thirty-three U.S. dollars). The differences in living standards between nuns and monks are the result of the fact that monks receive more support from their families and communities than nuns do. Despite the difficulties that the nuns face and the large difference in status between nuns and monks, the potential any nun has to reach enlightenment through various opportunities for high-quality instruction, serious study, and meditation is widely recognized and appreciated by the many lay practitioners who have visited Yarchen Monastery.

The natural and material conditions at Yarchen differ markedly from typical conditions in the surrounding towns and cities. Here, there is no electricity, no running water, and a scarcity of basic daily necessities. Many of the nuns rely on the roasted barley flour (*tsampa*) they brought from home for their sustenance. However, neither the rigors of practice nor the deficiencies of daily requirements can dissuade the nuns from their persistent pursuit of Dharma. Hindrances do not thwart their determination to do retreats, either—even in the poor mud huts in the dead of winter. The radiant smile on each nun's face reflects the tangible benefit of her Dharma practice and the understanding of life and human existence that practicing the Dharma brings. The tenacity and happiness of the nuns stand in a sharp contrast to the disappointment and disillusionment inherent in the indulgent lifestyles and material enjoyments of worldly people.

In 2011, I interviewed two nuns who told me that if they studied really hard and practiced well, they had a chance to become a *khenmo*. They were very, very excited about this. One of the nuns told me that she had studied extremely hard and really wanted to be a good practitioner and become a *khenmo* able to give Buddhist teachings. Unfortunately, she became sick and had to go to Chengdu to see a doctor, thus losing her chance to study and become a *khenmo*. She felt very sad about this. Her illness now requires her to visit Chengdu every single year. When I asked her whether she preferred to live in the monastery or in a big city like Chengdu, she was very clear that she preferred living in the monastery. Even under incredibly harsh conditions, thousands of nuns diligently pursue the essence of the Buddhadharma in order to realize their own Buddha nature. One cannot but admire the heroic spirit of perseverance of these Tibetan nuns.

The Circumstances for Creating Virtue

In 2007, I was able to trace the places of origin of the residents at Yarchen Monastery from the records in the operations office of the Bureau of Religion.

According to these records, most of the nuns and monks come from various areas of Tibet. The record for August 2007, for example, states that 2,531 of the residents of Yarchen Monastery were from Garze Prefecture, including 1,812 nuns from Xinrong, Derge, Padain, Sertar, Ritang, and Luhuo. A total of 692 residents were from nearby Baiyu County. Another 1,990 residents were from Qinghai Province, including 1,622 nuns from Nangchen, Yushu, and Golog. Another 1,711 residents were from the Tibetan Autonomous Region (TAR), including 1,548 nuns from Chamdo and Jomda. In addition, thirty-six residents were from Abje Prefecture, including five nuns. A small percentage of residents are not Tibetan. According to Yarchen Monastery's Web site, "In 2000 there were over a hundred disciples of Han origin in the four assemblies, and more than fifty of them were residential practitioners."[9] When I visited, I was told that there were at that time one hundred disciples of Han origin staying in retreat at Yarchen, mostly from Guangzhou, Jiangsu, Sichuan, and Shandong Provinces.

As mentioned before, to maintain the life and structure of the monastery, nuns are not only expected to uphold the precepts, but they are also required to participate in various kinds of physical labor around the monastery. In fact, the burden of the physical labor necessary to keep the monastery running falls mainly on the nuns rather than the monks. During the construction of the assembly hall for the nuns in 2006 and the assembly hall for the monks in 2008, the nuns took turns performing tasks such as carrying soil, stones, and sand on their backs. When I was at the monastery in August 2007, I saw only nuns performing physical labor. During my interviews, I specifically asked the nuns why no monks were carrying soil, stones, and sand on their backs. The nuns replied that they did not know and said that they were simply complying with what they had been asked to do.[10] One of the nuns told me that during the five years she had been at Yarchen, it was only in the last year that she had ever seen any monk carry soil.

At Yarchen Monastery, nuns have access to the very highest teachings, and they become great practitioners and often have profound realizations. The nuns appreciate having access to such great riches of Dharma and share the benefits of their knowledge and practice with society at large by dedicating the merit they accumulate. If there were other ways for them to pass their deep wisdom and compassion on to the wider community, it would bring great benefit to many people. However, as things stand now, it is more often the monks who are given the responsibility to teach large gatherings of people and to guide other monastics through their higher practices, while the nuns are generally requested to teach small groups in their own rooms, and to guide their fellow nuns through the preliminary and basic practices.

Envisioning Equality

On a conceptual level in Vajrayāna Buddhism, Tibetan women are given a lofty status. In daily life, however, these women face countless cultural and conventional restrictions to their spiritual potential. Tibetan women must overcome these impediments by learning how to become more aware of their social potential and as a result gain self-reliance in Dharma studies and practice. As they become more confident about the power of their own compassion and wisdom, these women will be better able to meet societal challenges and will make large gains in being recognized and affirmed by both religious institutions and society as a whole. In this androcentric culture, it is vital to construct a model of equality that allows women to pursue the same goals and education as men.[11] In the mid-1980s, Khenpo Jigme Phuntshok gave the title of *khenmo* to four nuns who had been studying with him for a long time. Thus, a new education system for Tibetan nuns was created in Kham that improved their status and opportunities. Akin to the *bodhisattva* Tārā, the nuns of Kham strive diligently to transcend the concepts of "man" and "woman" and to reach enlightenment in a woman's body in order to benefit sentient beings and empty the ocean of suffering. The global forces moving toward gender equity need to be mirrored in the monasteries to encourage and support female practitioners.

Tibetan Buddhism is replete with enlightened female figures. All Tibetans know the story of Princess Yeshe Dawa, who generated the great *bodhicitta*, achieved the wisdom of the Dharmakaya, and became Tārā, an enlightened being in female form. The thousands of nuns who live at Yarchen Monastery study diligently in their mud huts without electricity or any amenities. In Tibetan Buddhist belief, their devoted practice of compassion and wisdom will definitely lead them to attain the state of Buddhahood, just as Tārā did. To accomplish that, however, the nuns at Yarchen Monastery deserve much greater affirmation of their roles and status in the monastery's educational system and community organization. The living conditions and allocation of responsibilities in the *saṅgha* community need to be more equitably managed. The attainments of *khenmos* and *geshemas* need to be recognized and nurtured.[12] In their determination to uphold the precepts and practice the teachings, the nuns at Yarchen Monastery are eminent exemplars of the Buddhadharma. In a just and fair system, their courage and endurance in perpetuating the secret oral transmissions will surely yield fruit and be of ultimate benefit to all sentient beings.

My focus in this chapter has been the need to extend and enhance the education and status of Tibetan nuns that first started with Khenpo Jigme Phuntshok in the mid-1980s. In the twenty-first century, Tibetan women in general and Tibetan nuns in particular face the immense challenge of implementing in practical reality the high status that the Vajrayāna tradition has already accorded to them conceptually. Breaking through traditionally-established barriers will afford these women greater opportunity to make spiritual progress and also will enhance their self-confidence and self-reliance in studying and practicing the Dharma with compassion and wisdom. Providing nuns with greater opportunities for realization will move them closer to perfect awakening in their service to others.

Notes

1. 'Jam dbyangs sgrol ma, "General Introduction to the Study of Tibetan Women," *Tibetan Studies* 1(2008).
2. *Bodhicitta* is the "enlightened attitude" of wishing to become a Buddha and liberate all beings from suffering.
3. These pronouncements are recounted in Sarah Harding, *Machig Labdrön, Machik's Complete Explanation: Clarifying the Meaning of Chöd, A Complete Explanation of Casting Out the Body as Food* (Ithaca, NY: Snow Lion Publications, 2003), p. 23.
4. This research was conducted under the auspices of the Ministry of Education, General Project 10YJA730001 and SWUN 10XN07.
5. The term *khenpo* (*mkhan po*) is often interpreted to mean "abbot." In the Kagyü and Nyingma schools, it is also used to denote a recognized level of knowledge and authorization to teach, especially to monastics. Here, the term is used in the latter sense.
6. Achuk Rinpoche (1927–2010) was revered as an incarnation of the great treasure revealer (*terton*) Rigzin Longsal Nyingpo (1625–1682) of Kathok Monastery, himself believed to be an incarnation of Amitābha Buddha. Achuk Rinpoche was renowned as a Dzogchen master, having spent forty-three years in retreat with his teacher, Arik Rinpoche. Yed das 'od, *Sequence of Essential Practices of the Innate Wisdom of Great Perfection*, expounded by Lama Kun bzang tshul khrims and translated by Liu Liqian (Beijing: The Ethnic Publishing House, 2006).
7. The Tibetan term *tülku* (*sprul sku*, lit., "emanation body") refers to a person, usually male, who is believed to be the rebirth of a highly realized Buddhist teacher.
8. Do shes, *Masterpieces of Lama Tsong-kha-pa, with Detailed Commentaries* (Gansu: Gansu Ethnic Publishing House, 2002).
9. The "four assemblies" of a Buddhist society are *bhikṣus, bhikṣuṇīs, upāsakas* (laymen), and *upāsikās* (laywomen).
10. See Nyi ma bkra shes and Liu Yuan, "Tibetan Women's Traditional Silence and Modern Struggle," *Academic Journal of Chinese Women* 1(2007).
11. bDe skyid sgrol ma: *Study of Monastic Women in Tibetan Buddhism* (Beijing: Social Sciences Publishers, 2003).
12. The word *geshema* is the feminine of *geshe* (*dge bshes*), a scholarly title or degree traditionally conferred only on monks.

17

Nuns, Ḍākinīs, and Ordinary Women in the Revival of Mongolian Buddhism

Karma Lekshe Tsomo

According to *The Secret History of the Mongols,* the *khatun* (queens) of thirteenth-century Mongolia played significant roles and were often admired for their political acumen.[1] Accounts of ordinary Mongolian women in Mongolian historical literature are rare, however, and references to women in Mongolian Buddhist literature are almost entirely absent. Although Buddhism has been influential in Mongolia since the time of Činggis Khan in the thirteenth century, histories of Buddhism in Mongolia typically fail to mention women, except for brief references to slave women who were bought and sold[2] and wives who patronized Buddhism along with their spouses.[3]

Missing pieces to this puzzle of exclusion were discovered at the 10th Sakyadhita International Conference on Buddhist Women, held in Ulaanbaatar in 2008. Several hundred scholars, practitioners, social activists, and artists from Mongolia and around the world gathered in Ulaanbaatar to discuss "Buddhism in Transition: Tradition, Changes, and Challenges." Attention was focused on the contributions, challenges, and aspirations of Buddhist women. The theme of transition was, and remains, especially relevant to Mongolia because women there are shouldering major responsibilities in their struggle not just for survival, but also for the continuity of their unique cultural expressions in a time of radical social, economic, political, and religious change. The destruction and reconstruction of Mongolian Buddhist institutions over the past eighty years have deeply affected women and ushered in an era of serious questions and reevaluations of the existing social, economic, and religious structures.

The enthusiastic participation of women in Mongolian Buddhism is widely acknowledged but has received almost no scholarly attention. I am keenly interested in the roles women have traditionally played in Mongolian Buddhism and how those roles are changing in the post-Soviet era. My interest in Mongolian studies began at the East-West Center in Honolulu, where I met and interacted with classmates from Mongolia, and continued at the Institute of Buddhist Dialectics in Dharamsala, where I met Gabju Choijamts Demberel, now abbot of Gandantegchenling Monastery in Ulaanbaatar. In 1995, I visited Mongolia for the first time and, at the invitation of the abbot, stayed at Gandantegchenling Monastery. Kushok Bakula Rinpoche, whom I had known in India, was then serving as the Indian Ambassador to Mongolia. He invited me to travel with him to Tosontsengal, in the northwest of Mongolia, where I witnessed Mongolian religion and culture in the process of being revitalized.

Thereafter, I invited four young Mongolian nuns, each recommended by Bakula Rinpoche, to study Buddhist philosophy at Jamyang Chöling Institute in Dharamsala, which I directed. These young nuns, the first in Mongolian history to receive the precepts of a novice nun, belonged to two Buddhist women's centers in Ulaanbaatar: Dulmaalin and Narhajid. In 1997, I had visited these centers and two other Buddhist practice centers for women. In 2007 and 2008, I visited Mongolia to coordinate the 10th Sakyadhita International Conference on Buddhist Women in Ulaanbaatar and to edit the conference proceedings on the theme, "Buddhism in Transition: Tradition, Changes, and Challenges."[4] The conference included a panel on Buddhist Women of Mongolia, and these papers were included in the conference proceedings.[5] From 2010 to 2013, I traveled to Mongolia several times to complete research for this chapter.

My research focuses on the roles of women in the current revival and transformation of Buddhism in Mongolia. There is little or no mention of women in records of Mongolian Buddhism and no trace of nuns in the country's formerly vibrant monastic tradition. The monks' monasteries reportedly controlled nearly 20 percent of the capital in Mongolia, a concentration of wealth and power to which women were not granted access. During the period of Soviet domination, when Mongolian Buddhism was severely repressed and the order of monks nearly annihilated, many contend that Mongolian Buddhism survived largely because of the strong devotion and efforts of women. Women have been especially active in the revival of religious practice that has taken place throughout Mongolia since 1990. Now, women are allowed to enter the monasteries and attend public teachings, but they continue to lack access to monastic education, ritual training, and other aspects of the tradition. Their roles remain circumscribed and their many contributions unrecorded and unrecognized. My research project seeks to rectify this omission by documenting women's historical roles in Mongolian Buddhism as well as the current contributions they are making. The special focus is on rural *aimag*s (provinces) such as Zavkhan and Khuvsgul, where Buddhist culture is strong.

The issues raised by Mongolian scholars, practitioners, and social activists involved in the 10th Sakyadhita Conference illustrate that Mongolian women have the potential to become vibrant forces in a tradition that often neglects them. Women face numerous obstacles to achieving their aspirations. However, women have responded to the recent social, political, and economic changes in a variety of different ways: taking on increased responsibilities for their families, assuming new roles in business and government, speaking out against social injustice, and, most importantly for our discussion here, seeking new directions for spiritual development. Signs of women's enthusiasm for religious practices—Buddhism, shamanism, and increasingly Christianity—are evident in all corners of the country, yet it remains true that for women to become full participants in the revival of Buddhism in Mongolia, they will need to address centuries of their exclusion and clear a path for their future inclusion. Anachronistic arguments based on old stereotypes of women as unsuited, incapable, or uninterested in becoming major players in Mongolian Buddhist culture are being overshadowed by the strength, accomplishments, and sheer enthusiasm of modern Mongolian women. From my observations, based on interviews and fieldwork conducted from 1995 to 2013, Mongolian women are interested in learning about every aspect of Buddhism and are proving to be highly resourceful in pursuing their religious goals. Using the Sakyadhita conference as a reference point, I would like to explore the religious landscape of the Mongolian Buddhist resurgence from the perspective of Mongolian women and examine the varied perspectives that women bring to the revitalization of Buddhism in Mongolia, whether as full-time practitioners or as ordinary followers of a reawakening tradition.

Women in Mongolian Buddhist History

Perhaps the earliest reference to a Buddhist woman in Mongolian history is the story of Sain Uzesgelent, consort of Khubilai Khan, who is credited with fostering his devotion to Sakya Lama. Throughout Mongolian history, the consorts of *khan*s and other noblewomen have helped to elevate the status of the lamas (Buddhist teachers), *khampa*s (abbots), and *khutuktu*s (recognized reincarnate lamas). They encouraged the inception of the *datsans* (Buddhist monasteries and monastic universities), the building of shrines, the sponsoring of religious services, and the translation of texts. Women figure somewhat obliquely in historical accounts, such as in accounts of magical cures that helped to spread faith in Buddhism among commoners and aristocrats alike, for example, Neyiči Toyin's healing of an Ongniyud princess.[6] Other Mongolian women, such as Tsogt Dari in the mid-nineteenth century and Nomundari in the early twentieth century, were renowned for their support of Buddhist institutions. Several women have been popularized as emanations of Tārā, a highly revered *bodhisattva* in female form—a phenomenon documented as early as 1887 by the Russian scholar A. M. Pozdneev.[7]

Women continue to contribute substantially to the current flowering of Buddhist monasteries in Mongolia. Nevertheless, they still have no official status in Mongolian Buddhist institutions. In fact, prior to the 1990s, there was no order of ordained nuns, neither fully ordained *bhikṣuṇī*s nor novices. Although a woman might devote herself to religious practice nor shave her head after her husband died, her role was confined to being a devotee and donor. Women were banned from studying in the monasteries, the centers of religious literacy, so their access to the philosophical and ritual aspects of the tradition was severely limited. Excluded from studies, they engaged in devotional practices and the recitation of prayers that they had committed to memory. They told Buddhist stories that were transmitted from one generation to the next. Women quietly continued these practices during the period of Soviet domination of Mongolia, when overt demonstrations of religiosity went underground. Religion "led to problems" during Soviet times.[8]

Today, women assume one of three roles in the practice of Mongolian Buddhism: nun, "*ḍākinī*," or ordinary Buddhist laywoman. In the tantric tradition, the term *ḍākinī* denotes an emanation of enlightened energy in female form; in Mongolia, it is used for women practitioners who regularly perform tantric rituals and other religious activities. Here, I focus on three such women's practice centers (*datsans*) in Ulaanbaatar: Tugsbayasgalant, Narhajid, and Dulmaalin. All of these centers perform ritual practices, recitation of texts, and fasting rituals.

Preparing the Ground for an Order of Nuns

As Buddhism spread to Mongolia from the beginning of the thirteenth century, monastic communities developed for men, but not for women. The male domination of monastic institutions that existed in Tibet was replicated in Mongolia. Prior to the Soviet occupation of Mongolia, it was common for women to shave their heads and receive the five precepts of a Buddhist laywoman (Sanskrit: *upāsikā*; Tibetan: *dge bsnyen ma*).[9] These women lived celibate lives dedicated to Dharma practice, yet I have not found conclusive evidence of an order of nuns or a celibate monastic order for women in Mongolian history, although the term *gilam*, meaning "female lama" in Mongolian, may indicate the existence of women lamas in earlier times. Buddhist women practitioners, whether celibate or not, are often referred to as *handmaa* in Mongolian.

In 1990, Kushok Bakula Rinpoche, a highly respected lama from Ladakh, was appointed as the Indian Ambassador to Mongolia, a post that he held until his retirement in 2000.[10] In addition to his diplomatic and administrative duties, he began giving teachings on Buddhism and ordaining young Mongolian men as novice monks in an effort to revive the tradition of celibate monasticism that had nearly been eradicated by Soviet oppression. Early in 1993, Bakula Rinpoche conferred the thirty-six precepts of a novice nun (Sanskrit: *śrāmaṇerikā*; Tibetan: *dge tsul ma*) on eight women, and later that same year he gave these precepts to two more women. In 1994, Thubten Dolma and Thubten Kunze from Dumaalin and Thubten Chodron and Thubten Dechen from Narkhajid traveled to Dharamsala to study Buddhist philosophy and Tibetan language at Jamyang Chöling Monastery. These nuns, between twenty and twenty-five years of age, had already completed ten years of secular education and studied Buddhism privately for several years. After arriving in Dharamsala, they met H.H. Dalai Lama in a private audience and offered him blue *khatag* in the Mongolian style. His Holiness took a keen interest in the nuns—the first Mongolian nuns to study in India—and encouraged them to study well. Other Mongolian nuns studied at Kopan Nunnery (Khachoe Ghakyil Ling) in Nepal and at Ganden Chöling Nunnery in Dharamsala. By 2012, most had returned to Mongolia. Many of them have disrobed because of the lack of structural support for nuns in Mongolia, yet they continue to use their Buddhist education and language skills to contribute to the revival of their cherished cultural heritage.

Today, the number of actively engaged women practitioners has increased incrementally, yet there is still only one center specifically for celibate women practitioners, Dulmaalin (Tibetan: Dolma Ling), located on the outskirts of Ulaanbaatar. The monastery was built on the premises of a weathered Chinese temple known as Dara-Ekh, or Tārā Temple. Dulmaalin, established in 2002, has thirteen resident nuns who have taken the precepts of a novice nun. The center is linked with the Foundation for the Preservation of the Mahayana Tradition (FPMT), an international organization founded by the Tibetan lama Thubten Yeshe. It is under the spiritual direction of his disciple, the Nepali lama Thubten Zopa Rinpoche. The Dulmaalin nuns range

in age from sixteen to ninety-two. As at other FPMT centers, the nuns recite
texts, conduct *nyungne* fasting rituals,[1] and perform prayers for the benefit of
sentient beings and the local community. They chant in Tibetan, focus on the
recitation of *Lama Chöpa*, and study texts, especially the *Lamrim* (Graduated
Path to Enlightenment). The center also runs programs to promote environmental awareness and protection. Although celibate monasticism is favored
by some, who view it as necessary for stability, commitment, and discipline,
it is regarded by others as an unwanted Tibetan imposition in the Mongolian
Buddhist landscape.

Khandroma: A Uniquely Mongolian Category

Today, there are two active Buddhist practice centers for *khandroma*s (Sanskrit: *ḍākinī*; Tibetan: *mkha' 'gro ma*) in Ulaanbaatar: Tugsbayasgalant and
Narhajid. In Mongolia in recent times, the term *khandroma* has been used
to designate a *genen* or female lay practitioner with five precepts (Sanskrit:
upāsikā; Tibetan: *dge bsnyen ma*). Some of these practitioners have been nuns,
some are married to lamas, while others are otherwise ordinary laywomen
with a strong commitment to the practice and study of Buddhism. Women
in this category are competent to perform many different types of religious
services, including rituals and the reading of texts, which they do on a daily,
monthly, or annual basis. *Khandroma*s are respected for their understanding
of Buddhism and are also consulted, especially by women, for divinations and
advice regarding personal and family issues. The *khandroma*s at Tugsbayasgalant and Narhajid are also trained in rituals such as *chö* (*gcod*, "cutting"),
a visualization practice of offering one's body parts to satisfy the needs of
sentient beings. This visualization is accompanied by chanting, drums, and
thighbone horns.

The first center for *khandroma*s, Tugsbayasgalant, was founded in 1990
by Gantumur Natsagdorji, a married woman, near Ganden Monastery. Today,
the center has thirty *khandroma*s and a large congregation of lay followers
who attend services and request blessings and rituals. The center is associated with the lama Gurudeva, who was a well-known proponent of the
controversial Shugden practice.[2] Eight *khandroma*s from Tugsbayasgalant
studied at Zanabazar Buddhist University from 2002 and 2006. Since that
time, although courses on Buddhist topics are organized periodically, the
center's primary emphasis seems to be ritual activities that serve the needs
of the lay community.

The second center, Narkhajid, was founded in 1991 by Agvaanjantsan
Bassud, also a married woman. The temple is associated with the Nyingma

tradition and is dedicated to the female tantric deity Narkhajid (Sanskrit: Sarvabuddhaḍākinī; Tibetan: *Na ro mkha' spyod*). Of the center's thirty trained practitioners, twenty-six wear their hair long and practice as *ḍākinīs*, while four shave their heads and practice as novice nuns. The *khandromas* at these first two centers chant in the traditional Mongolian style known as *khüree*. In 1994, Narkhajid opened Naropa College in Mongolia to provide Buddhist education to children and young women.

Extraordinary Mongolian Buddhist Women Practitioners

Amaa was a revered 104-year-old Buddhist *yoginī*, an advanced female practitioner, from Khenti Province in northeastern Mongolia. In 2008, she voluntarily traveled two hundred miles over rough roads to attend the 10th Sakyadhita International Conference on Buddhist Women in Ulaanbaatar. At the opening ceremony, she was spontaneously invited to the stage to share her reflections with an audience of several hundred Mongolian and international Buddhist women. Memorably, she said, "I have been waiting for this moment my whole life." Everyone in the audience was very moved by this remarkable woman. Amaa's dedication to Buddhist practice began at a young age. When she was sixteen, she was the youngest of sixteen tantric practitioners who sought teaching and practice from the renowned Tibetan lama Zundui. The group stayed together for about two years in the remote countryside until the communists routed them, forcing them to flee. Nevertheless, Amaa practiced *chö* (*chod*) for more than seventy years. With undaunted determination, she persevered as a respected religious teacher and practitioner through seven decades of antagonistic communist rule. In the remote countryside in Khentii Province, she continued to be consulted daily for advice, prayers, and blessings until her death in 2011.

Another respected female religious practitioner is Jigmed Surenjav from Khovd Province. She is regarded as Green Tārā, a popular *bodhisattva* associated with healing and protection who is one of twenty-one Tārās in the Buddhist pantheon. At the age of forty, Jigmed Surenjav had an experience in which she "found purity." As a consequence, she discovered that she possessed special wisdom and supernormal abilities. Widely acknowledged as one of three Tārās from Khovd *aimag*, she founded and continues to direct a traditional healing and counseling center. With her extrasensory perception, special wisdom, and healing abilities, she has been helping people not only from Khovd, but also throughout Mongolia.

Mother Tārā Megjin Legzen is another Tārā from Khovd *aimag*. She was recognized at an early age by a renowned lama as an emanation of White

Tārā. Her father was also a lama. Even as a very young child, she was fond of performing prostrations and prayers. She is now sixty years old and has ten children. She describes her work in this way: "I personally do not do prayers. We have lamas in the temple. I ask them to do prayers. I help to heal sick children. I have helped many women to become pregnant and have also helped many people who underwent surgery in hospitals, but then did not receive further treatment. When I see a person, my instincts guide me. I do not believe in fortune telling. I think it is not true." Mother Tārā Megjin Legzen is also very actively involved in ecological concerns. She feels that the earth is being robbed of precious resources that are needed for its well-being. She has built a temple in Khovad Durgunsoum and has planted three thousand trees there in the past fifteen years. She teaches that human beings should love the earth like their own mother, reflecting the ecological concern that is endemic to the Mongolian worldview.

Ordinary Buddhist Women in a Time of Transition

In contrast to many cultures, women in Buddhist Mongolia have historically had the right to possess property and have had considerable economic, social, and sexual freedom. Women were valued both for their labor and as "reproducers of the nation," charged with the responsibility for ensuring both the biological and cultural continuity of the Mongol people.[3] They offered both their male children and the fruits of their labor to the monasteries. Today, many women in Mongolia are the sole or primary supporters of their families. Alcohol abuse, which has caused many men to be unreliable workers, is believed to be a major factor in the disproportionate responsibilities that Mongolian women currently shoulder.[4]

Factors impeding Buddhist women's development and leadership in Mongolia are similar to those affecting Buddhist women in other societies. Buddhist women's organizations are in need of support, but the major sources of that support are primarily in male hands—high-ranking Buddhist lamas, foreign organizations, and corporations. Mongolian Buddhist women receive the secular education they need to become breadwinners for their families, but they lack the Buddhist education they need to progress in their moral and spiritual life—educational resources that are also dominated by men.

In 2002, eight women were admitted to the Zanabazar Buddhist University, which was established in 1970 at Gandantegchenling, the largest monastery in Mongolia. After four years of studying Tibetan language, Mongolian language, and Buddhist texts, the women received diplomas certifying that they had completed the course. According to reports, for unknown reasons, women were not allowed to enroll in 2007 or 2008. In 2009, however, two of thirty students were women, and in 2010, four of seventy students were women. At present, ten of a total 150 students at the university are female. The number of female students seems to be curtailed, but I was unable to get a clear answer as to why.

It is also possible for women to study Buddhism at the National Mongolian University (NMU), either in the Department of Religious Studies in the School of Social Sciences, where 61 undergraduate and 32 graduate students are currently enrolled, or in the Center of Buddhist and Sanskrit Studies. Of the more than 160 students who have graduated from this department, more than 110 were women. Admission to the university is highly competitive, however, and expensive for most students. The curriculum is strongly oriented toward science and technology, and, as in many countries, the university is not structured to provide Buddhist education to a broad public. Buddhist women seek to learn about Buddhism not only because it will help them preserve their cultural heritage, but also because it will provide them with practical ways to deal with the enormous economic, social, and moral challenges they face in contemporary Mongolia. The Buddhist studies programs available at NMU, however, are accessible to only a few. Buddhism does not feature in the offerings of the School of Mongolian Language and Culture.

In their determination to learn more about Buddhism, Mongolian women are actively seeking alternatives. One example is Altentsetseg, a woman with a mission. She is determined to preserve Mongolia's Buddhist heritage in the remote countryside. She explains that Mongolia has 21 *aimag* (large provinces) and 368 *sum*s (smaller provinces). Zavkhan *aimag*, where she is from, has 24 *sum*s. Through a translator, she says,

> Almost ninety percent of the citizens in the countryside believe in the Buddha, but unfortunately they have lost the knowledge of how to protect the land, worship the local deities, and engage in Buddha training. After so many years of repression, people lack information and Buddhist practice centers. If they had information centers, it would not be difficult for them to develop themselves as the Buddha taught. My main purpose is to provide free education and opportunities for people in the countryside to develop themselves. I am ready to dedicate myself to humanity.
>
> Buddhism is the main ancient religion of Mongolia and we need to preserve it. Many people of other faiths now propagate their religions in Mongolia, especially in the cities and towns. They distribute clothes and food, and offer different kinds of training, in computer technology and English, free of charge. The Buddhists

do not have the good fortune to provide these resources, especially in the countryside, but there are many children who want
to learn. Few of them can afford to travel to the capital or larger
towns to study at the university. University studies are expensive
in Mongolia and herders in the countryside are poor.

Altentsetseg has set about assembling the resources she needs to propagate Buddhism in remote areas such as Zavkhan *aimag*. With the help of
friends, she applied for a donation of Buddhist books in English that are
published and distributed free of charge by the Buddha Educational Foundation in Taipei. Through sheer determination, she managed to get sponsorship
to attend the 13th Sakyadhita International Conference on Buddhist Women,
held in Vaishali, India, in January 2013. Without any knowledge of English
and on a shoestring budget, she traveled with three Mongolian friends to
learn more about the Buddhist teachings and how to present them to others.
Together, they chanted in Mongolian at the opening and closing ceremonies,
enthusiastically representing the Buddhist traditions of their country before
six hundred people from thirty-two countries.

The Future of Women in Mongolian Buddhism

Today in Mongolia, women are free to receive public Buddhist teachings,
to establish Buddhist organizations and centers, and to practice Buddhism,
whether as novice nuns, *ḍākinī*s, or ordinary laywomen. Full ordination as a
bhikṣuṇī, however, is still not an option.[5] Further, financial support for Buddhist women's endeavors is scarce, because all channels for development are
controlled by males, all of whom have their own priorities and would prefer
to have women support the temples and organizations that have already been
established by them, rather than branch out on their own. Historically, most
women have followed the path of least resistance and done exactly that.

Since Mongolia regained its national independence in 1990, however, a
number of women have asserted their independence and initiated Buddhist
practice centers of their own. These centers, located not only in Ulaanbaatar
but throughout the country, conduct services for the benefit of all sentient
beings and are situated squarely within the Mongolian Buddhist tradition. For
the most part, they are not advocating anything contrary to established Buddhist monasteries or organizations, but are simply seeking a more comfortable
place with greater opportunities within the traditional framework. They aspire
to create centers or temples where they can find their own voices, assert their
own agency, study Buddhist texts, and practice Dharma seriously, rather than
simply serve as donors and workers under the supervision of men.

Buddhist women have encountered many of the same challenges that other Mongolians have faced during the post-Soviet transitional period of political, economic, and social change. With "unemployment, poverty, growing disparities in income, declining educational, medical, and social welfare facilities, and reduced support for the arts, culture, and environmental protection,"[6] they have struggled to support their families and to achieve a level of income sufficient to survive the instability of a transitional economy. In charting an independent course, women have disproportionately experienced the burden of certain social problems: substance abuse, domestic violence, single parenting, and poverty. However, women in Mongolia enjoy some advantages that Buddhist women in other societies do not. Because women received free education during Soviet times, today 90 percent of women are reportedly literate. Women also gained representation in government, which empowered them.

At present, the centers and temples that women are creating are not perceived as being in competition with established monasteries and organizations. This is most likely because currently they are not yet powerful enough to be seen as threatening to male institutions. Even in the case of Dulmaaling, misgivings have more to do with protecting Mongolian Buddhist identity from Tibetan influences than with concerns about women's ascendancy. However, skepticism regarding the Buddhist clergy in the wake of moral lapses could increase the social and religious capital of well-behaved Buddhist women teachers and ritual specialists in the future. If and when women's practice centers become powerful enough to draw large numbers of Buddhist followers away from supporting traditional male monasteries and organizations, the dynamic will certainly change.

As of now, because of the limiting factors mentioned above, it is difficult to imagine women's practice centers becoming so powerful that they would be seen as threatening to monasteries. A far greater challenge is the appeal of well-funded, actively proselytizing Christian groups and nontraditional Buddhist organizations. Large, multinational Buddhist organizations such as Soka Gakkai International (SGI) and Friends of the Western Buddhist Order (FWBO) have strong international links and substantial funding and are already actively poised to become highly influential in Mongolia. If women are unable to gain access to Buddhist education and practice facilities and find comfortable spaces for their religious and social aspirations within the traditional Mongolian Buddhist framework, it is very likely that they will be attracted to international Buddhist organizations such as these, where their participation is valued as highly as men's. These well-organized, well-funded international groups are well aware of women's potential for the future development of Buddhism. In the face of these challenges, traditional Mongolian monasteries would do well to revise their thinking about women's participation. For their own survival, they must stop excluding women and limiting their access to material support by developing avenues for women to gain knowledge and take greater responsibility for the future of Mongolian Buddhism. To ignore this opportunity would be to squander the immense potential and genuine devotion of Mongolian women, a possibly fatal strategy for Mongolian Buddhist institutions.

As Buddhist institutions have regenerated and new monastic and cultural forms have emerged, Buddhist women have begun to take active roles in the religious and social renewal of their country. A host of unanswered questions remains, however, that necessitate a thorough study of Mongolian women's self-understanding in relation to Buddhist scholarship, practice, and institutions, including a survey of the resources currently available to women as well as what more will be required to ensure women's full participation in the regeneration of Buddhism in Mongolia. One starting point will be an examination of women's attitudes toward their historic exclusion from Buddhist institutions, with such questions as: In what ways are women aware of their systematic exclusion, in what ways are they complicit, and in what ways do they express resistance to the religious status quo? How are women currently working to transform their roles in Mongolian Buddhism in line with their newfound freedoms in a democratic society? In an age of religious pluralism, what attraction does Buddhism hold for women in Mongolia?

Although Mongolian women have never been in the Buddhist limelight before, that is beginning to change as they reenvision their roles within Mongolian Buddhism. Their struggle to gain access to the tools necessary for understanding their own religious traditions and their work to establish new religious communities by and for women will greatly increase their visibility. The methods used for this research project must combine ethnography with feminist analysis by asking such questions as: How do Mongolian women assess the extent of their own empowerment? How does the Buddhist establishment encourage or dissuade women in their activities? What are the main obstacles to women's advancement, and how can women become equal partners in reviving Mongolian Buddhist culture? How can women leverage democratization and the concomitant risks of cultural, economic, environmental, sexual, and religious upheaval and possible exploitation? The answers to these questions potentially hold the keys to ensuring Mongolian Buddhism's future.

Notes

1. Jeannine Davids-Kimball, "Katuns: The Mongolian Queens of the Genghis Khanite," in *Ancient Queens: Archaeological Explorations*, ed. Sarah Milledge Nelson (Walnut Creek, CA: Altamira Press, 2003), pp. 151–73.

2. C. R. Bawden, *The Modern History of Mongolia* (London: Kegan Paul International, 1989), pp. 139–41.

3. For example, Klaus Sagaster mentions that Jonggen Qatun and her husband, Sengge Dügureng, Qongtayji, who succeeded his father, Altan Khan, in 1582, invited the Dalai Lama from Eastern Tibet to Kökeqota to conduct the funeral services for his father. Klaus Sagaster, "The History of Buddhism among the Mongols," in *The Spread of Buddhism*, ed. Ann Heirman and Stephen Peter Bunbacher (Leiden: Brill, 2007), p. 399.

4. Karma Lekshe Tsomo, ed., *Buddhism in Transition: Tradition, Changes, and Challenges* (Ulaanbaatar: Sakyadhita, 2008).

5. Among the papers presented were: D. Burnee, "The Lives of Mongolian Buddhist Women, Past and Present"; Enkhmaa Chimed, "The Role of Buddhist Youth Organizations"; Tenzin Dolma, "The Older Generation of Mongolian Buddhist Nuns"; M. Gantuya, "Research on Mongolian Buddhist Women"; Thubten Kunze, "Mongolian Buddhist Women: 100 Years of History"; Danzan Narantuya, "Democratic Changes and the Conversion to Christianity;" D. Tungalag, "Mongolian Buddhist Families: Education and Tradition"; and Chuluuntsetseg Regzee, "The Role of the Media in Spreading Buddhist Thought."

6. Sagaster, "The History of Buddhism among the Mongols," in *The Spread of Buddhism*, ed. Ann Heirman and Stephen Peter Bunbacher (Leiden: Brill, 2007), pp. 403–4. Sagaster records that Buddhist stock went even higher when Neyiči Toyin cured a sick woman shaman and defeated another powerful shaman in the bargain.

7.

As far as female embodiments of Dara-ehe (Tārā) are concerned, I have seen only one of them, namely Tsagan-dara-ehe (White Tārā). The first encounter with this living goddess occurred in Uliastai [an important caravan town in western Mongolia, now in Zavkhan Province]. One day, while going along the street, I was surprised by a huge crowd around a Chinese shop. I was told that Dara-ehe visited this shop by invitation of the host. As this Chinese person was a good acquaintance of me, I passed easily to his room. Dara-ehe was sitting in the place of honor drinking tea and eating some sweets. This woman was about forty years old, not tall, and with a full figure; she was dressed in an ordinary robe made of blue cloth, with an ordinary head dress with a metallic *vajra* (Mongolian: *vachira*) at its center. After I sat down, I asked her about the purpose of her visit, where was she from, and so forth. She answered that her nomadic home was not far from Tzabhana, but that she had not been there for a long time since she was moving from place to place, by invitation, and was here because she wanted to buy a dress. After many other questions I discovered that she was an ordinary Mongolian woman without much education, even in Mongolian. She could not read or write, and by comparison with wives and daughters of the Khalkha princes, did not possess much knowledge.

None of my questions went unanswered, thanks to Lama Gelun, who accompanied her and helped respond to some of the questions.

For example, how do the Dörbets [a clan of the Oirat people] reconcile the existence of their Tsagan-Dara-ehe (White Tārā) with the fact that Tsagan-Dara-ehe is believed to reincarnate as the Russian tsars? When I asked her whether she had been to Russia, she was very surprised and looked toward the lama, who began to explain that this Tsagan-Dara-ehe is the physical embodiment of Dara-ehe that she reincarnated many times in Russia, and that was why, at those times, the Russian tsars were female. Now, the physical embodiment of Tsagan-Dara-ehe reincarnates among the nomadic Dörbets, but in Russia it is the spiritual embodiment of Tsagan-Dara-ehe that reincarnates and that is why the tsars became men. For the same reason, Naru-banchen-hutuhtu, who designated to the Dörbets the spiritual embodiments of Nogon-Dara-ehe (Green Tārā), could not designate to them the same embodiments of Tsagan-Dara-ehe (White Tārā), too.

The second encounter with Tsagan-Dara-ehe occurred on my way back to Russia. Near the Ulan-daba Pass in the Tsagan Shubutu Mountains, I saw six yurts, and two of them had a *ganchzhir* (a copper-gilded ornament usually found on top of *datsans*) for reference. The fringe on one of the doors was red, which indicated that it was a *kumirni*, the dwelling of an embodiment. The guide told me that it was the settlement of Tsagan-Dara-ehe. I approached with my acquaintance. In the yurt, I found Tsagan-Dara-ehe on her bed. Near the door, there were six ordinary Dörbets who had come to pay respect to her. Their conversation was quite ordinary: Tsagan-Dara-ehe asked each of them about their settlements, grass, cattle, the Dörbet people that she was acquainted with, recent events, and so on. Each Dörbet who entered the yurt first prostrated to Tsagan-Dara-ehe, then with great respect approached her for a blessing (*adiss*), just as they do with lamas. Each visitor presented her with a gift: one offered a sheep; another, a piece of butter; a third, a half block of green tea. The visitors were given cups of tea and ordinary conversation began. This may be the everyday life of Tsagan-Dara-ehe.

As I mentioned, there were six yurts: one of them was a *kumirni*; another was for Tsagan-Dara-ehe; in the third lived a *gelun* (monk); in the fourth were three *huvarak* (student monks); and in the fifth and the sixth were servants. In the *kumirni*, Tsagan-Dara-ehe performed prayer services if somebody requested her to. Tsagan-Dara-ehe herself does not read *noms* (sacred texts), but she is present at *khural* services, sitting on a special seat with five *olbokov* (carpets), flanked by a row of *burkhans* (sacred images) to her left.

This passage is introduced with an explanation about the history of the embodiments of White Tārā and Green Tārā among the Dörbets. These embodiments of "celestial virgins" were regarded as protectors or patrons of Buddhism. Some hoped that the Tārās would take male bodies, because women were not allowed to live in monasteries, but embodiment in female form was generally more successful. A. M.

Pozdneev, Очерки быта буддийских монастырей и буддийского духовенства в Монголии в связи с отношениями сего последнего к народу (Essays on the Life of Buddhist Monasteries and Buddhist Clergy in Mongolia and Relations of the Latter to the People) (St. Petersburg: Printing House of the Imperial Academy of Sciences, 1887; Reprint Elista, Kalmykia, Russian Federation: Kalmykskoye knizhnoye izdatel-stvo, 1993), pp. 235–38. English translation by Zhargal Aiakova.

8. Puntsag Dalam, quoted in Martha Avery, *Women of Mongolia* (Boulder, CO: Asian Art & Archaeology, 2000), p. 90.

9. Uradyn E. Bulag, *Nationalism and Hybridity in Mongolia* (Oxford: Clarendon Press, 1998), p. 123.

10. Kushok Bakula Rinpoche of Ladakh (1917–2003) was reputed to be the nineteenth incarnation of the *arhat* Bakula, one of Sakyamuni Buddha's sixteen core disciples. Bakula is one of the sixteen names included in the *Supplication to the Sixteen Arhats* text that is recited regularly in Tibetan monasteries and beyond. Before becoming the Indian ambassador to Mongolia, Bakula Rinpoche served as a member of the Indian Parliament, where he held a number of high posts, including head of the Minorities Commission. A young boy was recognized as his incarnation in Nubra, Ladakh, in 2005.

11. For more on *nyungne* (*smyung gnas*) practice and the remarkable nun who initiated it, see Ivette M. Vargas-O'Brian, "The Life of dGe slong ma dPal mo: The Experiences of a Leper, Founder of a Fasting Ritual, and Transmitter of Buddhist Teachings on Suffering and Renunciation in Tibetan Religious History," *Journal for the International Association of Buddhist Studies* 24:2(2001): 157–85.

12. Georges Dreyfus, "The Shuk-Den Affair: Origins of a Controversy," *Journal of the International Association of Buddhist Studies* 21:2(1998): 227–70.

13. Bulag, *Nationalism and Hybridity*, p. 149.

14. Inna, quoted in Avery, *Women of Mongolia*, p. 175.

15. Even in the more monastically inclined Tibetan tradition, which has been a source of Buddhist *vinaya* lineages for Mongolian monks since early times, there exists no lineage of *bhikṣuṇī* ordination to be transmitted.

16. Morris Mosabbi, *Modern Mongolia: From Khans to Commissars to Capitalists* (Berkeley: University of California Press, 2005), p. 8.

18

Mummy-la

The Life and Accomplishments of Freda Bedi

Tenzin Palmo

One of the complaints raised by women in contemporary Buddhist circles is the paucity of inspiring accounts of modern female practitioners. It was my privilege to have known an example of such a practitioner in Freda Bedi (Bhikṣuṇī Karma Khechog Palmo). It is unfortunate that, at the present time, her contributions are little remembered.

Freda was born in February 1911 in Derbyshire, England, to a middle-class family named Houlston. She was a bright and ambitious girl who attended Oxford University, where she obtained a master's degree in philosophy, politics, and economics. In her day, this was quite an accomplishment, because few young women were given the opportunity for a higher education. It is recalled that she helped a friend to study for the entrance exam to Oxford, then decided to sit for the entrance exam herself and passed! She was studying for a degree in economics when she met a fellow student named Baba Phare Lal Bedi, who was a scion of a notable Punjabi Sikh family that traced its ancestry back to the fifteenth-century spiritual leader Guru Nanak, founder of the Sikh tradition.

The young students fell in love and, despite opposition from both families, were determined to marry. Freda recalled that while the couple was making wedding plans, there was a debate in the British Parliament aimed at banning mixed-race marriages. The motion was vetoed.

During her time at Oxford, Freda had the opportunity to hear not only Mahatma Gandhi, who visited there in 1931, but also Rabindranath Tagore. Both of these figures, in their own unique ways, were deeply involved in the Indian movement to gain independence from British Colonial rule.

In the 1930s, Freda and Baba traveled to India, where they stayed for awhile with Baba's extended family. Later, she became a professor of English at a girls' college in pre-partition Lahore, now part of Pakistan. Both Freda and Baba were involved in Mahatma Gandhi's Satyagraha Indian National Independence movement and were imprisoned, along with their children, by the British authorities for leading demonstrations and other activities in the independence movement. Freda later wrote an account of her life in India and her days in jail titled *Behind the Mud Walls*.[1] In another book, *Bengal Lamenting*, she recounts her firsthand experience of the Bengal famine of 1943 that took more than one million lives.[2]

Following Indian independence, Freda Bedi went to work for the Indian government under Nehru, and in 1952, she was sent on a United Nations social services planning commission to Burma. She became enchanted by Burma and its Buddhist culture. She was fortunate to have the opportunity to study *vipassana* meditation under the great meditation masters Mahasi Sayadaw and U Thittila. During this time, her younger son, Kabir Bedi, who later became a well-known Bollywood film actor, received temporary ordination as a novice monk.[3]

In 1959, about eighty thousand refugees escaped from Tibet and settled in India and Nepal. In the beginning, many of these refugees stayed in Missamari Camp in Assam, a hot and steamy state on the northeastern border of India. The refugees arrived after having traveled for weeks and sometimes months over the high Himalayan mountain passes with little or no food and no road maps. At the camp in Missamari, they found themselves in a completely alien country, crowded together in extremely hot and unsanitary conditions. Many quickly succumbed to diseases such as dysentery, tuberculosis, and malaria. As the months went by, despair grew among the refugees, who questioned whether they would ever see an end to their suffering.

Finally, Freda Bedi, who was at that time in charge of the Central Government's Social Welfare Board, directed by Nehru, was dispatched to Missamari to sort out the chaos in the camps and start organizing an evacuation. Among the thousands of people crowded into these camps were many eminent Tibetan lamas (Buddhist teachers). At the time of this ordeal, no distinctions were made between high and low, rich and poor. All the refugees in the camps were leveled by their common predicament. Freda recognized that many of these refugees were important lamas. Years later, she could still recall their names, backgrounds, the histories of their escapes, and many interesting stories about their time in the camps. It is remarkable that in the confusion of those days and even with no knowledge of Buddhism or Tibetan Buddhist practice lineages, she could distinguish whom among them were the renowned lamas.

Freda dedicated herself to social welfare activities and had a great talent for organizing other people's lives for them. If people were undecided about what to do or where to go, "Mummy-la," as she became affectionately known, would arrange a connection with some distant acquaintance and help people start new lives, often in unexpected directions. With such a talent, she was the perfect person to reorganize and empty the camps. Every day she interviewed endless queues of people and arranged for them to be sent to friends or families in other towns in India, such as Kalimpong or Darjeeling. So many lamas and laypeople fondly remember Freda coming to their camps and arranging their transfer to more moderate climates. During this period, an Indian diplomat named Apa Pant urged Freda to meet His Holiness the 16th Gyalwa Karmapa. She became the Karmapa's devoted student.

In 1962, Freda founded the Young Lamas Home School in Delhi. She had the foresight to see that Buddhism would become a worldwide phenomenon even at a time when Tibetan Buddhism was generally seen as too exotic, esoteric, and complex to ever gain more than a limited appeal in the West. Western Buddhism at this time was still quite staid and orthodox, before the hippie era of the 1960s and 1970s when everyone seemed high on LSD and in love with colorful tantric visualizations. However, Freda believed that the Tibetan tradition of Vajrayāna Buddhism would spread in the West and that the people to transmit it there would be the *tülkus* (incarnate lamas), because they had been trained from early childhood to become Dharma teachers. To preach the Dharma, these young lamas would need to know English, because this is the global language. But it was of no use to simply send these young boys to English-medium schools, because they also needed to be trained in Buddhist philosophy and ritual. Recognizing this, Freda founded her own institute called the Young Lamas Home School, where young incarnate lamas of all lineages could stay and study with learned professors of their own traditions. At the same time, they could learn English from any backpacking Western volunteer, including the American beat poet Allen Ginsberg, who happened to turn up!

The school began in Delhi, with Chogyam Trungpa Rinpoche and Akong Rinpoche among the first students. Within a year or so, the school was transferred to the cooler climate of Dalhousie, a quiet Himalayan hill station in what was then the Punjab. In early 1964, I went to Dalhousie as a volunteer. For the next few months, I was Freda's secretary as well as an English teacher for the beginners' class. Lama Zopa Rinpoche was also a pupil at that time—indeed, many of the great lamas who later came to the West began their English lessons at the Young Lama's Home School.

In addition to this school for privileged *tülkus*, Freda also founded the first Buddhist nunnery for Tibetan women refugees in India. This nunnery was later transferred to Trilokpur, where it still exists. This was twenty years before anyone else thought about the plight of nuns, much less built nunneries for them. Again, Freda demonstrated her prescience and her talent for being ahead of the crowd.

Freda was tall and, by this time, heavily built. She wore a maroon sari and kept her well-oiled gray hair tied back in a bun. She had piercing blue eyes and was the quintessential *memsahib*, whose imperious manner quelled even high lamas. Nonetheless, she was kind, humorous, and very devoted to both the Dharma and the great lamas. At this time, she was affectionately known to all as Mummy-la.

In 1966, Freda received the novice (*śrāmaṇerikā*) ordination from the 16th Gyalwa Karmapa, who was living at Rumtek Monastery in Sikkim. Henceforth, she was known as Karma Khechog Palmo, or Sister Palmo, and dressed in the traditional robes of a nun. In 1972, Khechog Palmo went to Hong Kong and became one of the first English women to receive *bhikṣuṇī* ordination. Again, she demonstrated her fearlessness in taking what was at that time considered to be a most unusual step.

Karma Khechog Palmo moved to Rumtek Monastery, where she assisted Gyalwa Karmapa in his various projects and also translated some basic prayers and practices into English. She was instrumental in arranging for Gyalwa Karmapa to be invited to the West, especially to the United States, and accompanied him on his first visit there. This visit generated enormous interest, and many new centers were opened as a result. Further tours to Canada and Europe followed, including a meeting with Pope Paul VI in Rome. In addition, she visited South Africa on several occasions to spread the Dharma, and she is still fondly remembered there today.

During these early days of Buddhism spreading to the West, very few books on Tibetan Buddhism had been reliably translated into English, and very few lamas spoke fluent English. As a result, studying the Dharma was a challenge for Westerners, and especially for women, who were traditionally discounted and disregarded by the tradition. One reason why Karma Khechog Palmo was so wonderful was that no one could overlook *her*! Indeed, most lamas were somewhat in awe of her. She was not accustomed to being subservient and was usually the one to give the orders! Of course, by this time she was already an older woman, which made her dominance more socially acceptable. She was also great fun and a wonderful source of Tibetan lama gossip.

Khechog Palmo spent several years as the only woman in residence at Rumtek Monastery in Sikkim. There, she was close to Gyalwa Karmapa and the many high incarnate lamas who were studying at Rumtek. She spent her time in retreat and doing translation work. She was definitely a pioneer, and directly influenced the lives of many lamas of that earlier generation who contributed to the establishment of the Vajrayāna Buddhist tradition in the West.

Khechog Palmo passed away in March 1977. It is said that she has been reborn as the daughter of Beru Khyentse Rinpoche, a Karma Kagyu lama. This may be the only occasion of a Westerner taking rebirth as a Tibetan *tülku*, as opposed to a Tibetan lama being reborn as a Westerner.

Some time ago, Khechog Palmo's oldest son wrote to me suggesting that his mother's biography be written down and published. I recommended various possible authors, and eventually Vicki Mackenzie was selected as most suitable. Vicki has written several popular biographies of Buddhist teachers and is the author of my own biography, *Cave in the Snow*. She recently completed her work on this important biography of Khechog Palmo, who played such an integral part in the early narrative of the Tibetan refugee experience in India and whose contribution needs to be remembered.[4] Far too many accomplished Buddhist women have been lost to memory because their stories were never written down. Thankfully, such a fate does not await the extraordinary and important Dharma practitioner Khechog Palmo.

Notes

1. Freda Bedi, *Behind the Mud Walls* (Lahore: Unity Publications, 1940).
2. Freda Bedi, *Bengal Lamenting* (Lahore: Lion Publication, 1944).
3. A collection of the Indian nursery rhymes that she wrote for her older son has recently been published. Freda Bedi, *Rhymes for Rango* (Delhi: Random House India, 2010).
4. In the meantime, a biography of Khechog Palmo has been published. See Sheila Fugard, *Lady of Realisation: A Spiritual Memoir* (Bloomington, IN: Balboa Press, 2012).

BUDDHIST WOMEN IN
THE WEST

19

Bhikṣuṇī Ruimiao

An Embodiment of Transcultural Values

Malia Dominica Wong

Bhikṣuṇī Ruimiao is not well known in current history, but her life's work as a Buddhist nun has had a profound effect on myriad lives around the world. She worked tirelessly to realize her vision for global Buddhist education, and she never wavered in her effort to spread Buddhist education beyond the constraints of race, ethnicity, class, gender, generation, language, educational level, and even religion. Bhikṣuṇī Ruimiao's accomplishments provide us with a stunning example of how transculturalization can enrich the lives of people everywhere. She believed that the Dharma transcends all, meets in the hearts of all, is for the benefit of all, helps alleviate the suffering of all, and brings peace to society. Her teachings and goals are passed on today through the lives and activities of the many people she has educated and nurtured. This is the story of Bhikṣuṇī Ruimiao, the first Chinese *bhikṣuṇī* to teach Dharma in Manila and Hawai'i, presented here through the lenses of three different generations. The narrative explores the transcultural challenges she faced as well as the many triumphs she achieved and, above all, how the efforts of this outstanding Buddhist nun continue today through a contemporary legacy.

Early Influences

Bhikṣuṇī Ruimiao's roots extend back to her grandfather's village in Fujian, China. The successful tradition of overseas mercantilism in that region had sown the seeds of adventure and unlimited business possibilities in the local soil. The wealthy, culturally diverse port of Quanzhou nearby was known for its large size and many seafaring visitors, among them Marco Polo, as far back as the late thirteenth century. A strong tradition of education gave rise to many of China's most noteworthy scholars, statesmen, and military leaders during the Ming Dynasty (1368–1644) and Qing Dynasty (1644–1911). This was the world of her ancestors, which would foster the values of respect for diversity, breadth of vision, educational focus, and charismatic leadership that Bhikṣuṇī Ruimiao came to live by. However, there were also growing political tensions in the country, especially during the period between the Chinese Revolutions of 1911 and 1949.

Ruimiao's parents were enterprising and ran a successful business importing native goods and food products from the Philippines. After some years, they set sail for the Philippines, where they established a branch of their expanding business. In 1922, in Manila, Ruimiao was born as the youngest of six children (three boys and three girls) and spent her early childhood in the Philippines. As a young girl, however, she was sent to Hong Kong for education. In the course of her studies, she learned of the tumultuous aftermath of the Chinese Revolution of 1911: how warlords had divided the land into fiefdoms that were corrupt and exploitative and, as a result, how the majority of the Chinese people had become impoverished, which eventually led to the communist revolution. Listening to the stories of all these hardships profoundly influenced Ruimiao's gentle heart and instilled in her a wish to alleviate the sufferings of sentient beings.

Once her schooling was completed, Ruimiao returned to her grandfather's homeland of Fujian, where she began a career as an elementary school teacher. The young schoolchildren in her care not only gained academic knowledge from her, but also learned the subtle transcultural skills she had developed from the fusion of her experiences in the Philippines, Hong Kong, and China. She shared with the children the three different cultures, languages, and traditions that had broadened her perspective on life.

It was during this period that her desire to study Buddhism was kindled. One day, while on an outing with the students, she noticed a temple in the distance with a monk walking slowly by, his robe flowing on the breath of the wind. To her, he seemed to be at peace and in harmony with his surroundings, and the image stayed with her. Soon after, Ruimiao returned to Hong Kong and enrolled in a Buddhist college.

In Hong Kong, she had the privilege to study the *Huayen Sūtra* under the guidance of Master Hongyi's famous artist monk attendant, Miaolian. It was during a retreat under his guidance that she experienced moments of complete peace and serenity and became determined to become a nun. She took refuge with her teacher, Bhikṣuṇī Zhilin, the abbess of Cihang Jing Yuan in Hong Kong, and later furthered her studies in Buddhism at Dong Lian

Jue Yuan (Enlightenment Garden of the Eastern Lotus). After her novice (śrāmaṇerikā) ordination, she received bhikṣuṇī ordination in 1952 at the age of twenty-five.

In 1954, Bhikṣuṇī Ruimiao left Hong Kong and returned to the Philippines. Her goal was to introduce Buddhist education to the world by sharing the Buddha's teachings and helping people allay their suffering. She also wanted to build a Pure Land in this world by helping others learn to purify their minds, which would in turn bring peace to society. In a war-ravaged era, peace was a strong ideal.

After arriving in Manila, under the purple shadows of the Mariveles Mountains, Bhikṣuṇī Ruimiao began teaching high school students. In 1958, she made a public appeal for funds to establish a Buddhist temple and by 1960, utilizing the ethic of hard work instilled in her by her entrepreneurial parents, she realized her dream, and Che Wan Temple opened. As the first bhikṣuṇī ever in the Philippines, she was a pioneer, and her Chinese-Filipino following grew quickly. Sometimes more than three hundred people, hungry for the Dharma, would attend her dynamic teachings, and on special occasions, the numbers swelled to more than a thousand! Her motivation is beautifully captured in this verse from the Metta Sutta on how to cultivate "loving kindness towards all the world":

> One should cultivate an unbounded mind,
> above and below and across,
> without obstruction, without enmity, without rivalry.
> "Standing, or going, or seated, or lying down,
> as long as one is free from drowsiness,
> one should practice this mindfulness.
> This, they say, is the holy state here."[1]

Global Dharma Family

For Bhikṣuṇī Ruimiao, Che Wan Temple was only the beginning. She began to take the Buddha's teachings beyond established borders and became a builder of cultural bridges. By 1968, she ventured out over even more distant mountains and seas to visit California and observe yet another way of life. After a short time, her travels took her to Hawai'i, where she settled in a spot in Kaimuki on the island of Oahu, framed by the lush Ko'olau mountain range. Her global vision led her to construct a temple there, Jade Buddha Temple, a project that was formally completed in 1974.

Bhikṣuṇī Ruimiao's reputation as a teacher of Buddhism continued to grow and spread from Hawai'i. For example, one year she was invited to Taiwan to help lead a retreat and to be part of a quorum for an ordination ceremony.[2] There, she came to know a young devotee who was very conscientiously dedicated to temple service. With her previous teacher's blessing, this devotee became Bhikṣuṇī Jing Ping, Bhikṣuṇī Ruimiao's first disciple. Later, responding to a conference invitation in Malaysia, she met a laywoman (*upāsikā*) named Jing Ru who was serving the attendees by folding clothes. Though no words were exchanged, their eyes met each time Bhikṣuṇī Ruimiao passed the laundry room. On the third day, when Bhikṣuṇī Ruimiao was ready to depart for Manila, she asked Jing Ru if she would like to become a nun. Jing Ru responded positively and later followed Bhikṣuṇī Ruimiao to the Philippines, where she became known as Bhikṣuṇī Jing Ru. Later, three other women, from Malaysia, the Philippines, and Hong Kong, also dedicated themselves to the monastic path and received ordination, following in their teacher's footsteps.

As news of Jade Buddha Temple in Hawai'i spread, its membership grew. Followers from Taiwan, China, Hong Kong, Malaysia, and the Philippines found a Dharma home away from home. Even though Bhikṣuṇī Ruimiao spoke only a little English, Europeans, mainland Americans, and island locals were drawn to this humble and intriguing *bhikṣuṇī*. Koreans, Vietnamese, and Burmese were likewise drawn to her wise and compassionate, down-to-earth teachings, even when she mixed Tagalog, Cantonese, Mandarin, and English in the same breath!

Students at the University of Hawai'i campus in Manoa Valley and people of other faiths—Taoists, Christians, and Hindus—began to learn more about the Buddhist path through this approachable *bhikṣuṇī* in their midst. Bhikṣuṇī Ruimiao never turned people away and never saw anyone as being "different." At Jade Buddha Temple in Kaimuki, Bhikṣuṇī Ruimiao also received with most gracious hospitality many Dharma leaders from various traditions, including the 16th Gyalwa Karmapa; Master Xuanhua from the City of Ten Thousand Buddhas; Bhikṣuṇī Wuyin, the leader and founder of Xiangguang (the largest *bhikṣuṇī* training institute in Taiwan); and Karma Lekshe Tsomo, founder of Jamyang Foundation and Sakyadhita International Association of Buddhist Women. With her generous and inclusive vision, she also helped facilitate the opening of the Hawai'i branch of Tzu Chi Foundation, Taiwan's largest Buddhist charity.

The second generation of her new Dharma family in Hawai'i witnessed Bhikṣuṇī Ruimiao's global adaptability and cultural sensitivity as a pioneering citizen of the world. In dedicating herself fully to the spread of the Dharma, she overcame attachment to any one place and embodied her multicultural identity, touching hearts beyond ethnicity, age, creed, education, and language. All who had the good fortune to be in her presence recognized in her the possibility of a life without attachment to suffering and the ability of a human being to walk with serenity. Her principal teaching of *miao de*, the cultivation of wisdom to gain clear understanding, was the key to her spiritual attainment.

Not everyone is always able to transcend his or her own cultural bias or to step into the shoes of another in order to embrace the universality of Buddhist principles. Sometimes language and provincial thinking get in the way, and some of the second-generation followers dropped out. Disagreements arose over matters as simple as which foods to prepare. Some disciples returned to their home countries to begin their own temples. It is through the dynamism and devotion of Bhikṣuṇī Jing Ping and Bhikṣuṇī Jing Ru, her first two disciples, that Bhikṣuṇī Ruimiao's "Buddhism beyond borders" has continued at Jade Buddha Temple in Hawai'i.

Transcultural Path Makers

Buddhism itself is a transnational phenomenon and has migrated deftly from one culture to another.[3] Buddhist teachings such as the following are universal and seem to apply to all:

> Do not think of the past.
> Do not worry about the future.
> Things of the past have died.
> The future has not arrived.
> What is happening in the present
> should be observed deeply.
> The Wise Ones live according to this
> and dwell in stability and freedom.
> If one practices the teachings
> of the Wise Ones,
> why should one be afraid of death?
> If we do not understand this
> there is no way to avoid
> the great pain of the final danger.
> To practice diligently day and night,
> one should regularly recite
> the Bhaddekaratta Gatha.[4]

Bhikṣuṇī Jing Ping, with clarity of intention, left her homeland of Taiwan in 1986 to come to Hawai'i and study with Bhikṣuṇī Ruimiao. At Jade Buddha Temple, she and Bhikṣuṇī Jing Ru, along with a growing number of followers, helped spread the Dharma through a variety of civic and public programs that the temple organized and presented. Although, like Bhikṣuṇī Ruimiao, they spoke little English, they strongly communicated their ability to look beyond illusory cultural limitations and the occasional complications of language to the universality of Dharma. In the hustle and bustle of Honolulu's China-town, they founded Miao De (Wonderful Virtue) as an outreach project of Jade Buddha Temple. At Miao De, transcending mere words, they welcomed everyone to stop in for a cup of Dharma and find guidance through their suffering, based on the Buddha's way.

Bhikṣuṇī Ruimiao often expressed her dream of returning to the Philip-pines to build a school where young people could get a good education and also learn about Buddhism. Every year, she returned to lay the groundwork for the school and eventually devoted all her time to the project. With com-plete dedication and selflessness, she exhausted herself and went into a coma from which she never awoke.

Following Bhikṣuṇī Ruimiao's death at Che Wan Temple in the Philip-pines in 1998, Bhikṣuṇī Jing Ping stepped up as the new leader of the Buddhist group. In 2005, she fulfilled Bhikṣuṇī Ruimiao's dream to "spread the Dharma and teach ethics and values to Filipinos in their native land" by establishing Miao De Chan Temple in Tagaytay, a scenic spot an hour from Manila. Even though most of the population of the Philippines is Christian, the Buddha's teachings are for everyone. Because most Filipinos are poor and cannot afford education, Bhikṣuṇī Jing Ping's classes are free and the students are provided with good meals as well as lessons.

Over the years, Bhikṣuṇī Jing Ping has taken on the role of student, just as Bhikṣuṇī Ruimiao did, in trying to learn the language of the host culture. With a bit of English, she has adapted the *sūtra*s in Chinese to con-temporary melodies to make it easier for young Filipinos to learn Buddhism. Many students have already mastered both the English and Chinese chanting. Bhikṣuṇī Jing Ping teaches students in Chinese, interpreted into English, about the Buddhist principle of cause and effect and Pure Land thought. It is not easy to challenge patterns developed through a long history of coloniza-tion, identity struggle, social dislocation, poverty, and ethical contradictions. If a child's parents and relatives are in the habit of stealing and cheating to make a living, the child will have difficulty learning the difference between right and wrong. Lacking good moral examples, many children are inclined to perpetuate the unethical conduct and harm modeled by those around them.

How does she fund these programs? Jing Ping always says, "Just do it." Many devotees in Hawai'i have helped to support the programs and continue to do so. She is confident that the Buddhas and *bodhisattva*s will provide.

The programs that Bhikṣuṇī Jing Ping has initiated in the Philippines include three-day winter and summer training programs, a two-month sum-mer intensive Buddhist training, a Buddhist scholarship program for college students, a semimonthly community outreach education program for children and adults, and other group activities. She has also initiated a yearly citywide program of bringing Buddhism into the malls and closer to the people, and established two charity clinics that provide basic health care and dental care. These clinics distribute medicine to more than one hundred patients each week and also distribute groceries and rice to those in need twice a year. This highly educated nun who dearly cherished solitary meditation left the stillness of her own temple in Taiwan to make the Dharma more available in the Philippines. Her students continue to be inspired by her creativity and intelligence and are already becoming models of community service as volunteer teachers.

Bhikṣuṇī Jing Ping's own disciples, the third generation, hail from Vietnam, Burma, Taiwan, and China. All of them are familiar with the challenges of cultural identity and reorientation.[5] The stories of their immigration to the United States and other lands reveal some of the shifts and adaptations they made. "What's a carrot?" Bhikṣuṇī Yin Sheng asked when she arrived in the United States from Burma and found her first job in food services. Another, Bhikṣuṇī Yin Jue, recalled that as a child refugee arriving in Hawai'i from Vietnam, "I felt like an orphan dressed in Goodwill clothing." She adds, with a chuckle, "My friend Yin Liu from Taiwan was just curious when she heard that Yin Guan and I were going to cut our hair and become nuns. Once she came up to the temple on the mountaintop, though, she didn't want to leave. A few months later, she returned to the temple, but her parents came to take her home and locked her up. Then she ran away to the temple again!" This story reveals the cross-generational challenges that often face young women who want to become nuns when their parents have other plans for them. Unconventional by any definition, these third-generation nuns are now creating transcultural pathways of their own.

Traditionally, Asian temples in the United States have served two purposes: first, as cultural centers where immigrants gather to preserve their heritage, and second, as religious centers that minister to new arrivals' spiritual needs. At Jade Buddha Temple in Hawai'i, however, following Bhikṣuṇī Ruimiao's example, second- and third-generation nuns reach out to anyone who wants to learn more about Buddhism, and they serve a wide swath of the community. Members of the temple there are engaged in community service activities. For example, twice a month they visit Palolo Chinese Home to support elderly Buddhists in their Dharma practice, and they also contribute to many charitable foundations. The temple runs daily adult education classes for a small group and weekly classes for a larger group that incorporate study, chanting, meditation practice, and open dialogue about the *sūtra*s. Dharma cultivation (*ba guan zhai*) is held once a month to study the precepts. For the young, there are weekly classes (*di zi gui*) to learn Chinese and discuss good conduct. The temple has an extensive collection of Dharma videos that are available to the community at any time. Members of the temple work with the Buddhist Peace Fellowship and the Hawai'i Association of International Buddhists (with members from the Japanese, Tibetan, Theravāda, Chinese, Korean, American, Vietnamese, and other Buddhist traditions) to provide open public forums and Buddhist education to the public. The temple's activities are continually expanding. The temple also supports Sakyadhita International Association for Buddhist Women, whose conferences are transcultural experiences in themselves.

Transcending Time and Space

The path toward transculturation modeled by Bhikṣuṇī Ruimiao (the first generation) had as its clear goal the spread of Dharma to all who wished to learn. The guiding principle of Bhikṣuṇī Jing Ping (the second generation) was "Just do it," whether it be studying an unfamiliar language or devising new methods to communicate values. The style of the third generation is to develop confidence, ask questions, and express progressive ideas, for example, the idea of making things more eco-friendly and aesthetically pleasing. Buddhist women of this new generation are even more outgoing and intrepid than their predecessors. These heirs of a uniquely transnational, female Dharma lineage are not afraid to speak broken Chinese, English, Korean, Vietnamese, or Tagalog. They are comfortable discussing the Dharma in many diverse settings with all kinds of people. They take time to stroll serenely, letting the wind gently blow them and the seeds of Dharma into new and unimagined spaces. In Hawai'i, we say,

> A'ohe hana nui ka alu'ia.
> No task is too big when done together.

Notes

1. The popularly recited *Metta Sutta* is found in the Sutta Nipata, translated into English by K. R. Norman, *The Group of Discourses* (2nd ed.) (Oxford: Pali Text Society, 2001), pp. 143–52.
2. For the ordination of a *bhikṣuṇī* in the Chinese Dharmagupta *vinaya* tradition, a quorum of ten *bhikṣus* and ten *bhikṣuṇīs* is required. For the ordination of a *bhikṣu*, only a quorum of ten *bhikṣus* is required.
3. Surprisingly little research has been done on the transmission of Buddhism to Hawai'i, especially Chinese Buddhism. Partial accounts include Louise H. Hunter, *Buddhism in Hawaii: Its Impact on a Yankee Community* (Honolulu: University of

Hawai'i Press, 1971); and Michihiro Ama, *Immigrants to the Pure Land: The Modernization, Acculturation, and Globalization of Shin Buddhism, 1898–1941* (Honolulu: University of Hawai'i Press, 2011). The introduction of Buddhism to Hawai'i is also documented in "Aloha Buddha," a video produced by Lorraine Minatoishi and directed by Bill Ferehawk and Dylan Robertson (2011).

4. Thich Nhat Hanh, *Awakening of the Heart: Essential Buddhist Sutras and Commentaries* (Berkeley: Parallax Press, 2012), p. 257.

5. A new genre of literature is developing around stories of cultural location and dislocation. See, for example, Larry Yu and Valerie Katagiri, eds., *Where Are You From? An Anthology of Asian American Writing* (Portland: Thymos, 2012). Also see Carol E. Kelly, *Accidental Immigrants and the Search for Home: Women, Cultural Identity, and Community* (Philadelphia: Temple University Press, 2013).

20

What Is a Relevant Role Model?

The Example of an Ordinary Woman Who Achieved Enlightenment

Rita M. Gross

When we think of notable Buddhist women, we tend to think of famous women who stand out and are unusual in their accomplishments, so unusual that they have been remembered by later generations. When we think about it, we realize that most women have no chance of becoming such notable women, that is, of doing something so outstanding or extraordinary that they will be remembered for generations to come.

Yet throughout the current Buddhist women's movement, there has been a longing for female role models, for stories of women practitioners that would stand beside all the stories of the great male practitioners who have been remembered throughout Buddhist history. The longing for such stories is especially relevant for practitioners of Tibetan Buddhism because it has an especially strong tradition of retelling spiritual biographies and autobiographies and then relying on them for personal inspiration. We want these stories because we intuitively recognize the importance of learning about people who have actually completed the Buddhist path as inspiration for our own practice.

As women, we not only want such stories about women, but *need* them because they reassure us that this practice tradition is not just for men—that it is truly relevant for women who are not content to play only subsidiary roles as donors and supporters; women who are not content merely to be mothers and consorts of revered male saints, but want to have some input into the unfolding of Buddhist practice and tradition. We want these stories to assure ourselves that Buddhism's promised fruition of enlightenment is possible for women. We desperately need these stories because so many texts and so many threads of the tradition have told us that women have an "unfortunate rebirth," and that the best we can do in our lives as women is to accrue the karma to attain a future, more fortunate rebirth as a male in which practicing for realization would be more realistic. But what self-respecting woman who appreciates her "precious birth as a human being" would give her life energy to such a religious system? The stories of men, who have never had to face rampant prejudice against them as practitioners simply because of their sex, are only of limited relevance to women, who *do* have to face such prejudice. Given those realities, stories about men simply are not sufficiently inspiring for us. We need to solve the problem of the seeming lack of suitable, inspiring stories about female role models.

Part of the problem stems from the fact that the very few stories we do have about women are about incredibly outstanding women such as Yeshe Tsogyel[1] and Machig Labdron.[2] What could be wrong with that situation, one might wonder? These women were truly outstanding practitioners and innovators. It could be claimed that Yeshe Tsogyel was the first Tibetan to become enlightened and that she had as much to do with the establishment of Buddhism in Tibet as anyone. It is sometimes said of Machig Labdron that she was the only Tibetan to initiate practices that went back to India. Such outstanding women are surely worthy and inspiring role models. What more could women possibly want or need? Indeed, in my quest for female role models, I have written extensively about Yeshe Tsogyel[3] and to a lesser extent about Machig Labdron as great heroes of Tibetan Buddhism, as role models who could encourage us on our own paths. Yeshe Tsogyel in particular has been very inspiring to me in the way that she solved several problems that present great difficulties for contemporary women.

But is there some contradiction between our longing for stories of notable Buddhist women—our longing for female role models—and the reality of our own, ordinary lives? After all, very few of us have the capability to "make history" to any great extent. Yeshe Tsogyel, Machig Labdron, and others like them may have been women, but how realistic are they as role models for us? They were also outstanding practitioners whose accomplishments match those of the most outstanding male heroes of the tradition, such as Milarepa, Longchenpa, or Jigme Lingpa, and are far above the expectations most of us could have for ourselves. What about us? Does Buddhist tradition only provide a few stories about women who are so outstanding that they are not realistic role models for most of us?

For women, who have few role models beyond women such as Yeshe Tsogyel and Machig Labdron, the existence of those few outstanding role models can easily become mere tokenism, which is in some ways worse than having no stories at all about such women. Tokens hold out the false promise that people like us might be able to emulate their success, even though an impenetrable glass ceiling for more ordinary women is firmly in place. Furthermore, with a few tokens in place, those in power often claim that there are no problems with the system at all, that it is perfectly fair and open and that if we were good enough, we too could somehow penetrate the glass ceiling and enter the realms of the Yeshe Tsogyels and Machik Labdrons. I have often heard the feminist call for the transformation of Buddhist institutions so that they would be more equitable for all those rejected on just such grounds. It is claimed that the existence of a few token female role models proves that there is nothing wrong with male-dominated Buddhist institutions, and nothing but my own inadequacies prohibits me from joining their ranks.

Is there a record of women who, while not as outstanding as Yeshe Tsogyel or Milarepa, nevertheless are counted as worthy practitioners who became enlightened and contributed to the development of their lineages? Contemporary scholars, many of them women, are much more interested in that question than were previous generations of scholars and practitioners. Each year, more materials emerge from obscure manuscript sources and contemporary field research. Given the amount of information that turns up when scholars search for it in a concerted way, one can only wonder how much more has been lost, presumably forever in the more distant past. What difference do such materials make for contemporary Buddhist women?

I have always been keenly interested in the topic of female role models and have frequently declared that the presence of female role models and teachers is the litmus test for whether or not Buddhism is overcoming its sexist past in its current manifestations.[4] A new development is that recently, in workshops on female role models in Tibetan Buddhism, along with highlighting stories about Yeshe Tsogyel, I have begun to focus on the autobiography of a much more ordinary but nevertheless realized practitioner, a woman named Orgyen Chökyi. I do this because I have begun to believe that part of the problem with a lack of female role models is that our expectations for these role models are unrealistically high.

These two narratives contrast significantly, and it is interesting to contemplate which woman is more inspiring to oneself, and why. Some continue to prefer the glamour and magic of Yeshe Tsogyel, whose life would undoubtedly make the more dramatic feature film, but others react with relief to the story of a woman who is very much like ourselves in many ways but who, nevertheless, achieved realization during her relatively short life, even though she was never famous and was virtually forgotten soon after her death. I am comforted by having found a story of a woman who shared many of the frustrations I have experienced in my own life. I find that I can actually identify much more with such a role model than with someone like Yeshe Tsogyel.

Orgyen Chökyi lived from 1675 to 1729 in present-day Nepal. But who is she? Though several manuscripts of her life story survived in Himalayan libraries and she was somewhat well known in her home region, she was completely unknown to Westerners until the recent translation of her autobiography, *Himalayan Hermitess*, by Kurtis Schaeffer.[5] Her story first surfaced to a Western scholar in 1961. In an account published in 1975, the anthropologist Cornielle Jest narrates that while he was doing fieldwork in the Dolpo region of Nepal, a local Buddhist leader told him about a locally well-known woman, "Ani Chökyi," who had lived some time ago. (How long ago was unknown to the local leader, and the anthropologist did not inquire further about her.) The local leader told a story about her that matches to some extent the narrative found in her autobiography but differs from it in other significant details and glamorizes her life more than does her own autobiography.[6] Beyond mentioning the conversation, the anthropologist did nothing more with her story and did not follow up on local leads as to where a copy of the manuscript of her autobiography could be found. By the time Kurtis Schaeffer was doing his research, a number of manuscript copies of her autobiography had been located and preserved.

Setting her story side by side with that of Yeshe Tsogyel is a study in contrasts.[7] There is no narrative about her previous lives, and she was not blessed with a miraculous conception and birth, nor did she enjoy a privileged childhood, as did Yeshe Tsogyel. She was the daughter of parents who wanted a son, and, because of their disappointment in getting a daughter instead, they treated her badly, beginning with the name she was given—Kyilo, or "Happiness Dashed." Both her father and her mother abused her so severely that local monks and nuns intervened and reprimanded her parents on several occasions. Her mother tried to teach her to weave, but she was not very successful at learning weaving and was punished for her failures.

Then, when she was eleven, she was sent to herd goats, *dzomo* (a cross between a yak and a cow), and, at age twenty, horses. During her experiences of herding animals, she frequently witnessed the death of animals under her care and grieved bitterly over the suffering both of young animals seized by eagles or leopards and the suffering of the bereft mother animals. Two themes emerged from these experiences. First, the local monastics commented that because she had so much spontaneous pity for the animals, she had the capacity to develop great compassion if she received religious training. In fact, apparently while still a teenager, she entered the religious life and her hair was cut, though she continued to herd animals as well. Second, watching these animal mothers and children filled her with great revulsion for the female form and gender role, a theme that persisted in a very strong manner almost until the end of her life. Two examples of her songs of revulsion regarding femaleness are clear:

> When I ponder our female bodies
> I am sorrowful: impermanence rings clear.
> When men and women couple—creating more life—
> Happiness is rare, but suffering is felt for a long time.
> May I not be born again in a female body.
> May the mare not be born as a mare.
> The steed follows yet another mare.
> When I see the shamelessness of men,
> [I think] May I be born in a body that will sustain the precepts.[8]

A page later, she is even clearer:

> I could do without this female body with its misery. . . .
> The female body is itself *samsāra*—the round of existence.
> May I attain a male body and keep the vows.
> May I never again be born in the body of a woman![9]

Like Yeshe Tsogyel, Chökyi did have some spiritual vocation. As already narrated, she joined a local religious community in her youth, but unlike Yeshe Tsogyel, she had no glamorous teacher and consort who singled her out for special treatment and thorough training. Nevertheless, she did receive instruction in the fundamentals of Tibetan Buddhist meditation techniques, up through and including teachings on the Great Seal and the Great Perfection, and did experience some relief from her sufferings as she practiced these teachings. She also went on an extensive pilgrimage to Kathmandu Valley and Mount Kailash. Nevertheless, through all of these experiences, she continued to end every practice session with a prayer never to be reborn again as a female, whereas Yeshe Tsogyel, once she escaped from mundane marriage, rarely expressed dissatisfaction with her lot as a woman, perhaps because she had such an intimate and intense relationship with her guru-consort.

For many years after returning from her pilgrimage, Orgyen Chökyi was required to spend most of her time doing menial work in the kitchen or other work involved in running a large monastery. During this time, she does not seem to have received much further training and was often extremely frustrated with her lot. She wrote frequently about her unhappiness and depression and her longing to be in solitude and to practice intensively. She made many requests to do so, which were always denied. Her guru also told her that there was no benefit to all the suffering she was creating in her mind by her reactions to her experiences and gave her meditation practices that could act as antidotes to her depressed state of mind.[10]

Only after many years and numerous requests, toward the end of her life at the age of about fifty, was she finally granted her own meditation cave and the provisions needed to live a solitary life. The tenor of her songs changed from depression and complaint to joy and contentment. However, speaking as a practitioner who has experienced a similar transformation, I suspect that her happy meditation cave was the result of transformations that had already taken place by following her guru's instructions rather than the immediate cause of her contentment and happiness. A depressed mind easily goes with a meditator into a solitary cave. Nevertheless, her songs shift markedly in their tone, and there are no further complaints about the woes of female birth. Instead, she celebrates her friendships with other female renunciants. For example:

> Hearing the teachings of the Master and Buddha,
> Gaining experience with this beggar woman's strong faith,
> Experiencing the joy of non-conceptual radiant bliss—
> These are mine, Chökyi's joyous spiritual experience.
> Solitary, alone and looking after reality,
> Free from the chatter of common people,
> Serving religious women of a similar religion—
> These are mine, Chökyi's signs of joy.[11]

Soon after this, she was told by her guru that there was no further need for her to engage in religious practices, and she seems to have died not long thereafter when a roof beam fell down and wounded her in the head during a religious ceremony.

One of the saddest incidents in her whole autobiography is the reaction of her guru when Chökyi, thinking that there was good reason for her joys and sorrows to be recorded despite the fact that she could not write, asked her teacher to write her story for her. He replied, "There is no reason to write a liberation tale for you—a woman."[12] Without intending to solve a great puzzle for modern Buddhist women, her guru also demonstrated why we have so few records of female role models throughout Buddhist history! She cried about the fact that she could not write her story herself. In contrast, Tsogyel is represented as not only having written her own autobiography but also as having recorded and hidden many of Padmasambhava's *terma* (treasure texts). She certainly was not illiterate! However, somehow Orgyen Chökyi did manage to record her life story. She explains, "Later when I was dying, amazing omens of my death arose and I thought, 'I have been struck with the spiritual instruction of the *ḍākinī*.' The impediment of not being able to write disappeared and I wrote."[13]

Chökyi died in accordance with traditional signs from Great Perfection literature: the sky was clear, there was a rainbow, and flowers fell from the sky. Her body remained in a meditation pose for seven days, and when she was finally cremated two weeks after her death, her cremation pyre caught fire spontaneously.[14] In traditional Tibetan understanding, these are signs commonly associated with the death of an accomplished practitioner.

In my estimation, Orgyen Chökyi's autobiography provides a very interesting and relevant counterpoint to the religious autobiography of Tibet's most famous woman—Yeshe Tsogyel. For one thing, Chökyi's story is definitely relevant for the realism with which she discusses what it was like to be a woman, especially a woman with a religious vocation, in traditional Tibetan Vajrayāna Buddhist culture. She frequently laments not only her lot but the situation faced by all females, whether human or non-human. Much of her frustration with being female is based on biology. She identifies strongly with the suffering of animal mothers who lose their young and has some strong negative comments about the indifference of the males of a species to this suffering. But one suspects that her sensitivity to the suffering of female animals is a way of expressing her frustration with her own lot, with the abuse she suffered from her parents for not being a boy and with the lack of opportunity for significant training during much of her life. (It is unlikely that a monk with some aptitude for meditation would have been kept in the kitchen for as long as she was.) It is clear that her prejudices and values regarding female birth are deeply imbedded in her culture. She is not reflecting an idiosyncratic personal viewpoint but the prevailing cultural attitude toward women. For those who are skeptical of Buddhist feminist claims that Buddhism does not have a stellar record concerning gender issues, such comments in the "native" voice, a voice that could not possibly have been influenced by Western feminists, are important. They provide a significant reality check. They also provide a counterbalance to those who claim that Vajrayāna praise of the "feminine principle" translates easily or directly into positive circumstances for women.

However, regarding her opinions about women and the female gender role, it is important to note that toward the end of her life, things changed. In the last prayer in her autobiography, she prays:

> May I, Orgyen Chökyi, a beggar with no wants,
> Be born healthy and active
> Rebirth upon rebirth
> In an empty valley with no people.
> I pray that I meet with women friends of a similar religion.[15]

This change of heart regarding being female, and presumably possibly being reborn as a woman, which is implied by her prayer to meet with "women friends of a similar religion," is very significant, even though Orgyen Chökyi neither explains this change of heart nor even seems to notice it. But this change of heart represents the most important way in which she is a relevant role model for today's women. She achieved peace and contentment with her life despite the obstacles she encountered, especially her own dissatisfaction with the female gender role and her own depression and frustration. This does not mean that we, as modern Buddhist women, should simply accept the limitations that Buddhist institutions still place upon us, but that we must find personal peace and contentment in spite of those obstacles. Only then will we have the resources to deal with them skillfully and effectively.

All in all, the lives of Yeshe Tsogyel and Orgyen Chökyi are not very similar. Compared with the traditional story of Yeshe Tsogyel's life, Orgyen Chökyi's life was not outstanding or remarkable. She was not seen as someone predestined for high spiritual accomplishment, and she did not have an outstanding teacher who immediately recognized her potential and trained her individually. Unlike Yeshe Tsogyel, she did not have many students, if any, and did not leave a large legacy, nor was she widely remembered. And though her death was dramatic, it was not very dramatic compared with the death narrated in Tsogyel's autobiography. However, in many ways, Orgyen Chökyi is a more realistic role model than Yeshe Tsogyel precisely because she is more ordinary and because she suffered the same indignities of a difficult family situation and frustration over the liabilities of the female gender role that many of us suffer. She was ignored for much of her life and struggled for everything she ever achieved, including being able to record her own struggle. For much of her life she was very unhappy, something that resonates with many of us. Nevertheless, Orgyen Chökyi persevered and came to be regarded as someone who had attained Buddhism's goal of liberation from samsara despite all her obstacles. To me, she seems a lot more like I am than does Yeshe Tsogyel, and her very ordinariness is more encouraging to me than Tsogyel's impossibly fortunate circumstances.

A major question of this chapter is what it might mean for contemporary Buddhist women like us to see ourselves as both empowered and self-determined as well as relatively ordinary. What a relief to realize that we do not all have to be Yeshe Tsogyels in order to accomplish the Buddhist path, even though her life story might make a better epic movie than our own, or the life of Orgyen Chökyi. A deeper Dharma point shines forth from these stories. The dramatic and the extraordinary may be entertaining and exciting, but true enlightenment lies in the sacred outlook that can see through the deception of evaluating the ordinary as mundane and irrelevant. "Things-as-they-are," *dharmatā*, may not be all that dramatic or different from what we already are and have. Yet all teachings tell us that it is in appreciating things as they are that we find freedom and peace. We must also ask whether we may have been co-opted in longing for stories of extraordinarily accomplished women who may not be realistic role models. Perhaps when we are young we all think that we could be Yeshe Tsogyel, but with age we may come to the realization that being Orgyen Chökyi is just fine.

This chapter also brings up two major questions. Why does the Tibetan Buddhist tradition consistently reject and marginalize stories of women like Orgyen Chökyi while honoring men who are no more outstanding than she was? What can we do about that value system? Nothing is more discouraging or infuriating to a woman like myself than Orgyen Chökyi's teacher's statement that, though she was a credible student, because she was a woman, and only because she was a woman, her story was not worth recording. No wonder that less than one percent of all Tibetan biographical and autobiographical literature is by or about women![16] Because her teacher was not unusual in this prejudice, the effect is that in every generation, each woman who has any spiritual vocation at all must reinvent the wheel by herself, wondering why there are so few realistic female role models and questioning the validity of her own aspiration. Her doubt is intensified when everyone else tells her that she should be content to be a donor and supporter of men, perhaps the mother or the consort of an important male teacher, but never a serious practitioner in her own right who seeks realization or, heaven forbid, even seeks to influence the development of Buddhist tradition as a teacher!

How different is the situation for men. Buddhist records include many, many stories about men who, while not as noteworthy as Milarepa or Longchenpa, nevertheless did achieve a great deal in terms of meditation or scholarship and did influence developing Buddhist traditions. These stories are routinely collected, treasured, contemplated, and used for personal inspiration. The sheer volume of such stories about men reassures any male aspirant that he is doing something worthy and valued, rather than something unusual and not especially encouraged, as is the case for female aspirants. A male seeker need only pick up one of several very large volumes containing many, many stories about highly regarded practitioners, and he will find that almost all of the stories are about people who look like him—other men. Take, for example, Dudjom Rinpoche's monumental *The Nyingma School of Tibetan Buddhism*.[17] The content volume weighs in at 973 pages and contains at least 137 stories. In those stories, a few women are mentioned from time to time, but even Yeshe Tsogyel does not receive a full chapter discussing her life in full; instead, she appears in several chapters in which the achievements of Padmasambhava are discussed. There is also a page-long list of seventeen women "who were also accomplished masters."[18] Almost as massive is Nyoshul Khenpo's *A Marvelous Garland of Rare Gems: Biographies of*

Masters of Awareness in the Dzogchen Lineage.[19] This book contains at least 204 biographies. At most, a half dozen of them are biographies of women, including a chapter on Yeshe Tsogyel. Add to those volumes all the books on Kagyu, Sakya, and Gelug lineages, which are at least as male dominated as the Nyingma and Dzogchen lineages. The result is a huge literature about outstanding practitioners meant to be inspiring to people practicing on the path. But how inspiring can this body of literature be to women? Even as a Westerner who takes Tibetan models seriously, I find this literature depressing rather than inspiring and take my inspiration not so much from these stories as from the fact that such male dominance is utterly at variance with the liberating Dharma. Imagine the impact of this literature on someone who treasures it as her charter for liberation!

It is often pointed out that there are many more women who practice seriously and achieve a level of realization that brings them respect even from prominent male teachers than make it into the records. One example is the previous Khandro Rinpoche, who nets about half a page in Tulku Urgyen Rinpoche's autobiography *Blazing Splendor*.[20] As a very young woman, she was chosen to be a consort of the fifteenth Karmapa when it was determined that his life could be extended only if he took her as a consort. She is credited with having extended his life for three years and later became a highly regarded practitioner in her own right. Of her, Tulku Urgyen says, "Khandro Chenmo was treated with immense respect as though she were a great lama. Word would spread wherever she went and thousands of people would go to meet her. . . . At special ceremonies, she was usually placed on a throne as high as Khyentse or Kongtrul." However, to my knowledge, there is no spiritual autobiography or other lengthy report of her life and accomplishments. Traditionally, such women almost never took public teaching roles and even rebuffed those who sought their advice informally. Often, they cited their femaleness as a disqualification for their ability to give advice about meditation practice, even though they were widely admired as meditators.[21]

However, being admired as a skilled meditator and someone who has something to contribute to the ongoing tradition but not making it into the records is a dead end that leaves the next generation of women practitioners stranded. It is fine to point out that the memories of such women may circulate orally for generations in a limited geographical region. People often claim that oral tradition is important, even determinative, in Tibetan Buddhism, so it doesn't matter too much if outstanding women are remembered only orally. Indeed, oral transmissions and oral tradition is central to the transmission of Vajrayāna Buddhism. But usually, the oral transmissions concern commentary on material that is already written down, though the written texts may be highly restricted. Furthermore, if oral tradition were sufficient for keeping records about inspiring practitioners, then we have to ask why the stories of men are written down while male teachers refuse to have stories about their capable female students recorded. Something is deeply amiss here. Furthermore, if oral transmission alone is relied upon, any given woman's story will only be narrowly known and will eventually be lost to the collective memory and inspiration of the tradition.

I claim that the current generation of practitioners, both women and men, has a great responsibility to undo and correct the mistakes made by previous generations of practitioners that are so evident in this chapter. The remarkable achievements of Western women Dharma practitioners who now constitute about half of the recognized North American Dharma teachers are certainly a major step in that direction. Such women are not shy about teaching publicly if they have the training and ability to do so. They confirm what we have always known: if given the training and the recognition, women are at least as capable of spiritual achievements as men. Also noteworthy is the example of my guru, the current Khandro Rinpoche, whose official title is Her Eminence Mindroling Jetsun Khandro Rinpoche. She teaches more widely and more publicly in Asia, Europe, and North America than any other Tibetan woman and also more than many male teachers. It is hard to imagine that historical reports about our era will be able to write her out of their accounts!

It is also important for this generation of practitioners to correct the massive oversight on the part of previous generations of practitioners that left us so bereft of the stories of accomplished women practitioners. We can do this by recording as many stories of outstanding women as we can and by retrieving as many stories from forgotten libraries and manuscript collections as we can, as has been done in this book about notable Buddhist women. It is hard to think of any activity that could be of more benefit to the survival and flourishing of Dharma in our world.

Notes

1. For a biography of Yeshe Tsogyal, see Gyalwa Changchub and Namkhai Nyingpo, *Lady of the Lotus-Born: The Life and Enlightenment of Yeshe Tsogyal* (Boston: Shambhala Publications, 1999).

2. For a translation of Machik Labdron's biography, see Sarah Harding, *Machik's Complete Explanation: Clarifying the Meaning of Chöd* (Ithaca, NY: Snow Lion Publications, 2003).

3. Rita M. Gross, "Yeshe Tsogyel: Enlightened Consort, Great Teacher, Female Role Model," in *A Garland of Feminist Reflections: Forty Years of Religious Exploration* (Berkeley: University of California Press, 2009), pp. 263–80.

4. Ibid., pp. 281–90.

5. Kurtis R. Schaeffer, *Himalayan Hermitess: The Life of a Tibetan Buddhist Nun* (Oxford: Oxford University Press, 2004).

6. Ibid., pp. 3–4.

7. To some extent, this chapter presupposes some familiarity with the traditional life story of Yeshe Tsogyel. Her story has been translated three times, the most accessible translation being Padmakara Translation Group, *Lady of the Lotus Born* (Boston: Shambhala Publications, 2002).

8. Schaeffer, *Himalayan Hermitess*, p. 142.

9. Ibid., p. 143.

10. Ibid., p. 165.

11. Ibid., p. 171.

12. Ibid., p. 131.

13. Ibid., p. 132.

14. Ibid., p. 182.

15. Ibid., p. 178.

16. Ibid., p. 4.

17. Dudjom Rinpoche, *The Nyingma School of Tibetan Buddhism: Its Fundamentals and History* (Boston: Wisdom Publications, 1991).

18. Ibid., p. 536.

19. Nyoshul Khenpo, *A Marvelous Garland of Rare Gems: Biographies of Master of Awareness in the Dzogchen Lineage* (Junction City, CA: Padma Publishing, 2005).

20. Tulku Urgyen Rinpoche, *Blazing Splendor* (Boudhanath: Rangjung Yeshe Publications, 2005), pp. 56–57. The present Khandro Rinpoche's teachings on the four elemental realities of life can be found in Khandro Rinpoche, *This Precious Life: Tibetan Buddhist Teachings on the Path to Enlightenment* (Boston: Shambhala, 2003).

21. For example, Tulku Urgyen Rinpoche tells many stories about his grandmother in his autobiography, *Blazing Splendor*. According to his account, she knew more about ritual, torma making, and many other topics than any lama. Yet when lamas would come to ask her advice, she would refuse to see them and would reprimand them, saying, "What kind of lamas are you—bowing down to this old woman?" Ibid., p. 81.

Bibliography

Adiele, Faith. *Meeting Faith: The Forest Journals of a Black Buddhist Nun*. New York: W. W. Norton & Company, 2005.

Allione, Tsultrim. *Women of Wisdom*. London: Routledge and Kegan Paul, 1984.

Ama, Michihiro. *Immigrants to the Pure Land: The Acculturation of Shin Buddhism in Hawaii and North America, 1898–1941*. Honolulu: University of Hawai'i Press, 2011.

Anālayo, Ven. "Attitudes Towards Nuns: A Case Study of the Nandakovāda in the Light of Its Parallels." *Journal of Buddhist Ethics* 17(2010): 331–400.

Anālayo, Ven. "Mahāpajāpatī's Going Forth in the Madhyama-āgama." *Journal of Buddhist Ethics* 18(2011): 167–317.

Arai, Paula. *Bringing Zen Home: The Healing Heart of Japanese Women's Rituals*. Honolulu: University of Hawai'i Press, 2011.

Arai, Paula Kane Robinson. "An Empowerment Ritual for Nuns in Contemporary Japan." In *Women's Buddhism, Buddhism's Women: Tradition, Revision, Renewal*. Edited by Ellison Banks Findly, pp. 119–30. Boston: Wisdom Publications, 2000.

Arai, Paula Kane Robinson. "Sōtō Zen Nuns in Modern Japan: Keeping and Creating Tradition." In *Religion & Society in Modern Japan*. Edited by Mark Mullins, Shimazono Susumu, and Paul Swanson, pp. 203–18. Berkeley: Asian Humanities Press, 1993.

Arai, Paula Kane Robinson. *Women Living Zen: Japanese Soto Buddhist Nuns*. New York: Oxford University Press, 1999.

Avery, Martha. *Women of Mongolia*. Boulder, CO: Asian Art & Archaeology, 2000.

Bancroft, Anne. "Women Disciples in Zen Buddhism." In *Women As Teachers and Disciples in Traditional and New Religions*. Edited by Elizabeth Puttick and Peter B. Clarke, pp. 91–96. Lewiston: E. Mellen Press, 1993.

Barnes, Nancy Schuster. "Buddhist Women and the Nuns' Order in Asia." In *Engaged Buddhism: Buddhist Liberation Movements in Asia*. Edited by Christopher S. Queen and Sallie B. King. Albany: State University of New York Press, 1996.

Barnett, Robert. "Women and Politics in Contemporary Tibet." In *Women in Tibet*. Edited by Janet Gyatso and Hanna Havnevik, pp. 285–366. New York: Columbia University Press, 2005.

Bartholomeusz, Tessa. *Women under the Bo Tree: Buddhist Nuns in Sri Lanka*. New York: Cambridge University Press, 1994.

Batchelor, Martine, and Son'gyong Sunim. *Women in Korean Zen: Lives and Practices*.

New York: Syracuse University Press, 2006.

Blackstone, Kathryn. *Women in the Footsteps of the Buddha: Struggle for Liberation in the Therīgāthā*. Surrey, UK: Curzon Press, 1998.

Bodhi, Bhikkhu. *The Revival of the Bhikkhunī Ordination in the Theravāda Tradition*. Penang, Malasia: Inward Path Publisher, 2011.

Boucher, Sandy. *Dancing in the Dharma: The Life and Teachings of Ruth Denison*. Boston: Beacon Press, 2005.

Boucher, Sandy. *Discovering Kwan Yin, Buddhist Goddess of Compassion: A Path toward Clarity and Peace*. Boston: Beacon Press, 1999.

Boucher, Sandy. *Hidden Spring: A Buddhist Woman Confronts Cancer*. Somerville, MA: Wisdom Publications, 2000.

Boucher, Sandy. "The Net of Indra: A Writing Workshop on Women's Global Connectedness." In *Buddhist Women in a Global Multicultural Community*. Edited by Karma Lekshe Tsomo, pp. 282–94. Kuala Lumpur: Sukhi Hotu Press, 2008.

Boucher, Sandy. *Opening the Lotus: A Woman's Guide to Buddhism*. New York: Ballantine Books, 1997.

Boucher, Sandy. *Turning the Wheel: American Women Creating the New Buddhism*. Boston: Beacon Press, 1993.

Brown, Sid. *The Journey of One Buddhist Nun: Even Against the Wind*. Albany, NY: State University of New York Press, 2001.

Cabezón, José Ignacio, ed. *Buddhism, Sexuality, and Gender*. Albany: State University of New York Press, 1992.

Campbell, June. *Traveller in Space: In Search of Female Identity in Tibetan Buddhism*. New York: George Braziller, 1996.

Caplow, Zenshin Florence, and Reigetsu Susan Moon. *Record of the Hidden Lamp: 100 Stories and Koans from Twenty-Five Centuries of Awakened Women*. Boston: Wisdom Publications, 2013.

Changchub, Gyalwa, and Namkhai Nyingpo. *Lady of the Lotus-Born: The Life and Enlightenment of Yeshe Tsogyal*. Boston: Shambhala Publications, 1999.

Chayat, Roko Sherry, ed. *Subtle Sound: The Zen Teachings of Maurine Stuart*. Boston: Shambhala Publications, 1996.

Cheng, Wei-yi. *Buddhist Nuns In Taiwan and Sri Lanka: A Critique of the Feminist Perspective*. Richmond, Surrey: RoutledgeCurzon, 2007.

Cheng, Wei-yi. "Luminary Buddhist Nuns in Contemporary Taiwan: A Quiet Feminist Movement." *Journal of Buddhist Ethics* 10(2003): 39–56.

Cho, Eun-su. *Korean Buddhist Nuns and Laywomen: Hidden Histories, Enduring Vitality*. Albany: State University of New York Press, 2011.

Chodron, Thubten. *Blossoms of the Dharma. Living as a Buddhist Nun*. Berkeley: North Atlantic Books, 1999.

Collette, Alice. "Buddhism and Gender: Reframing and Refocusing the Debate." *Journal of Feminist Studies in Religion* 22:2(2006): 55–84.

Day, Terence P. "The Twenty-one Taras: Features of a Goddess-Pantheon in Mahayana Buddhism." In *Goddesses in Religions and Modern Debate*. Edited by L. Hurtado, pp. 83–122. Atlanta: Scholars Press, 1990.

Derris, Karen. "When the Buddha Was a Woman: Reimagining Tradition in the Theravāda." *Journal of Feminist Studies in Religion* 24.2(2008): 29–44.

DeVido, Elise A. "'Buddhism for This World': The Buddhist Revival in Vietnam, 1920–1951, and Its Legacy." In *Modernity and Re-enchantment: Religion in Post-revolutionary Vietnam.* Edited by Philip Taylor, pp. 250–96. Lanham, MD: Lexington Books, 2008.

Devine, Carol. *Determination: Tibetan Women and the Struggle for an Independent Tibet.* Toronto: Vauve Press, 1991.

Diemberger, Hildegard. *When a Woman Becomes a Religious Dynasty: The Samding Dorje Phagmo of Tibet.* New York: Columbia University Press, 2007.

Dobbins, James C. *Letters of the Nun Eshinni: Images of Pure Land Buddhism in Medieval Japan.* Honolulu: University of Hawai'i Press, 2004.

Dowman, Keith. *Sky Dancer: The Secret Life and Songs of the Lady Yeshe Tsogyel.* London: Routledge and Kegan Paul, 1984.

Dresser, Marianne. *Buddhist Women on the Edge.* Berkeley: North Atlantic Books, 1996.

Drolma, Delog Dawa. *Delog: Journey to Realms Beyond Death.* Junction City, CA: Padma Publishing, 1995.

Eck, Diana L., and Devaki Jain, eds. *Speaking of Faith: Global Perspectives on Women, Religion, and Social Change.* Philadelphia: New Society Publishers, 1987.

Edou, Jerome. *Machig Labdron and the Foundations of Chod.* Ithaca, NY: Snow Lion, 1995.

Falk, Monica Lindberg. *Making Fields of Merit: Buddhist Female Ascetics and Gendered Orders in Thailand.* Seattle: University of Washington Press, 2007.

Falk, Nancy Auer. "The Case of Vanishing Nuns: The Fruits of Ambivalence in Ancient Indian Buddhism." In *Unspoken Worlds: Women's Religious Lives in Non-Western Culture.* Edited by Nancy Auer Falk and Rita M. Gross, pp. 207–24. San Francisco: Harper & Row, 1980.

Falk, Nancy Auer. "An Image of Women in Old Buddhist Literature: The Daughters of Mara." In *Women and Religion:* Edited by Judith Plaskow and Joan Arnold Romero, pp. 105–112. Missoula, MT: Scholars Press, 1974.

Farrer-Halls, Gill. *The Feminine Face of Buddhism.* Wheaton, IL: Quest Books, 2002.

Faure, Bernard, and Stephen F. Teiser, eds. *The Power of Denial: Buddhism, Purity, and Gender.* Princeton: Princeton University Press, 2003.

Feldman, Christina. *The Quest of the Warrior Woman: Women as Mystics, Healers and Guides.* London: Aquarian, 1994.

Feldman, Christina. *Woman Awake: A Celebration of Women's Wisdom.* London: Penguin/Arkana, 1990.

Findly, Ellison Banks. "Women and the Arahant Issue in Early Pali Literature. *Journal of Feminist Studies in Religion* 15:1(1999): 57–76.

Findly, Ellison Banks. *Women's Buddhism, Buddhism's Women: Tradition, Revision, Renewal.* Boston: Wisdom Publications, 2000.

Friedman, Lenore. *Meetings with Remarkable Women: Buddhist Teachers in America.* Boston: Shambhala Publications, 1987.

Friedman, Lenore, and Susan Moon. *Being Bodies: Buddhist Women on the Paradox of Embodiment.* Boston: Shambhala Publications, 1997.

Fugard, Sheila. *Lady of Realisation: A Spiritual Memoir.* Bloomington, IN: Balboa Press, 2012.

Grant, Beata. *Daughters of Emptiness: Poems of Chinese Buddhist Nuns.* Somerville, MA: Wisdom Publications, 2003.

Grant, Beata. *Eminent Nuns: Women Chan Masters of Seventeenth-century China.* Honolulu: University of Hawai'i Press, 2008.

Grant, Beata. "Female Holder of the Lineage: Linji Chan Master Zhiyuan Xinggang (1597–1654)." *Late Imperial China* 17:2(1996): 51–76.

Grant, Beata. "The Red Cord Untied: Buddhist Nuns in 18th Century China." In *Buddhist Women Across Cultures: Realizations.* Edited by Karma Lekshe Tsomo. Albany: State University of New York Press, 1999.

Grant, Beata. "Through the Empty Gate: The Poetry of Buddhist Nuns in Late Imperial China." In *Cultural Intersections in Later Chinese Buddhism.* Edited by Marsha Weidner, pp. 87–113. Honolulu: University of Hawai'i Press, 2001.

Gregory, Peter N., and Susanne Mrozik. *Women Practicing Buddhism: American Experiences.* Somerville, MA: Wisdom Publications, 2007.

Grewal, Inderpal, and Caren Kaplan. eds. *Scattered Hegemonies: Postmodernity and Transnational Feminist Practices.* Minneapolis: University of Minnesota Press, 2002.

Grimshaw, Anna. *Servants of the Buddha: Winter in a Himalayan Convent.* Cleveland: Pilgrim Press, 1994.

Gross, Rita M. *Buddhism after Patriarchy: A Feminist History, Analysis, and Reconstruction of Buddhism.* Albany: State University of New York Press, 1993.

Gross, Rita M. *A Garland of Feminist Reflections: Forty Years of Religious Exploration.* Berkeley: University of California Press, 2009.

Gross, Rita M. "Helping the Iron Bird Fly: Western Buddhist Women and Issues of Authority in the Late 1990s." In *The Faces of Buddhism in America.* Edited by Charles S. Prebish and Kenneth K. Tanaka, pp. 238–52. Berkeley: University of California Press, 1998.

Gross, Rita M. "I Will Never Forget to Visualize That Vajrayogini Is My Body and Mind." *Journal of Feminist Studies in Religion* 3(Spring 1987): 77–89.

Gross, Rita M. *Soaring and Settling: Buddhist Perspectives on Social and Theological Issues.* New York: Continuum Press, 1998.

Gross, Rita M., and Rosemary Radford Reuther. *Religious Feminism and the Future of the Planet: A Buddhist-Christian Conversation.* New York: Continuum Press, 2001.

Gunawardena, R. A. L. H. "Subtile Silks of Ferreous Firmness: Buddhist Nuns in Ancient and Early Medieval Sri Lanka and Their Role in the Propagation of Buddhism." *The Sri Lankan Journal of the Humanities* 14:1–2(1988): 1–59.

Gutschow, Kim. *Being a Buddhist Nun: The Struggle for Enlightenment in the Himalayas.* Cambridge: Harvard University Press, 2004.

Gutschow, Kim. "The Delusion of Gender and Renunciation in Buddhist Kashmir." In *Everyday Life in South Asia,* pp. 264–71. Bloomington: Indiana University Press, 2002.

Gutschow, Kim. "What Makes a Nun? Apprenticeship and Ritual Passage in Zangskar, North India." *Journal of the International Association of Buddhist Studies* 24:2(2001): 187–216.

Gyatso, Janet. "One Plus One Makes Three: Buddhist Gender, Monasticism, and the Law of the Non-excluded Middle." *History of Religions* 43:2(2003): 89–115.

Gyatso, Janet, and Hanna Havnevik. *Women in Tibet*. New York: Columbia University Press, 2005.

Haas, Michaela. *Dakini Power: Twelve Extraordinary Women Shaping the Transmission of Tibetan Buddhism in the West*. Ithaca, NY: Snow Lion Publications, 2013.

Harding, Sarah. *Machik's Complete Explanation: Clarifying the Meaning of Chöd*. Ithaca, NY: Snow Lion Publications, 2003.

Harding, Sarah. *Niguma, Lady of Illusion*. Ithaca, NY: Snow Lion Publications, 2010.

Harris, Ian, ed. *Buddhism and Politics in Twentieth Century Asia*. New York: Printer, 1999.

Havnevik, Hanna. "On Pilgrimage for Forty Years in the Himalayas: The Female Lama Jetsun Lochen Rinpoche's (1865–1951) Quest for Sacred Sites." In *Pilgrimage in Tibet*. Edited by Alex McKay. Richmond, Surrey: Curzon Press, 1998.

Havnevik, Hanna. *Tibetan Buddhist Nuns: History, Cultural Norms and Social Reality*. New York: Oxford University Press, 1989.

Higham, John. "Multiculturalism and Universalism: A History and Critique." *American Quarterly* 45(1993): 195–219.

Holmes-Tagchungdarpa, Amy. *The Social Life of Tibetan Biography: Textuality, Community and Authority in the Lineage of Tokden Shakya Shri*. New York: Lexington Books, 2013.

Horner, Isaline Blew. *Women under Primitive Buddhism*. Delhi: Motilal Banarsidas, 1990.

Hsieh, Ding-hwa. "Images of Women in Ch'an Buddhist Literature of the Sung Period." In *Buddhism in the Sung*. Edited by Peter N. Gregory and Daniel A. Getz Jr. Honolulu: University of Hawai'i Press, 1999.

Htun, Rawe. *The Modern Buddhist Nun*. Translated by San Lwin. Yangon: Parami Bookshop, 2001.

Huang, C. Julia. *Charisma and Compassion: Cheng Yen and the Buddhist Tzu Chi Movement*. Cambridge: Harvard University Press, 2009.

Huang, Chien-Yu Julia, and Robert P. Weller. "Merit and Mothering: Women and Social Welfare in Taiwanese Buddhism." *Journal of Asian Studies* 57:2(May 1998): 379–96.

Hunter, Louise H. *Buddhism in Hawaii: Its Impact on a Yankee Community*. Honolulu: University of Hawai'i Press, 1971.

Hüsken, Ute. " 'Gotamī, Do Not Wish to Go from Home to Homelessness!' Patterns of Objections to Women's Asceticism in Theravāda Buddhism." In *Asceticism and Its Critics: Historical Accounts and Comparative Perspectives*. Edited by Oliver Freiberger. New York: Oxford University Press, 2006.

Hüsken, Ute. "The Legend of the Establishment of the Buddhist Order of Nuns in the Theravāda Vinaya-Pitaka." *Journal of the Pali Text Society* 26(2000): 43–69.

Ito, Tomomi. "Questions of Ordination Legitimacy for Newly Ordained Bhikkhunī in Thailand." *Journal of Southeast Asian Studies* 43:1(2012): 55–76.

Jaini, P. S., trans. *Apocryphal Birth Stories*. 2 vols. London: Pali Text Society, 1986.

Jayawardena, Kumari. "Some Aspects of Religious and Cultural Identity and the Construction of Sinhala Buddhist Womanhood." In *Religion and Political Conflict in South Asia: India, Pakistan, and Sri Lanka*. Edited by Douglas Allen, pp. 161–80. Delhi: Oxford University Press, 1992.

Jikun, Abbess Kasanoin. *In Iris Fields: Remembrances and Poetry*. Kyoto: Tankosha, 2009.

Jordt, Ingrid. "Bhikkhunī, Thilashin, Mae-Chii: Women Who Renounce The World in Burma, Thailand and the Classical Pali Buddhist Texts." *Crossroads: An Interdisciplinary Journal of Southeast Asian Studies* 4:1(1988): 31–39.

Kabilsingh, Chatsumarn. *Thai Women in Buddhism* Berkeley: Parallax Press, 1991.

Kabilsingh, Chatsumarn. "The Future of the *Bhikkhunī Samgha* in Thailand." *Speaking of Faith: Global Perspectives on Women, Religion, and Social Change*. Edited by Diana L. Eck and Devaki Jain. Philadelphia: New Society Publishers, 1987.

Kajiyama, Yuichi. "Women in Buddhism." *Eastern Buddhist* 15:2(1982): 53–70.

Kawahashi, Noriko. "Jizoku (Priests' Wives) in Soto Zen Buddhism: An Ambiguous Category." *Japanese Journal of Religious Studies* 22(Spring 1995): 161–83.

Kawanami, Hiroko. "The Bhikkhunī Ordination Debate: Global Aspirations, Local Concerns." *Buddhist Studies Review* 24:2(2007): 226–44.

Kawanami, Hiroko. "Buddhist Nuns in Transition: The Case of Burmese *thilá-shin*." In *Indian Insights: Buddhism, Brahmanism and Bhakti*. Edited by Peter Connolly and Sue Hamilton, pp. 209–24. London: Luzac Oriental, 1997.

Kawanami, Hiroko. "Patterns of Renunciation: The Changing World of Burmese Nuns." In *Women's Buddhism, Buddhism's Women: Tradition, Revision, Renewal*. Edited by Ellison Banks Findly, pp. 159–71. Somerville, MA: Wisdom Publications, 2000.

Kawanami, Hiroko. "The Religious Standing of Burmese Buddhist Nuns (*thilá-shin*): The Ten Precepts and Religious Respect Words." *Journal of the International Association of Buddhist Studies* 13:1(1990): 17–39.

Kaza, Stephanie. "Acting with Compassion: Buddhism, Feminism, and the Environmental Crisis." In *Ecofeminism and the Sacred*. Edited by Carol J. Adams, pp. 50–69. New York: Continuum International, 1993.

Kelly, Carol E. *Accidental Immigrants and the Search for Home: Women, Cultural Identity, and Community*. Philadelphia: Temple University Press, 2013.

Khaing, Mi Mi. *The World of Burmese Women*. London: Zed Books, 1984.

Khema, Ayya. *Be An Island: The Buddhist Practice of Ayya Khema*. Somerville, MA: Wisdom Publications, 1999.

Khema, Ayya. *I Give You My Life: The Autobiography of a Western Buddhist Nun*. Translated by Sherab Chodzin Kohn. Boston: Shambhala Publications, 1998.

Khong, Chan, Cao Ngoc Phuong, and Maxine Hong Kingston. *Learning True Love: How I Learned and Practiced Social Change in Vietnam*. Berkeley: Parallax Press, 1993.

King, Sallie B., trans. *Passionate Journey: The Spiritual Autobiography of Satomi Myodo*. Boston: Beacon Press, 1995.

Klein, Anne C. *Meeting the Great Bliss Queen: Buddhists, Feminists, and the Art of the Self*. Ithaca, NY: Snow Lion Publications, 2008.

Klein, Anne C. "Primordial Purity and Everyday Life: Exalted Female Symbols and the Women of Tibet." In *Immaculate and Powerful: The Female in Sacred Image and Social Reality*. Edited by Clarissa Atkinson, Constance Buchanan, and Margaret Miles, pp. 111–38. Boston: Beacon Press, 1985.

Klein, Anne C. "Presence with a Difference: Buddhists and Feminists on Subjectivity." *Hypatia* 9:4(1994): 112–30.

Korte, Anne-Marie. "Women and Miracle Stories: Introduction." In *Women and Miracle Stories: A Multidisciplinary Exploration.* Edited by Anne-Marie Korte. Brill: Leiden, 2001.

Krey, Gisela. "On Women as Teachers in Early Buddhism: Dhammadinnā and Khemā." *Buddhist Studies Review* 27:1(2010): 18.

Kunsang, Erik Pema. *Dakini Teachings: Padmasambhava's Oral Instructions to Lady Tsogyal.* Boston: Shambhala Publications, 1990.

Kusuma, Bhikkhunī. "Inaccuracies in Buddhist Women's History." In *Innovative Buddhist Women: Swimming Against the Stream.* Edited by Karma Lekshe Tsomo. Surrey, UK: Curzon Press, 2000.

LaMacchia, Linda. *Songs and Lives of the* Jomo *(Nuns) of Kinnaur, Northwest India: Women's Religious Expression in Tibetan Buddhism.* Delhi: Sri Satguru Publications, 2008.

Lang, Karen Christina. "Images of Women in Early Buddhism and Christian Gnosticism." *Buddhist Christian Studies* 2(1982): 95–105.

Lang, Karen Christina. "Lord Death's Snare: Gender Related Imagery in the *Theragāthā* and the *Therīgāthā.*" *Journal of Feminist Studies in Religion* 2(1986): 63–79.

Lang, Karen Christina. "Shaven Heads and Loose Hair: Buddhist Attitudes Toward Hair and Sexuality." In *Off with Her Head! The Denial of Women's Identity in Myth, Religion, and Culture.* Edited by Howard Eilberg-Schwartz and Wendy Doniger. Berkeley: University of California Press, 1995.

Levering, Miriam L. "The Dragon Girl and the Abbess of Mo-shan: Gender and Status in the Ch'an Buddhist Tradition." *Journal of the International Association of Buddhist Studies* 5:1(1982): 19–36.

Levering, Miriam L. "Lin-chi (Rinzai) Ch'an and Gender: The Rhetoric of Equality and the Rhetoric of Heroism." In *Buddhism, Sexuality, and Gender.* Edited by Edited by José Ignacio Cabezón, pp. 248–52. Albany: State University of New York Press, 1992.

Levering, Miriam. "Stories of Enlightened Women in Ch'an and the Chinese Buddhist Female Bodhisattva/Goddess Tradition." *Women and Goddess Traditions.* Edited by Karen L. King, pp. 248–52. Minneapolis: Fortress Press, 1997.

LeVine, Sarah. "At the Cutting Edge: Theravāda Nuns in the Kathmandu Valley." In *Innovative Buddhist Women: Swimming against the Stream.* Edited by Karma Lekshe Tsomo, pp. 13–29. Surrey, UK: Curzon Press, 2000.

LeVine, Sarah. "Dharma Educations for Women in the Theravāda Buddhist Community of Nepal." In *Buddhist Women and Social Justice: Ideals, Challenges, and Achievements.* Edited by Karma Lekshe Tsomo, pp. 137–54. Albany: State University of New York Press, 2004.

LeVine, Sarah. *The Saint of Kathmandu and Other Tales of the Sacred in Distant Lands.* Boston: Beacon Press, 2008.

LeVine, Sarah E., and David N. Gellner. *Rebuilding Buddhism: The Theravada Movement in Twentieth Century Nepal.* Cambridge: Harvard University Press, 2005.

Lottermoser, Friedgard. "Buddhist Nuns in Burma." *Sakyadhita Newsletter* 2:2(1991).

Mackenzie, Vicki. *Cave in the Snow: Tenzin Palmo's Quest for Enlightenment.* New York: Bloomsbury Publications, 1995.

Makley, Charlene E. "The Body of a Nun: Nunhood and Gender in Contemporary Amdo." In *Women in Tibet*. Edited by Janet Gyatso and Hanna Havnevik, pp. 259–84. New York: Columbia University Press, 2005.

McGranahan, Carole. "Narrative Dispossession: Tibet and the Gendered Logics of Historical Possibility." *Comparative Studies in Society and History* 52:4(2010): 768–97.

McGranahan, Carole. "Truth, Fear, and Lies: Exile Politics and Arrested Histories of the Tibetan Resistance." *Cultural Anthropology* 20:4(2005): 570–600.

Meeks, Lori R. *Hokkeji and the Reemergence of Female Monastic Orders in Premodern Japan*. Honolulu: University of Hawai'i Press, 2010.

Minamato, Junko. "Buddhist Attitudes: A Woman's Perspective." In *Women, Religion and Sexuality*. Edited by Jeanne Beche, pp. 154–71. Philadelphia: Trinity Press International, 1991.

Mohanty, Chandra Talpade. *Feminism without Borders: Decolonizing Theory, Practicing Solidarity*. Durham: Duke University Press, 2003.

Mohr, Thea, and Jampa Tsedroen. *Dignity & Discipline: Reviving Full Ordination for Buddhist Nuns*. Somerville, MA: Wisdom Publications, 2010.

Morrell, Sachiko Kaneko, and Morrell, Robert E. *Zen Sanctuary of Purple Robes: Japan's Tōkeiji Convent Since 1285*. Albany: State University of New York Press, 2006.

Mrozik, Susane. "A Robed Revolution: The Contemporary Buddhist Nun's Movement." *Religion Compass* 3:3(2009): 360–78.

Murcott, Susan. *The First Buddhist Women: Translations and Commentaries on the Therigatha*. Berkeley: Parallax Press, 1991.

Narayan, Uma. *Dislocating Cultures: Identities, Traditions, and Third World Feminism*. New York & London, Routledge, 1997.

Neumaier-Dargyay, Eva K. "Buddhist Thought from a Feminist Perspective." In *Gender, Genre and Religion*. Edited by Morny Joy, E. K. Neumaier-Dargyay, and Mary Gerhart, pp. 145–70. Waterloo, Ontario: Wilfrid Laurier University Press, 1995.

Nissan, Elisabeth. "Recovering Practice: Buddhist Nuns in Sri Lanka." *South Asia Research* 4:1(1984): 32–49.

Obeyesekere, Ranjini. *Yasodhara, the Wife of the Bodhisattva: The Sinhala* Yasodharavata *(The Story of Yasodhara) and the Sinhala* Yasodharapadanaya *(The Sacred Biography of Yasodhara)*. Albany: State University of New York Press, 2009.

O'Halloran, Maura. *Pure Heart, Enlightened Mind: The Zen Journal and Letters of Maura "Soshin" O'Halloran*. Boston: Charles E. Tuttle, 1994.

Palmo, Jetsunma Tenzin. *Into the Heart of Life*. Ithaca, NY: Snow Lion Publications, 2011.

Park, Pori. *Trial and Error in Modernist Reforms: Korean Buddhism under Colonial Rule*. Berkeley: Institute of East Asian Studies at University of California, 2009

Paul, Diana Y. "Kuan Yin: Saviour and Savioures in Chinese Pure Land Buddhism." In *Book of the Goddess: Past and Present*. Edited by Carl Olsen, pp. 161–75. New York: Crossroad, 1983.

Paul, Diana Y., and Frances Wilson. *Women in Buddhism: Images of the Feminine in Mahayana Tradition*. Berkeley: University of California Press, 1985.

Pittman, Don A. *Toward a Modern Chinese Buddhism: Taixu's Reforms*. Honolulu: University of Hawai'i Press, 2001.

Rhys Davids, Caroline A. F., trans. *Poems of Early Buddhist Nuns: Therigatha*. Boston: Wisdom Publications, 1989.

Richman, Paula. "Gender and Persuasion: The Portrayal of Beauty, Anguish, and Nurturance in an Account of a Tamil Nun." In *Buddhism, Sexuality, and Gender*. Edited by José Ignacio Cabezón. Albany: State University of New York Press, 1992.

Richman, Paula. "The Portrayal of a Female Renouncer in a Tamil Buddhist Text." In *Gender and Religion: On the Complexity of Symbols*, eds. Caroline Walker Bynum, Stevan Harrell, and Paula Richman, pp. 143–65. Boston: Beacon Press, 1985.

Ruch, Barbara. *Engendering Faith: Women and Buddhism in Premodern Japan*. Ann Arbor: University of Michigan Center, 2002.

Sakya, Jamyang, and Julie Emery. *Princess in the Land of Snows: The Life of Jamyang Sakya in Tibet*. Boston: Shambhala Publications, 1988.

Salgado, Nirmala S. "Religious Identities of Buddhist Nuns: Training Precepts, Renunciation Attire, and Nomenclature in Theravāda Buddhism." *Journal of the American Academy of Religion* 72:4(2004): 935–53.

Salgado, Nirmala S. "Ways of Knowing and Transmitting Religious Knowledge: Case Studies of Theravāda Buddhist Nuns." *Journal of the International Association of Buddhist Studies* 19:1(1996): 61–79.

Schaeffer, Kurtis R. "The Autobiography of a Medieval Hermitess: Orgyan Chokyi (1675–1729)." In *Women in Tibet*. Edited by Janet Gyatso and Hanna Havnevik. New York: Columbia University Press, 2005.

Schaeffer, Kurtis R. *Himalayan Hermitess: The Life of a Tibetan Buddhist Nun*. Oxford: Oxford University Press, 2004.

Schmidt, Amy. *Dipa Ma: The Life and Legacy of a Buddhist Master*. Katonah, NY: BlueBridge, 2005.

Schuster [Barnes], Nancy. "Striking a Balance: Women and Images of Women in Early Chinese Buddhism." In *Women, Religion, and Social Change*. Edited by Yvonne Yazbeck Haddad and Ellison Banks Findly. Albany: State University of New York Press, 1985.

Scott, Rachelle M. "Buddhism, Miraculous Powers, and Gender: Rethinking the Stories of Theravāda Nuns." *Journal of the International Association of Buddhist Studies* 33:1–2(2011): 489–511.

Sharma, Arvind. "How and Why Did the Women in Ancient India Become Buddhist Nuns?" *Sociological Analysis* 38(1977): 239–51.

Shaw, Miranda. *Passionate Enlightenment*. Princeton: Princeton University Press, 1994.

Shaw, Miranda. "Worship of Women in Tantric Buddhism: Male Is to Female as Devotee Is to Goddess." In *Women and Goddess Traditions*. Edited by Karen L. King, pp. 111–36. Minneapolis: Fortress Press, 1997.

Shih, Bhikkhunī Juo-Hsüeh. *Controversies over Buddhist Nuns*. Oxford: Pali Text Society, 2000.

Shih, Pao-Ch'ang. *Lives of the Nuns: Biographies of Chinese Buddhist Nuns from the Fourth to Sixth Centuries: A Translation of the Pi-Ch'Iu-Ni Chuan*. Translated by Kathryn Ann Tsai. Honolulu: University of Hawai'i Press, 1994.

Smith, Kendra. "Sex, Dependency, and Religion: Reflections from a Buddhist Perspective." In *Women in the World's Religions, Past and Present*. Edited by

Ursala King, pp. 219–31. New York: Paragon House, 1987.

Somers, Robert M. "Biography of the Nun An-Ling-Shou." *Harvard Journal of Asiatic Studies* 15:1.2(June 1952): 193–96.

Sorensen, Clark. "The Myth of Princess Pari and the Self Image of Korean Women." *Anthropos* 83(1988): 403–19.

Spiro, Melford. *Gender, Ideology and Psychological Reality*. New Haven: Yale University Press, 1997.

Sponberg, Alan. "Attitudes toward Women and the Feminine in Early Buddhism." In *Buddhism, Sexuality, and Gender*. Edited by José Ignacio Cabezón. Albany: State University of New York Press, 1992.

Tsomo, Karma Lekshe. "Buddhist Feminist Reflections." In *Buddhist Philosophy: Selected Primary Texts*. Edited by Jay Garfield and William Edelglass, pp. 437–48. New York: Oxford University Press, 2009.

Tsomo, Karma Lekshe, ed. *Buddhist Women across Cultures: Realizations*. Albany: State University of New York Press, 1999.

Tsomo, Karma Lekshe, ed. *Buddhist Women and Social Justice: Ideals, Challenges, and Achievements*. Albany: State University of New York Press, 2004.

Tsomo, Karma Lekshe, ed. *Buddhist Women in a Global Multicultural Community*. Kuala Lumpur: Sukhi Hotu Press, 2008.

Tsomo, Karma Lekshe. "Global Exchange: Women in the Transmission and Transformation of Buddhism." In *Trans-Buddhism: American Perspectives on the Transmission, Translation, and Transformation of Buddhism in the Global Arena*, pp. 209–36. Amherst: University of Massachusetts Press, 2009.

Tsomo, Karma Lekshe, ed. *Innovative Buddhist Women: Swimming Against the Stream*. Surrey, England: Curzon Press, 2000.

Tsomo, Karma Lekshe. "Lao Buddhist Women: Quietly Negotiating Religious Authority." *Buddhist Studies Review* 27:1(2010):85–106.

Tsomo, Karma Lekshe. *Sisters in Solitude: Two Traditions of Buddhist Monastic Ethics for Women: A Comparative Analysis of the Chinese Dharmagupta and the Tibetan Mūlasarvāstivāda Bhikṣuṇī Prātimokṣa Sūtras*. Albany: State University of New York Press, 1996.

Uchino, Kumiko. "The Status Elevation Process of Soto Sect Nuns in Modern Japan." In *Speaking of Faith*. Edited by Diana L. Eck and Devaki Jain, pp. 159–73. Philadelphia: New Society Publishers, 1987.

Van Esterik, John. "Laywomen in Theravada Buddhism." In *Women of Southeast Asia*. Edited by Penny Van Esterik, pp. 55–78. DeKalb: Northern Illinois University, Center for Southeast Asian Studies, 1982.

Van Esterik, John. "Women Meditation Teachers in Thailand." In *Women of Southeast Asia*, Center for Southeast Asia Monograph Series. Edited by Penny Van Esterik, pp. 42–54. Dekalb: Northern Illinois University Press, 1982.

Vargas-O'Bryan, Ivette. "The Life of dGe slong ma dPal mo: The Experiences of a Leper, Founder of a Fasting Ritual, and Transmitter of Buddhist Teachings on Suffering and Renunciation in Tibetan Religious History." *Journal for the International Association of Buddhist Studies* 24:2(2001): 157–85.

Von Furer-Haimendorf, Christoph. "A Nunnery in Nepal." *Kailash: Journal of Himalayan Studies* 4:2(1976): 121–54.

Walters, Jonathan S. "A Voice from the Silence: The Buddha's Mother's Story." *History of Religions* 33(1994): 358–79.

Watkins, Joanne C. *Spirited Women: Gender, Religion, and Cultural Identity in the Nepal Himalaya.* New York: Columbia University Press, 1996.

Wijayaratna, Mohan. *Buddhist Nuns: The Birth and Development of a Women's Monastic Order.* Kandy, Sri Lanka: Buddhist Publication Society, 2010.

Willis, Jan D. *Dreaming Me: Black, Baptist, and Buddhist—One Woman's Spiritual Journey.* Somerville, MA: Wisdom Publication, 2008.

Willis, Janice D. *Feminine Ground: Essays on Women and Tibet.* Ithaca, NY: Snow Lion Publications, 1989.

Willis, Janice D. "Nuns and Benefactresses: The Role of Women in the Development of Buddhism." In *Women, Religion, and Social Change.* Edited by Yvonne Yazbeck Haddad and Ellison Banks Findly. Albany: State University of New York Press, 1985.

Willson, Martin. *In Praise of Tara: Songs to the Saviouress.* London: Wisdom Publications, 1986.

Wilson, Liz. *Charming Cadavers: Horrific Figurations of the Feminine in Indian Buddhist Hagiographical Literature.* Chicago: University of Chicago Press, 1996.

Wilson, Liz. "Seeing through the Gendered 'I': The Self-Scrutiny and Self-Disclosure of Nuns in Post-Aśokan Buddhist Hagiographic Literature." *Journal of Feminist Studies in Religion* 11:1(1995): 41–80.

Yi, Hyangsoon. "Pomunjong and Hanmaŭm Sŏnwŏn: New Monastic Paths in Contemporary Korea." In *Out of the Shadows: Socially Engaged Buddhist Women.* Edited by Karma Lekshe Tsomo, pp. 228–34. Delhi: Sri Satguru Publications, 2006.

Young, Katherine K., and Arvind Sharma. *Images of the Feminine—Mythic, Philosophic and Human—in the Buddhist, Hindu, and Islamic Traditions: A Bibliography of Women in India.* New York: New Horizons, 1974.

Young, Serinity. *Courtesans and Tantric Consorts: Sexualities in Buddhist Narrative, Iconography, and Ritual.* New York: Routledge, 2004.

Yü, Chün-fang. *Kuan Yin: The Chinese Transformation of Avalokiteśvara.* New York: Columbia University Press, 2001.

Yu, Larry, and Valerie Katagiri, eds. *Where Are You From? An Anthology of Asian American Writing.* Portland: Thymos, 2012.

Yuichi, Kajiyama. "Women in Buddhism." *The Eastern Buddhist* 15:2(Autumn 1982): 53–70.

Contributors

Kalzang Dorjee Bhutia completed his graduate education in Buddhist Studies at the University of Delhi with a thesis on the response of Buddhist intellectuals and institutions to modernity and colonialism in the Eastern Himalayan state of Sikkim. His research interests include Buddhist history and culture in the eastern Himalayan state of Sikkim, transnational Buddhist networks, and indigenous environmentalisms in the Himalayas.

Cristina Bonnet-Acosta was born and raised in San Juan, Puerto Rico. She received her B.A. in Communications from the University of Puerto Rico, an M.A. in Buddhist Studies from the School of Oriental and African Studies in the U.K., and an M.A. in Literature Studies at Stanford University. She spent more than a year doing research in South and Southeast Asia and has been writing on gender, feminism and Buddhism since 2003. She currently works for the United Nations in Vienna, Austria.

Eun-su Cho taught in the Department of Asian Languages and Cultures at the University of Michigan before accepting a position as an associate professor in the Department of Philosophy at Seoul National University. She received her Ph.D. in 1997 from the University of California, Berkeley. She has published articles ranging from Indian Abhidharma Buddhism to Korean Buddhist thought and history. She edited an anthology on Korean Buddhist nuns, *Korean Buddhist Nuns and Laywomen: Hidden Histories, Enduring Vitality*, and co-translated (with John Jorgensen) the *Jikji: The Essential Passages Directly Pointing at the Essence of the Mind.*

Karen Derris is an associate professor of Religious Studies at the University of Redlands. She received a Ph.D. from Harvard University in Religious Studies with a disciplinary focus in Buddhist Studies. Her research focuses on Buddhist ethics and literature, particularly in the Theravadin traditions of South and Southeast Asia. She is co-editor (with Natalie Gummer) of *Defining Buddhisms: A Reader.*

Elise Anne DeVido received a Ph.D. in History from Harvard University. She taught world history and women's history as an associate professor in the Department of History at National Taiwan Normal University for many years. Her publications include *Taiwan's Buddhist Nuns* and numerous articles on Taiwanese Buddhism. She is currently an associate professor in the Department of History at St. Bonaventure University, New York, and is researching 20th-century Vietnamese Buddhism.

Bhikkhunī Dhammananda (Chatsumarn Kabilsingh) received an M.A. in Religion from McMaster University in Canada and a Ph.D. in Buddhism from Magadha University in India. She was a professor of Philosophy at Thammasat University in Bangkok for many years. She received *sāmaṇerī* ordination in 2001 and *bhikkhunī* ordination in 2003, both in Sri Lanka. Currently, she devotes her energy to training programs for nuns at Songdhammakalyani Temple and works to establish the lineage of full ordination for women in Thailand.

Rita M. Gross was a professor of Comparative Studies in Religion at the University of Wisconsin, Eau Claire, for many years. She has also taught widely as a Dharma teacher, especially in the Shambhala *mandala* and at Jetsun Khandro Rinpoche's center, Lotus Garden, in Stanley, Virginia. She is the author of *Buddhism after Patriarchy: A Feminist History, Analysis, and Reconstruction of Buddhism* and other books on Buddhist women.

Punyawati Guruma holds a B.A. and an M.A. in Buddhist Studies from the Graduate Institute of Pali and Buddhist Studies, Kelaniya University, Sri Lanka. She practices and teaches at Dharmakirti Vihara in Kathmandu, Nepal. Currently she is establishing a new monastery called Shakya Muni Kirti Vihar on the outskirts of Kathmandu.

Amy Holmes-Tagchungdarpa is an assistant professor of Buddhist cultural history in the Department of Religious Studies at Grinnell College. Her research interests include the culture and history of the Sino-Tibetan borderlands and the Himalayas, and more broadly, intersections between literary and material history, interpersonal networks, cultural production and gender studies between East, Inner and South Asia. She is the author of 'The Social Life of Tibetan Biography: Textuality, Community and Authority in the Lineage of Togden Shakya Shri' (2014).

Tomomi Ito is an associate professor in the Graduate School of Intercultural Studies, Kobe University, Japan. She received her Ph.D. in Southeast Asian Studies in 2002 from Australian National University, focusing on Buddhist debates in 20th-century Thailand, especially the ideas proposed by Bhikkhu Buddhadasa. Her major research interest is social history of Thai Buddhism and Thai Buddhist women. In recent years, she has been conducting ethnographical research on the restoration of Theravāda *bhikkhunī saṅgha* in Thailand and Sri Lanka.

Yu-chen Li is an associate professor in the Department of Chinese Literature at National Tsing Hua University, Taiwan. Her research interests include the gender issues in religious studies, Buddhist literature, and the Chinese religious novels. She is author of *Tadai da Biquiuni* (*Bhiksuni*s of the Tang Dynasty) and *Cooking and Religious Practice,* and editor of *Women and Religion: An Interdisciplinary Perspective* (Funu yu zongjiao: kualingyu de shiye).

Thích Nữ Như Nguyệt (Nguyen Thi Thu Ha) graduated with a Ph.D. from the Department of Buddhist Studies, University of Delhi, with research on the origin and development of the Bhikkhunī Saṅgha in Vietnam. Currently, she is a member of Board of Foreign Affairs of the Vietnamese Bhikkhunī Saṅgha and was vice-secretary general of the Vietnamese Conference Planning Committee for the 11th Sakyadhita International Conference. She is currently a lecturer in the Department of World History at Van Hanh University, Ho Chi Minh City. She also teaches at various monasteries in Vietnam and abroad.

Thích Nữ Huong Như (Hoang Thi Phuong Thao) received a Ph.D. in the Department of Buddhist Studies at the University of Delhi in 2005 with research on Buddhism and psychotherapy. She is currently a lecturer at the Buddhist University in Ho Chi Minh City.

Padma'tsho (Baima cuo) is a professor in the Tibetan Studies Department at Southwest University for Nationalities in Chengdu, China, where she teaches Tibetan Buddhism and Tibetan culture. She received her Master's degree from the Nationalities Department and the Department of Tibetan Studies at the Central Nationalities University in Beijing and completed her Ph.D. in the Department of Religious Studies at Sichuan University.

Tenzin Palmo spent 18 years practicing in the remote Himalayan region of Lahaul. In 1973, she traveled to Hong Kong to receive the *bhiksuni* ordination. She is the founder of Dongyu Gatsal Ling, a monastery for the training of *togdenmas* (female yogic practitioners) near the community of Tashi Jong in northern India. Her story has been documented in *A Cave in the Snow.* She is the author of *Reflections On A Mountain Lake: Teachings on Practical Buddhism.*

Alyson Prude is a Ph.D. candidate in Religious Studies at the University of California, Santa Barbara. Her current research is a contemporary ethnography of Buddhist revenants ('*das log*), focusing on issues surrounding the body, death and dying, gender and religious authority in eastern Tibet and Tibetan Buddhist Nepal.

Hyeseon Sunim joined the monastic life in 1985 and practices at the Hanmaum Seonwon in Korea under the tutelage of Seon Master Daehaeng. She received a Ph.D. in Buddhist Studies from Dongguk University in 2006 with a dissertation on "The Hanmaum Teaching and Seon Practice Method."

Karma Lekshe Tsomo is a professor of Theology and Religious Studies at the University of San Diego. She received a doctorate in Philosophy from the University of Hawai'i at Manoa. She is past president of Sakyadhita: International Association of Buddhist Women and director of Jamyang Foundation, an educational initiative for women in developing countries. Her publications include *Buddhist Women Across Cultures: Realizations*; *Innovative Buddhist Women: Swimming Against the Stream*; and *Buddhist Women and Social Justice: Ideals, Challenges, and Achievements*.

Malia Dominica Wong, O.P., is on staff at Chaminade University of Honolulu and an adjunct professor in the Religious Studies Department. She received a D.Min. from the University of Creation Spirituality in 2000 with a thesis entitled, "The Gastronomics of Learning From Each Other: Parallels in Spiritual Practices." She has been involved with Buddhist-Christian practices since 1986 and has been steadfastly working to build bridges of harmony among peoples of all denominations. She is grateful to be a member of Sakyadhita and to be at its service.

Hyangsoon Yi is a professor of Comparative Literature and director of the Korean Language and Literature program at the University of Georgia. She received her Ph.D. in English (with a minor in Film Studies) from Pennsylvania State University. Her book *Piguni wa Han'guk munhak* (Buddhist Nuns and Korean Literature) was selected by the Korean Academy of Sciences as an outstanding scholarly book. She co-authored *Welcome to Korean!* and has published extensively on Korean literature and film, and the history of Korean Buddhist nuns.

Index